W9-CCN-560

Dover Memorial Library
Gardner-Webb University
P.O. Box 836
Boiling Springs, N.C. 28017

Export Restraint and the New Protectionism

Export Restraint and the New Protectionism

The Political Economy of Discriminatory Trade Restrictions

Kent Albert Jones

Ann Arbor

THE UNIVERSITY OF MICHIGAN PRESS

HF
1414.5
.J66
1994

Copyright © by the University of Michigan 1994
All rights reserved
Published in the United States of America by
The University of Michigan Press
Manufactured in the United States of America
∞ Printed on acid-free paper

1997   1996   1995   1994   4   3   2   1

A CIP catalogue record for this book is available from the British Library.

Jones, Kent Albert.
    Export restraint and the new protectionaism : the political economy
of discriminatory trade restrictions / Kent Jones.
        p.   cm.
    Includes bibliographical references and index.
    ISBN 0-472-10527-2 (alk. paper)
    1. Export controls.   2. Restraint of trade.   3. Protectionism.
I. Title.
HF1414.5.J66   1994
382'.64—dc20   94-31943
                                                            CIP

This study is dedicated to the memory of
Jan Tumlir
(1926-1985)
and
Gerard Curzon
(1921-1989)
Teachers, Mentors, GATT Scholars

Contents

Preface and Acknowledgments

Nothing is more damaging to a new truth than an old error.

—Goethe

As the major trading countries of the world again run the danger of succumbing fully to the siren call of protectionism, the very system of trading rules designed to prevent such disasters is crumbling. The most salient example of this development is the proliferation in recent years of discriminatory export restraint agreements, pledges by exporters or their governments to place quantitative limits on export deliveries of specific goods to specific importing countries. Designed to remedy import "disruption," formal voluntary export restraint (VER) agreements have been applied to a large number of manufactured goods in contravention of the spirit, if not the letter, of the GATT, including textiles and apparel, carbon steel products, consumer electronics, nonrubber footwear, automobiles, and machine tools. Other products not covered by GATT disciplines, particularly in agriculture, are also subject to voluntary export restraint and other forms of negotiated trade restrictions. In addition, the intimidating character of unfair trade law enforcement often leads to price or quantity "undertakings" by exporters as a means of terminating such cases. Such instances of negotiated or induced export restraint have distorted trade patterns, discriminated against the most efficient producers, and seem designed to spread and at the same time poison trade relations. Negotiated export restraint has therefore come to represent a major threat to the world economic order, and became the subject of intense negotiations at the Uruguay Round of trade negotiations.

In a broader sense, most major trade issues today involve a conflict among or between nations over discrimination in the conduct of commercial relations, and the problem of export restraint can best be understood in this context. The recent trend toward strengthening regional trading blocs has raised questions, for example, about the relevance of nondiscrimination as a principle of trade policy as applied to specific commodities. In the Uruguay Round of trade negotiations, the negotiations focused on the question of whether to make selective export restraint agreements fully legal or illegal under GATT rules. Similarly, trade disputes over the use of unfair trade laws generally involve allegations that such statutes are manipulated to tilt enforcement measures against specific low-cost suppliers. Recent attempts to phase out long-standing export restraint agreements in steel and textiles have met with vehement political opposition among domestic producers of the goods.

The problem of export restraint and other discriminatory trade policies as vehicles for international conflict has thus driven trade policy to a critical juncture. Many critics of the existing system of trading rules point to the recent trends in bilateralism and market-sharing trade restrictions as evidence that "the GATT is dead" and that the era of managed trade has begun, that free trade and nondiscrimination are dead letters in trade policy. In the new era of "enlightened" economic nationalism, trade relations will be governed, according to this scenario, by negotiated quantitative agreements on trade flows at the sectoral and even at the aggregate level. Trade imbalances will be correctable through tightly managed trade policy. Governments will be in a position to guarantee that their producers gain a fair share of output and trade in world markets, especially in strategic or sensitive products. Trade policy will become industrial policy.

Such a vision of managed trade based on the assertion of national economic and political interests is not entirely new, as the following pages will show, but their continual reemergence in altered forms gives testimony to the persistence of protectionism. Government policymakers, the international business community, and the public at large would do well to consider thoroughly the origins and consequences of VERs and other managed trade policy devices before rejecting the admittedly troubled GATT in favor of the new protectionism. This study sets out to guide the reader through the main policy issues. Why, for example, have VERs replaced tariffs as the major form of protectionism? How do VERs differ from tariffs and import quotas in terms of market effects and political economy? Why are VERs so prominent and long-lasting in steel and textiles? What are the linkages between VERs, unfair trade law, and competition (antitrust) law? Finally, what is the best way to reform the trading system, in terms of both the GATT and domestic trade policy making structure? In this regard, it is necessary to take a hard look at the alternatives. Do VERs and other forms of export restraint, however objectionable, represent the lowest-cost means of maintaining an otherwise open trading system?

Scope of the Study

This study focuses on the distorting effects of VER agreements on world trade patterns and their disruptive effects on trade relations. Chapter 1 gives a historical account of the use of voluntary export restraint and its development under the GATT system. Chapters 2 presents the theory of the market effects and political economy of VERs, including their tendency to divert export trade to third countries and to cause value escalation in the makeup of restricted trade, while chapter 3 presents a review of empirical evidence of these phenomena and estimates of the cost of VERs. Chapters 4 and 5 examine the relationship between VERs and other forms of trade restriction, particularly trade law devices, that together form a system of export restraint. Chapter 4 concentrates on the process of policy choice and how it has become skewed toward devices that induce export restraint, while chapter 5 presents evidence that changes in legislation regarding unfair trade have systematically changed the incentive structure of unfair trade law filings. Chapter 6 focuses on the conflict between competition law and trade law that exists in steel export restraint agreements, while chapter 7 considers the effects of export restraint on the interests of developing countries. The final two chapters address public policy issues associated with export restraint and the prospects for policy changes. Chapter 8 focuses on the GATT reform and includes an assessment of Uruguay Round developments. Chapter 9 proposes a legislatively mandated economic impact statement for trade policy and trade law measures as a means of increasing public awareness of their effects and of promoting nonprotectionist solutions to trade disputes.

I wish to thank the Babson College Board of Research and Robert Madden for financial support during the research stages of this study, and David Savage, Toshi Kinugawa and Ebru Ipecki, who provided valuable assistance in preparing the tables and graphs. Special thanks go to my wife, Tonya Price, for her expertise in electronic publishing and the preparation of the text for publication. I am also indebted to the Visiting Scholar's program at the U.S. Department of State for use of its facilities in pursuing this research project and debating it with many highly informed colleagues there. Several scholars from academia, government and law have contributed comments to various portions of the study, including Rachel McCulloch, Jeffrey Schott, Ingo Walter, Thomas Grennes, Gary Horlick, Steven Marks, Roberto Bonifaz, Robert McAuliffe, Henry Goldstein, Marshall Casse, William DeWald, Jane Bradley, Richard Jones, Michael Ulan, Ken Abbott, Tracy Murray, and Gerald Rosen. The usual caveat applies: while I have benefited from their advice, I have not always taken it, so that any remaining errors in analysis or ignorance of policies and laws are my responsibility alone.

A final acknowledgment is due to two GATT scholars whose deaths have left the world much poorer in its ability to understand the workings of the world trading system. Jan Tumlir, formerly director of research at the GATT Secretariat, and Gerard Curzon, formerly professor of international economics at the Graduate Institute of International Studies at the University of Geneva, jointly conducted seminars on trade policy at which I received my first useful lessons in the political economy of trade and the GATT. Any contribution that I can offer to the understanding of voluntary export restraint and its role in the GATT system is due largely to their lessons and influence on my thinking. It is only appropriate that this study be gratefully dedicated to their memory.

CHAPTER 1

Export Restraint, the New Protectionism, and the Gatt's Dilemma

In the field of trade...discrimination in any form is likely to lead to more discrimination...in the long run all countries will suffer from the inevitable distortion of trade patterns which will arise out of discrimination.... [T]he only way to prevent a country or a pair of countries from making the move that will set off this chain reaction is to obtain the simultaneous pledge of the largest possible number of trading countries that they will not discriminate against each other.

—John W. Evans, Director of Commercial Policy, GATT, 1956

The Problem

History has shown, and current experience continues to show, that significant shifts in the competitive structure of the world economy create political pressure for trade restrictions as groups with incomes tied to the economic performance of declining industries seek to protect their wages and profits through reduced import competition. Corden (1984a) has noted that trade policy in recent years has focused mainly on the "conservative social welfare function," assuring that economic events do not reduce the welfare of specific groups, particularly those with political power, even at the expense of overall national economic welfare. In the era prior to the signing of the General Agreement on Tariffs and Trade (GATT), "old protectionism" was usually carried out with the use of directly imposed tariffs and import quotas. With the elimination of tariffs and quotas by the GATT as the major instruments of trade policy, however, it has become evident that surges in protectionist sentiment tend to lead to more innovative means of trade restriction. Crisis conditions and disorderly international markets in the industries mentioned above have created particularly strong protectionist feelings in the United States and the European Community (EC), causing trade officials there to turn increasingly to voluntary export restraints (VERs) as an alternative to the traditional instruments of trade control. In this manner, VERs and related devices have become the most significant policy tools of the "new protectionism."

Yet, notwithstanding its designation as a new trade policy device, VER agreements represent only a new form of long-standing protectionist practices, "old wine in new bottles" as Bhagwati (1985) has put it. Their appearance is part of what Jan Tumlir called the "cycle of learning and unlearning" that has characterized trade relations in this century: lessons of the economic and political damage of escalating protectionism seem to be acknowledged for a time, particularly in the wake of catastrophic events, and then forgotten. Specifically, VERs and other instruments of induced export restraint embody many of the disturbing characteristics of the protectionist mentality that have often dominated national trade policy formulation in the past, and which the GATT signatories had hoped to control. First, they represent a renewal of national tendencies toward mercantilism, the belief that national wealth is automatically enhanced by reducing imports. The political context of VER agreements suggests that governments regard the successful negotiation of reduced foreign deliveries to their markets as a victory vis-à-vis the foreigner. Closely linked with this idea is the concept that national power is directly related to the country's balance on current account: surplus countries are strong; deficit countries are weak. A powerful country can and should, according to this philosophy, compel foreigners to reduce exports to its markets in order to redress a trade deficit. The use of political and economic power is a necessary ingredient in concluding most export restraint agreements. More than two hundred years of trade theory, beginning with Adam Smith's *Wealth of Nations*, have attempted to dispel the mercantilist arguments with the evidence of the benefits of the efficient allocation of resources under a liberal trade regime, along with the political advantages of a system of open trade. VERs show in renewed form the tenacity and political appeal of protectionism.[1]

Secondly, VER agreements reveal the traditional preference, especially of large countries or trading blocs, for discriminatory trade policies.[2] Governments have been particularly vulnerable to this type of thinking in times of domestic or international economic instability, or when shifts in the international structure of competition result in increased import competition from specific countries. By reducing trade relations to a set of bilateral agreements, individual countries can be isolated for rewards or punishment while restricting the scope of potential retaliation. Again, political power is given an enticingly larger role when (especially smaller) trading partners can be singled out and, if need be, bullied into agreements deemed desirable by the importing country. The GATT, citing the history of escalating protectionism, reduced trade, and lower economic welfare associated with discriminatory trade policy regimes, consciously sought to replace them wherever possible with a multilateral system of rules, but VERs have successfully evaded these provisions.

Finally, VER agreements show the underlying fascination of governments with managed trade, particularly with cartel-like agreements. Like any other market-driven phenomenon, international trade is not always predictable, and left unrestricted thus forces national economies to adjust to changing conditions of supply, demand, competitiveness, and comparative advantage. Adjustment may involve transitional unemployment in declining sectors, regionally focused hardship, and embarrassing plant closures—events that, to be sure, can result from several types of market disturbances, not just from imports. Yet it is tempting for governments to attempt to remove the sting of international competition by negotiating market-sharing agreements with foreign firms if this relieves the immediate political distress of adjustment. VERs typically involve such a restriction on competition by requiring the exporting country to form a cartel among existing export-supplying firms, the market effects of which will be shown in chapter 2. Yet this seemingly modest initial attempt to manage markets may result in the expansion of the VER to include an entire network of exporting countries and increasingly detailed and tightened product coverage, creating a worldwide export cartel. Such cartels in manufactured goods had already been attempted in the 1920s and 1930s, particularly in steel, to the detriment of economic welfare and trade relations. Their revival through VERs bodes ill for the consumer and for world economic growth.

Defining Export Restraint

Voluntary export restraint is a form of trade restriction distinguished by the fact that the exporting country controls the limitation on trade. Such action is termed *voluntary* in the sense that the exporting country formally imposes it unilaterally and could technically modify or eliminate it. In reality, however, a country typically restrains exports under a VER agreement only in response to pressures from an importing country. In its most visible form, export restraint occurs as a bilaterally negotiated agreement, even if it is the exporting country that announces the policy. The announcement of ostensibly voluntary restraint by the exporter alone has variously served the purpose of allowing the importing country to deny that it has induced the action as a protectionist policy and providing it with a legal fiction that helps it to avoid possible charges of antitrust violations. Even when formal export restraint is imposed unilaterally by the exporting country (known as autolimitation in GATT parlance), it is typically the result of protectionist pressures in the importing country. In any case, the political economy of export restraint agreements, as will be shown in chapter 2, makes clear that truly independent and voluntary export restraint would not typically require any agreement with importing countries, since the exporters or their government would initiate such profit-maximizing measures on their own.

Export restraint may take other forms of a less formal nature, however. Export forecasts, import surveillance, price monitoring, bilateral consultations, industry-to-industry arrangements, and import licensing requirements, for example, provide a framework for monitoring deliveries to an import market from a specific exporter, with the clear implication that surges in deliveries may lead to more drastic action (Kostecki 1987). Export restraint may also take the form of an agreement on minimum prices. Finally, the enforcement and administration of antidumping, countervailing duty, and other trade laws, as well as threatened trade legislation, may also induce exporters to restrain deliveries through their intimidating effects, a subject to be discussed in more detail in chapters 4 and 5. In this context, governments can induce export restraint through the announcement of reference or trigger prices, which establish criteria for avoiding unfair trade investigations. Often, such informal means of induced export restraint are precursors to formal export restraint arrangements.

Historical Background

The earliest documented use of export restraint as a tool of commercial policy occurred in the early 1930s, as Belgium and France transferred the rights to issue licenses on goods subject to bilaterally negotiated quotas to exporters (Heuser 1939, 112). These arrangements were an extension of the industrial ententes, or international industry-to-industry cartel arrangements that were popular during the period and enjoyed the assent and at times cooperation of governments. Supporters of such collusive agreements viewed them as a means of establishing order in the chaotic markets of the 1930s. They covered a variety of agricultural and manufactured goods, as well as coal, but were not without controversy, as importers often protested the transfer of the quota profits to the foreign exporter. Even during these early export restraint arrangements, contemporary observers recognized the dangers to consumer welfare of promoting export cartels in this manner (ibid., 114-15, 119).

The first major use of voluntary export restraint as a means of settling a trade dispute appears to be the agreement concluded in 1936 limiting Japanese textile exports to the United States. Japanese deliveries of cotton textiles had risen sharply from 1.22 million square yards in 1929 to 7.29 million square yards in 1936. By the end of that year, bookings for 1937 had already reached 150 million square yards. At this point American textile producers sought a quick means by which to stem the surge in Japanese competition. Negotiations between representatives of producers from both countries, which were concluded in late 1936, resulted in a gentlemen's agreement between the two national industries (Dietrich 1940; Farley 1940) and apparently had the consent of both governments. It set yearly limits of 155 million square yards of cotton goods deliveries in 1937 and 100 million square yards in 1938. In late 1938 the agreement was renewed for two more years, allowing for 100 million square yards per year in 1939 and 1940. Separate quota agreements were also concluded on cotton rugs, velveteens and corduroys, and cotton hosiery (Farley 1940).

Institutional factors also appeared to play a significant role in the Japanese textile VER. The United States had changed the legislative basis for commercial policy in the Reciprocal Trade Agreements Act of 1934, which transferred direct control over tariff policy and trade negotiations from Congress to the executive branch. The circumstances of the textile negotiations suggest that the VER agreement was motivated at least in part by the desire of U.S. trade officials to isolate the textile issue from congressional protectionist pressure, which could have unraveled the general reforms of the 1934 trade act. This "nesting" aspect of VERs (Aggarwal 1985), in which the bilaterally negotiated trade restriction is designed to carve out a politically sensitive trade dispute in order to protect the larger trading system from protectionist attack, would re-emerge twenty years later in the series of textile agreements with Japan and less-developed countries, which were negotiated outside normal GATT disciplines.[3]

Japan negotiated similar agreements with Burma (Dietrich 1940), India, Australia, and the United Kingdom during the 1930s. The arrangements reportedly involved the quid pro quo of tariff reduction, pledges not to raise tariffs, and in some cases reciprocal barter agreements. In the case of India, for example, the Japanese export limit was dependent on levels of Japanese purchases of Indian goods (Farley 1940). This was another version of the bilateral clearing arrangement that was a popular aspect of trade policy during the economic turmoil of the 1930s.

Bhagwati (1986) suggests that the concept of export restraint is closely connected to the Japanese cultural trait of avoiding confrontation by means of self-initiated compromise. While it has become clear over the years that the incentive structure of export restraint operates equally well outside Japanese culture, it is noteworthy that export restraint as a tool of commercial diplomacy appears to have developed primarily in Japan. An earlier precedent for export restraint had already appeared in 1907, when diplomatic tension between the United States and Japan arose over the large influx of Japanese immigrants to California. Anti-Japanese sentiment had developed there due to a combination of labor competition and racism, creating conflicts remarkably similar to those that would arise over trade decades later. Public anger had given rise to threats of unilateral actions by local authorities, including a ban on admitting Japanese immigrants to public schools. The crisis was finally settled when President Theodore Roosevelt concluded a gentlemen's agreement with the Japanese government limiting the number of passports issued to Japanese emigrants to U.S. territory (Esthus 1966). Through "voluntary" emigration restraint, Japan thus avoided the unilateral restrictions on immigration that were imposed on other countries in the years before general immigration quotas of the 1920s.

Yet the historical record of voluntary export restraint goes on to show that such cooperative trade agreements in no way represented lasting solutions to the underlying conflicts they sought to resolve. Japanese trade policy resorted to such agreements in the face of increasing frustration in gaining access to export markets, especially in Asia. The resulting tensions contributed to the rise of economic and territorial expansionism in Japan, culminating in the Japanese military aggression of the 1930s and 1940s.

The worldwide state of suspicion and instability caused by discriminatory trade agreements in the 1930s, based on jealously guarded bilateral pacts and the often rigid exclusion of competitive goods through quotas, can be linked in part to the deterioration of diplomatic relations that led to World War II. This fact was not lost on the founders of the GATT. After the cessation of hostilities, the allies had fresh memories of the disastrous international economic policies of the previous decade, and sought in the International Monetary Fund (IMF) and the GATT to establish institutions guaranteeing international monetary stability and a framework of multilateral trade policy rules to maintain open trading markets, respectively. Nondiscrimination and transparency were to provide the foundation of an international economic order.

VERs and the GATT

Export Restraint and the Content of the GATT

The GATT, concluded in 1947, is a set of rules governing trade policies among its members. Its provisions define the constraints under which its members (contracting parties) can impose trade restrictions, and therefore have played a large role in the development of the VER as a tool of trade policy. The main activities of the GATT, for example, have been to reduce the tariff levels applicable to trade among its members. In trade negotiations, each country must submit schedules of concessions (tariff reductions) and is bound by those schedules according to the provisions of articles I and XXVIII. These provisions effectively prohibit GATT members from unilaterally raising tariffs, and have thereby severely restricted tariff increases as a policy option when confronted with pressure for trade restrictions.

Even in cases where a contracting party can claim that emergency action to restrict imports is necessary, the GATT rules impose strict requirements on any increase in trade barriers, including thoroughgoing consultations, compensation to affected exporters, and a nondiscriminatory application of the emergency protection measure. In this regard, article XIX, the escape clause, was so designed to make any increase in trade restrictions a politically expensive proposition. Any such action would have to be applied across the board, to all imports, thereby increasing the scope for compensation. For these reasons the original architects of the GATT clearly expected the escape clause to be used only on rare occasions.

In addition, the GATT calls for the general elimination of quantitative restrictions in article XI, subject to certain exceptions, principally in cases of balance-of-payments deficits (art. XII and XVIIIB). Since import quotas were the major form of quantitative restriction in use at the time the GATT was negotiated, early GATT activity focused on the removal of existing import quotas and a ban on the introduction of new import quotas. This constraint thus also generally eliminated import quotas from the arsenal of acceptable trade policy devices.

A preliminary examination of VER agreements shows that they are designed to circumvent the GATT restrictions on the use of tariff increases and import quotas, and on the severe constraints of the escape clause (although in some cases, VER-type agreements have also been concluded under escape clause actions). Yet their increasing popularity has undermined the basic principles of the GATT. A closer examination of certain GATT articles reveals these conflicts. For example, the single most important idea of the GATT is nondiscrimination, set forth in article I, the most favored-nation (MFN) clause, which reads in part:

> any advantage, favor, privilege or immunity granted by any contracting party to any product originating in or destined for any other country shall be accorded immediately and unconditionally to the like product originating in or destined for the territories of all other contracting parties.

In other words, access to the import market of any contracting party by any other contracting party shall be accorded on a nondiscriminatory basis; all members of the GATT club receive the same treatment as the most-favored nation. This principle is so central to the entire foundation of the GATT that it can be amended only by a unanimous vote of the contracting parties.

Another important aim of the GATT is the general elimination of quantitative restrictions, found in article XI:

> No prohibitions or restriction other than duties, taxes or other charges, whether made effective through quotas, import or export licences or other measures, shall be instituted or maintained by any Contracting Party on the importation of any product of the territory of any other Contracting Party or on the exportation or sale for export of any product destined for the territory of any other Contracting Party.

The purpose of eliminating all nontariff barriers (NTBs) was tied to the issue of transparency. Aside from limiting trade restrictions to the form most compatible with the price system and least damaging to economic welfare, article XI also had the practical purpose of establishing a system of straightforward, visible means of government intervention in trade that would facilitate negotiations for reductions in the level of protection.

VER agreements contradict the MFN principle and the goal of eliminating NTBs by establishing a quantitative trade restriction that discriminates against certain exporters. They do not violate the letter of the GATT insofar as the GATT only prohibits discriminatory import tariffs and quotas in restricting foreign trade entering the country. A close reading of article XIII (on the nondiscriminatory administration of quantitative restrictions), however, casts further doubt on the validity of VERs under the GATT:

No prohibition or restriction shall be applied by any contracting party on the importation of any product of the territory of any other Contracting Party or on the exportation of any product destined for the territory of any other Contracting Party, unless the importation of the like product of all third countries or the exportation of the like product to all third countries is similarly prohibited or restricted.

Strict adherence to the letter of article XIII would appear to prohibit any contracting party from limiting exports except on an MFN basis. The original purpose of this provision was to prevent countries from independently restricting exports in a discriminatory manner, to the detriment of the targeted importing country. Since the GATT did not envision the widespread use of export restrictions as a means to satisfy protectionist demands of the importing country, this rule has conveniently been ignored in VER agreements. In fact, enforcement of this provision would hold the victim of VER agreements (the exporting country) guilty of the infraction, whereas in reality it is the importing country that is responsible for causing it. Article XIII does not, therefore, hold much promise as a means by which VER agreements can be controlled.

GATT and the Paradigm of Discrimination

Among the many frustrations of the early GATT negotiations was the difficult task of eliminating the vestiges of discriminatory and quantitative restrictions. The provisions banning quantitative restrictions allowed exceptions in some cases for agricultural goods and severe balance-of-payments deficits (art. XII and XVIIIB). The agricultural exemptions from quantitative restrictions, in particular, have haunted the GATT ever since its inception, and still represent a major source of conflict among its members. Thus, political constraints have compromised the original ambitious purposes of the GATT from its very beginnings.

Yet other sources of the erosion of GATT principles are contained in the GATT itself, especially regarding the principle of nondiscrimination. While the erosion of the MFN principle has reached critical proportions only in recent years, the content of the GATT itself has helped to undermine it in at least three ways: (1) through the stated exceptions to the MFN rule, especially in articles VI, XVIIIB, and XXIV; (2) through the view of trade-liberalizing measures as concessions and the emphasis on reciprocity; and (3) by creating the prohibitively high political cost of escape clause protection.

The GATT compromised the principle of nondiscrimination in several instances. The most prominent general exceptions to MFN dealt with the formation of customs unions and free trade areas in article XXIV and the special treatment of less-developed countries (LDCs) in part IV, which provided the underpinnings for the Generalized System of Preferences (GSP). The GSP provides for preferential tariff treatment toward less-developed countries and operates under a waiver of GATT article I (Pomeranz 1988, 11-13). In addition, LDCs enjoy special and differential treatment in their own import policies. Article XVIIIB, which allows LDCs to impose selective trade restrictions for balance-of-payments reasons, has been a conduit for openly discriminatory, protectionist policies and represents a serious source of trade friction between the developed and less-developed members of the GATT. In addition, article VI allows discriminatory tariffs to be applied in cases of dumping and export subsidies. Further exceptions to MFN are contained in articles XIV (rules for deviating from MFN for balance-of-payments purposes) and XXXV (nonapplication of the GATT to particular countries, to be discussed in greater detail below).

In defense of the drafters of the GATT, these measures served the purpose of providing a political modus vivendi that was probably necessary to achieve a consensus on the final document and the subsequent adherence of new GATT members. In particular, customs unions could be viewed as a vehicle for movement toward freer trade—at least in an institutional sense—and the GSP and article XVIII made GATT membership more attractive to less-developed countries. The various exceptions to MFN based on balance of-payments problems or other special circumstances provided contingency measures that would, in theory, not interfere with the general application of the MFN principle. Article VI formed the basis of the widely accepted rules of fair trade that were politically necessary in many countries to gain domestic consensus on more open trade.

At the same time, the GATT's tolerance for discrimination, however narrowly it attempted to circumscribe it, has weakened its ability to prevent the signatories from violating Article I in practice. If article VI can allow discriminatory tariffs against unfairly traded goods, it is but a small step to the conclusion that discrimination should also be allowable against unfairly disruptive imports. And if the GATT allows countries to favor certain trading partners in customs union or free trade arrangements, is it not also justifiable to show preference toward traditional trading partners by using VERs to restrict the access of newly competitive interlopers in your domestic market? The resulting inner conflict within the GATT appeared most clearly in its 1959 decision to use market disruption as a criterion for protection in textiles trade (Dam 1970, 269-300).

Similarly, the GATT's emphasis on reciprocity and references to tariff concession also created an internal contradiction by misstating the gains-from-trade argument. Even as economic theory shows the benefits of unilateral tariff reductions, the GATT's language suggests that the benefits are actually sacrifices, and has reinforced the traditional mercantilist view that access to domestic markets is the property right of governments, to be shared only in exchange for reciprocal measures. This makes it all the easier for governments to rationalize a withdrawal of concessions as a reasonable response to any increase in imports that heightens the political cost of the trade agreement. If import disruption can be traced to specific exporters, it then appears equally reasonable to discriminate against them in applying trade restrictions.

The principal means within the GATT of holding the long-standing and deep-rooted mercantilist tendencies of governments at bay fell to article XIX, the escape clause. The purpose of this provision was to act as the main safety valve for protectionist pressure, guaranteeing general adherence to GATT principles while allowing for special cases of temporary protection. As noted earlier, it is generally accepted that trade protection under article XIX must be administered in a nondiscriminatory fashion, and when combined with the requirements of an injury test and compensation to affected exporters, this means that GATT-consistent protection comes at a high political price. The rarity of escape clause action suggests that this price is usually prohibitive. In view of these constraints placed by the GATT on trade policy, surges in protectionist pressures have consequently followed paths of lower resistance to the VER solution, highlighting the failure of article XIX to fulfill its designated role as a safety valve.

In retrospect, it is clear that the role of the MFN principle in trade relations under the GATT could be only as strong as the political will to maintain it. It was, perhaps, too much to expect that a broad, contractual arrangement among countries, in itself, could provide the means by which governments could shield trade policies from the eventual incursion of mercantilism and special interest politics. In the early postwar period, to be sure, the environment for enlightened trade policy was unusually good. Postwar recovery and rapid economic growth, with the (usually) self-confident United States dominating the world economy and leading the way on trade negotiations, facilitated the political recognition of the gains from trade among GATT member countries. Yet the international consensus on the GATT's objective of trade liberalization, and on the MFN principle in particular, began to weaken as the postwar recovery ran its course and structural change in the world economy revealed new patterns of comparative advantage. By abandoning the systematic rules of a world trading order for VER regimes in politically sensitive products, governments had to negotiate the minutiae of international export cartel arrangements from one crisis period to the inevitable next.

VERs in the GATT Period

In defense of the political compromises on the MFN clause, it can be said that for practical purposes they have not generally prevented the overall level of protection among GATT members from declining, which after all was the underlying goal of the GATT. During the first two decades of the GATT, however, serious problems of consistent and multilateral adherence to GATT principles arose over the fears of many countries regarding potential trade disruption, especially from Japan, a situation that enhanced the political importance of VERs. Article XXXV allows a contracting party to remain in the GATT and yet suspend GATT in its trade relationship with particular countries. Several countries invoked this article against Japan (Curzon 1965, 37). In addition, Italy "grandfathered" a VER agreement on Japanese automobile deliveries to its market (OECD 1985, 32). The resurgence in Japanese textile exports in the 1950s renewed protectionist sentiment in the United States, Canada, and Europe and caused these countries to go outside the GATT framework to limit Japanese exports. Export restraint agreements were, in fact, the quid pro quo required by several (especially European) countries for a disinvocation of GATT article XXXV (Patterson 1966, 285-300).

Japan continued to be perceived as the disruptive exporter throughout the postwar period, and the ensuing diplomatic efforts to create a cooperative method of trade restriction in the GATT era led to the establishment and increasingly widespread use of export restraint as a tool of commercial policy. The United States negotiated an informal textile export restraint agreement with Japan in 1956, which was in effect from 1957 to 1961. This arrangement was followed by the Short-Term and Long-Term Agreements negotiated by the United States, Canada, and Europe with Japan and other textile-producing countries. These export restraint agreements were the forerunners of the present Multifibre Arrangement (MFA).

The textile VER agreements were significant because they represented the first major instance of the abandonment of GATT principles in a dispute over trade in manufactured goods. In a declining sector of the established industrial countries, protectionist sentiment was strong enough to override the discipline of GATT rules and focus trade restrictions against specific countries with increasing comparative advantage in the protected good. Since most GATT members had actually welcomed the discipline and international obligations of GATT rules as a useful buffer between domestic protectionist pressure and protectionist policies, the textiles case suggested that further measures to evade GATT rules would occur in disputes over trade in politically sensitive industries. The targets of such discriminatory measures would generally be those countries with emerging comparative advantage. The policy tool would be voluntary export restraint.

Following textiles, the next major industrial sector that came under protectionist pressure was steel. The United States concluded its first set of steel VER agreements with Japan and the EC in 1968, and by 1984 most steel trade was covered by a web of VERs imposed by the United States, the EC, and other countries. From the limited coverage of early VER agreements, renewed export pacts have tended to increase the scope of restrictions and restrain trade in greater and greater detail. In the case of textiles and steel, in fact, the VER agreement networks have represented virtual cartels of international trade in those products, covering most exports of most major suppliers to the world market.[4]

The proliferation of VERs within product categories and to other industries in recent years is remarkable. A 1990 GATT study (GATT 1990a) counted some 249 gray area export restraint agreements among GATT members in force in September 1989, covering such diverse sectors as steel, footwear, automobiles, machine tools, agricultural products, electronics goods, textiles, clothing, and other products. Aside from formal quantitative VERs and orderly marketing arrangements, the GATT tally of export restraint devices included export forecasts, discriminatory import systems, nongovernmental industry-to-industry agreements, and unilateral export restraint by governments. This large number of discriminatory trade restrictions did not include price undertakings to terminate antidumping actions, arrangements that often have the character of export restraint, as will be shown in chapter 4. It also does not include the thousands of highly detailed quotas under the MFA, which are technically within the ambit of the GATT, since the original MFA negotiations occurred under GATT auspices. Of the 249 export restraint measures, 36 (14 percent) were long-standing arrangements that had begun before 1975, but 105 (42 percent) had begun since 1985 (GATT 1990a, 21). While most (130) measures restricted exports from developed countries, export restraint arrangements tended to affect LDC (82) and East European (37) exports disproportionately, since the volume of exports from these countries was less than one-third the size of developed country exports. The GATT report also noted that 60 percent of the existing export restraint arrangements at that time had no expiration date (ibid., 12).

Recent events reveal the protean nature of export restraint arrangements. Despite efforts to eliminate formal VERs in steel, for example, the trade policy crisis in this sector persists. The United States ended its formal steel export restraint program in March 1992, but U.S. domestic producers filed unfair trade petitions almost as soon as the quotas expired, and some form of continued export restraint is likely, as will be shown in chapter 6. Similarly, VERs covering automobile exports to the United States and the EC have changed shape over the years. While the United States has officially opposed the continuation of Japanese automobile export restraint to its market since 1985, Japanese automobile exporters and the Japanese government have concluded that unilateral export restraint is still necessary as a means of forestalling protectionist legislation and unfair trade law petitions in the United States. Continued protectionist pressure from the U.S. automobile industry prompted the Japanese government to reduce its informal automobile export restraint policy from 2.3 million to 1.65 million units from March 1992 to March 1993 (*Financial Times*, 20 March 1992). The EC has consolidated national automobile export restraint measures administered by its member countries against Japan into an EC-wide residual quota, while the issue of whether to include automobiles produced in Japanese transplant facilities in EC in the quota is still hotly debated.

TABLE 1. Voluntary Restraints, Surveillance and Similar Measures Affecting Imports: Situation as of Mid-1990

Exporter/Importer	Product	Measures
Agriculture		
All suppliers/EC	Sheep/goat meat	VER/duty free access
Argentina, Australia, Chile, New Zealand, South Africa/EC	Dessert apples	Export forecasts
Korea Rep./EC (Italy)	Frozen squid	Reference prices
Australia/U.S.	Bovine meat	VRA on export volume
New Zealand/U.S.	Bovine meat	VRA on export volume
Footwear		
Korea Rep., Taiwan/EC	Footwear(excl. slippers)	Prior EC surveillance/VER
China/France	Slippers and sandals	Autolimitation
Korea, Rep. of /Ireland	Footwear	Industry-to-industry arrangement
Czech & Slovak Rep., Romania, Poland/ U.K.	Footwear	Industry-to-industry arrangement
Korea Rep. /U.S.	Footwear	Autolimitation
Textiles		
Bulgaria/EC	MFA textiles/clothing	VERs (1987–91)
Soviet Union/EC	MFA textiles/clothing	VERs (1987–91)
Japan/EC	Certain textiles/clothing	Export ceilings[a]
Cyprus/EC	Certain textiles/clothing	Informal restraint
Egypt/EC	Certain textiles/clothing	Informal restraint
Malta/EC	Certain textiles/clothing	Informal restraint
Morocco/EC	Certain textiles/clothing	Informal restraint
Tunisia/EC	Certain textiles/clothing	Informal restraint
Turkey/EC	Certain textiles/clothing	Informal arrangement with Turkish manufacturers
Yugoslavia/EC	Certain textiles/clothing	Informal restraint arrangements
Chile, Bolivia, Paraguay Honduras, Venezuela, Costa Rica, Cuba, Ecuador, El Salvador, Nicaragua/EC	Certain textiles/clothing	Exchange of letters

(*continued*)

TABLE 1—*Continued*

Exporter/Importer	Product	Measures
El Salvador/U.S.	Cotton yarn	Export quotas
Fiji/U.S.	Cotton, man-made fiber	Export quotas
Haiti/U.S.	Cotton, man-made fiber	Export quotas
Mauritius./U.SA	Certain cotton and non-MFA textile products	Export quotas
Nepal/U.S.	Certain cotton goods	Export quotas
Nigeria/U.S.	Cotton goods	Export quotas
Soviet Union/U.S.	Cotton sheeting and printed cotton cloth	Export quotas
Taiwan/U.S.	Textiles and apparel	Export quotas
Trinidad & Tobago/U.S.	Selected textiles/apparel	Guaranteed access levels
UAR/U.S.	Selected textiles/apparel	Export quotas
Steel and Steel Products		
Austria/EC	Steel	Consultation mechanism
Brazil/EC	Pig iron and steel	VER/price monitoring
Bulgaria/EC	Steel	VER/price monitoring
Czech & Slovak Rep./EC	Steel	VER/price monitoring
Finland/EC	Steel	Consultation mechanism
Hungary/EC	Steel	VER/price monitoring
Japan/EC	Steel	Export cartels
Poland/EC	Steel	VER/price monitoring
Romania/EC	Steel	VER/price monitoring
Sweden/EC	Steel	Consultation mechanism
All other suppliers/EC	Steel	Basic Price Mechanism[b]
EC/U.S.	Steel & steel products	VRAs[c]
Australia/U.S.	Steel & steel products	VRAs[c]
Austria/U.S.	Steel & steel products	VRAs[c]
Brazil/U.S.	Steel & steel products	VRAs[c]
China/U.S.	Steel & steel products	VRAs[c]
Czech and Slovak Federal Republic/U.S.	Steel & steel products	VRAs[c]
EC/U.S.	Steel & steel products	VRAs[c]
Finland/U.S.	Steel & steel products	VRAs[c]
German D.R./U.S.	Steel & steel products	VRAs[c]

TABLE 1—*Continued*

Exporter/Importer	Product	Measures
Hungary/U.S.	Steel & steel products	VRAs[c]
Japan/U.S.	Steel & steel products	VRAs[c]
Korea Rep./U.S.	Steel & steel products	VRAs[c]
Mexico/U.S.	Steel & steel products	VRAs[c]
Poland/U.S.	Steel & steel products	VRAs[c]
Romania/U.S.	Steel & steel products	VRAs[c]
Trinidad & Tobago/U.S.	Steel & steel products	VRAs[c]
Venezuela/U.S.	Steel & steel products	VRAs[c]
Yugoslavia/U.S.	Steel & steel products	VRAs[c]
Canada/U.S.	Steel & steel products	Export monitoring/ export permits[d]
Machinery		
Japan/EC	Machine tools for planing, gear cutting, etc.	EC surveillance/export monitoring/moderation
Japan/EC	Machining centers	EC surveillance/export monitoring/moderation
Japan/EC	NC lathes	EC surveillance/export monitoring/moderation
Japan/EC	Forklift trucks	EC surveillance/export monitoring/moderation
Japan/EC	Ball bearings	Export restraints[a]
Japan/EC (France)	Machine tools (machining centers, NC lathes)	Restraint arrangement
Japan/EC	Electropneumatic drills	EC surveillance
Japan/U.S.	Machine tools	VRA: market share limits for each category
Taiwan/U.S.	Machine tools	VRA: market share limits for each category
Brazil/U.S.	Machine tools	U.S. request for restraint
Germany/U.S.	Machine tools	U.S. request for restraint
Italy/U.S.	Machine tools	U.S. request for restraint
Korea Rep./U.S.	Machine tools	U.S. request for restraint
Singapore/U.S.	Machine tools	U.S. request for restraint
Spain/U.S.	Machine tools	U.S. request for restraint
Sweden/U.S.	Machine tools	U.S. request for restraint

(continued)

TABLE 1—*Continued*

Exporter/Importer	Product	Measures
Switzerland/U.S.	Machine tools	U.S. request for restraint
U.K./U.S.	Machine tools	U.S. request for restraint

Electrical and Electronic Household Equipment

Japan/EC	Color TV sets	EC surveillance/ export monitoring
Japan/EC	Color TV sets	EC surveillance/ export monitoring
Japan/EC	Video tape recorders	EC surveillance/ export monitoring
Korea Rep./EC	Microwave ovens	Export moderation (industry)
Korea Rep./EC	Video tape recorders	EC surveillance/export monitoring/moderation
Japan/EC (Germany)	Color TV sets	Export moderation
Japan/EC (France)	TV tubes	Industry-to-industry arrangement
Japan/EC (France)	Video tape recorders	Industry-to-industry arrangement
Japan/EC	Personal computers	EC surveillance
Japan/U.S.	Semiconductors	Bilateral gov't arrangement on dumping/market access to Japan
Korea Rep./U.S.	VCRs, microwave ovens, TV sets (color/B&W)	Autolimitation: floor price & unit volume restraints

Road Motor Vehicles

Japan/EC	Passenger cars	EC surveillance/export monitoring
Japan/EC	Commercial vehicles	EC surveillance (light commercial vehicles)/ export monitoring
Japan/EC	Motorcycles	EC surveillance (machines > 380 cc) export monitoring
Japan/EC (UK)	Passenger/commercial/ 4-wh. drive vehicles	Industry-to-industry arrangement
Japan/EC (Belgium)	Automobiles	Price fixing subj. to admin. authorization
Japan/USA	Passenger cars	Autolimitation[e] (adjusted yearly)

TABLE 1—*Continued*

Exporter/Importer	Product	Measures
Japan/Canada	Automobiles	Informal understanding of export levels
Korea/Canada	Automobiles	Informal understanding of export levels
Other Products		
Japan/EC	Metal flatware	Export restraint[a]
Korea Rep./EC (Benelux countries)	Metal flatware	Industry-to-industry[f]
Singapore, Taiwan, Thailand/EC (France)	Umbrellas arrangements	Industry-to-industry
Japan/EC (UK)	Pottery	VERs
China/USA	Tungsten products	Orderly marketing arrangement
Korea Rep./USA	Stuffed toys, pianos, leather bags, fishing rods, tarpaulin products, brassware	Autolimitation

Source: GATT 1990b, 1991

[a] The EC Commission was unaware of these measures. [b] Basic prices establish minimum theshold prices below which antidumping or other restrictive measures may be taken. [c] VRAs were formally terminated in march 1992; however, antidumping and countervailing duty investigations commenced against many steel products shortly thereafter. [d] The U.S. government has denied knowledge of the existence of the Canadian measure. [e] The U.S. government is on record as opposing the coninuation of Japanese automobile restraint after bilateral VRAs ended in 1985. [f] The governments of Belgium and the Netherlands informed the GATT Secretariat that they were not aware of these measures.

Export restraint therefore represents a continuing threat to the GATT, not least because its tentacles can spread easily through administrative and trade law channels to restrict and distort trade in new and creative ways. The GATT has noted, for instance, that the four leading enforcers of antidumping laws, the United States, the EC, Canada, and Australia, initiated over 1,000 investigations from 1980 to 1989, resulting in over 500 cases of verifiable trade restrictions.[6] Many of the cases were terminated by VERs (Finger and Murray 1990), while others involved price undertakings that are a form of export restraint. Meanwhile, U.S.-Japan export restraint negotiations on semiconductors expanded to encompass market-opening measures imposed under threat of its revised section 301 statute. Such measures have already led to the phenomenon of "voluntary import expansion" (see Bhagwati 1988, 83-84), in which the foreign importing country diverts the source of imports in favor of suppliers from the threatening country. Export restraint regimes thus also threaten to expand to create general bilateral managed trade regimes covering both imports and exports, which would institutionalize discrimination and effectively destroy the GATT.

VERs and the Spread of Trade Disputes

The record of VERs shows that such agreements in their most damaging form typically begin as government policies with modest objectives and temporary scope, but grow into self-perpetuating institutional arrangements of increasingly restrictive measures. The early voluntary export restraint agreements with Japan on textiles in the 1930s and 1950s, for example, were viewed by many as a necessary expedient of commercial diplomacy that would not hamper the long-run adjustment of the industry according to market principles. The first multilateral textile arrangements, with their stated emphasis on market-driven adjustment and expanding trade opportunities, were similarly received with optimism that they would promote a world trading order based on comparative advantage (see Curzon 1965, 256-58). Yet once the quantitative, discriminatory machinery of restricting trade was in place, the framework was established that made possible perpetual protection in textiles, with more comprehensive product coverage, trade restrictions against new suppliers, new collective surge provisions, and lowered quota growth.

The path and evolution of particular export restraint agreements have been driven largely by the international conflict they engender. Because the agreements are by design discriminatory, restrained exporters will often seek to avoid the quota restrictions by transshipping the goods or by setting up production and exporting facilities in countries not covered by the agreement, devices that will be examined in chapter 2. Similarly, the discriminatory nature of the agreement creates opportunities for nonrestrained exporters to enter the protected market, a phenomenon that has been common in steel, textiles, and automobiles. Finally, VERs may cause trade diversion by redirecting exports from restrained suppliers toward unprotected markets, leading to surges in imports of the protected goods in third markets that remain open to trade. In addition to the resentment this phenomenon creates against the original restraint-inducing country, the rebounding exports tend to renew the protectionist cycle as the third country introduces trade restrictions. These market effects imply that, if the agreement is to have any restrictive force beyond the short term, and if it is to create an orderly world market, it must be extended to cover all major existing and potential suppliers of the protected good. Actual or feared trade diversion was a major factor establishing the comprehensive MFA in textiles and clothing, and this fear has also contributed heavily to the vitriolic trade relations in steel between the United States and the EC. The anticipation of rebounding automobile exports from Japan was especially significant in the early 1980s, when the VER negotiated by the United States with Japan prompted Canada and several EC countries to conclude preemptive export restraint arrangements of their own with Japan, or to tighten existing VER quotas. In this manner the initially limited protective measure often expands into a comprehensive global arrangement.

VERs have caused further distortion and conflict through their value-escalation effect—the shifting by exporters of deliveries from lower-value to higher-value items within the quota constraint. As this shift occurs, the latter product categories become subject to surges in the import market and new calls may arise for protection in the form of more detailed and rigidly defined quota categories. Value escalation has been observed in several export restraint agreements, most prominently in automobiles, textiles, clothing, and steel, leading to highly detailed export cartels in these products. Such value shifting is particularly troubling because of its regressive income distribution effects: by raising the price and limiting the supply of lower-value items, the welfare of poorer income groups is more severely damaged by VER agreements.

Induced export restraint has poisoned trade relations and the integrity of the GATT in other, more subtle ways. The use of trade law petitions and administration as a method of inducing export restraint has often undermined the original purpose of those measures, which was to act as a safety valve for protectionist pressure. This phenomenon has been most prominent in steel trade, where governments and domestic import-competing firms have used trade law harassment in order to get recalcitrant exporters to the export restraint bargaining table. A similar tactic was used by the U.S. semiconductor industry in getting the Japanese government to conclude an official price-floor agreement with the U.S. government in 1986, resulting in higher prices and lower exports to the United States. In many cases antidumping or countervailing duty petitions filed by domestic firms over trade in a narrowly defined product category have the effect of inducing exporters to negotiate VERs covering much broader categories. Trade law thereby loses credibility as a legitimate device regulating trade according to transparent, mutually recognized, and accepted rules. It is not that trade law petitions are without merit in each case, but only that strict trade law enforcement measures on unfairly traded goods would be less damaging to economic welfare than the VERs that often result from the petitions (see Levine 1985).

Finally, agreements on export restraint typically represent the assertion of political and economic power of larger over smaller countries, and thereby undermine the credibility of the GATT and of the goal of an orderly, nondiscriminatory world trading order. In addition, some exporting countries, particularly Japan and the newly industrializing countries (NICs) have welcomed VERs as a means of locking in market shares, to the detriment of market newcomers, particularly the poorer LDCs. In general, the reduced market risk associated with a guaranteed VER quota is particularly attractive to exporting countries whose comparative advantage in the product is declining and has tended to create a coalition for VER protection, especially in textiles. In this manner, VERs have locked many LDCs into a system of rigid, anticompetitive export market shares, in which earlier market entrants and larger exporters with more political clout are favored in market share allocations. The failed prospect of equal access to opportunities for trade and growth through GATT rules has been a bitter disappointment for many LDCs, and the promise of preferential treatment through the GSP and other GATT measures has been in many cases deprived of substance by VERs against goods in which LDCs have comparative advantage, particularly in textiles, clothing, and steel. Even though the VER provides some compensation to the exporter in the form of a transfer of the scarcity premium of the trade restriction, for many LDCs such agreements involve a net loss in welfare because they misallocate resources and stifle economies of scale and domestic competition (see Trela and Whalley 1988). The distortion of market signals through VERs only compounds the problem of deficient internal economic policies in many LDCs. Moreover, the politics of trade discrimination are based on the assertion of power; small countries almost never gain from these arrangements when compared to the outcome from a nondiscriminatory trading system based on multilateral rules.[7]

Summary

The use of voluntary export restraint in commercial relations first appeared as a means of isolating and defusing potentially damaging trade disputes in politically sensitive industries, allowing otherwise normal trade relations to proceed. Since World War II, developments in the GATT system have strongly influenced the evolution of export restraint. To the extent that such agreements removed textiles, automobiles and steel as roadblocks to GATT-sponsored multilateral trade negotiations and liberalization, for example, they have facilitated world trade. However, the market effects of negotiated, discriminatory quantitative restrictions have had implications for the world trading system that the early practitioners of VERs apparently did not contemplate. In short, export restraint agreements have tended to create a framework for extended protectionism and conflict. If the import disruption problem does not disappear in a timely manner, for example, the importing country is likely to seek a renewal of the VER. If nonrestrained countries enter the protected import market, or if restrained exporters shift deliveries toward higher value-added goods within the quota categories, then the importing country may decide that a more comprehensive, detailed, cartel-like agreement is necessary. If some exporters are reluctant to conclude such an agreement, then the importing country may use or manipulate unfair trade laws either to induce export restraint informally or to leverage a negotiated VER.

The increasing use of induced export restraint as an instrument of trade policy has often denied the most efficient or emerging suppliers their economically determined share of export markets; caused consumers, especially in low-income groups, to suffer welfare losses, stifled world economic growth, especially in the LDCs; and undermined trade relations through the constant renewal and perpetuation of trade disputes. The foregoing review of the history of export restraint has shown that the GATT, which attempted to establish a politically viable set of trade policy rules for multilateral trade liberalization, ironically contained the seeds of the poisoned growth of trade discrimination. While emphasizing the importance of the MFN clause, it not only left open the loophole of export restraint as a means of protectionism and provided in several articles the foundation for preferential and discriminatory treatment, but also tolerated the early departure from MFN in textiles.

With the entire GATT system under attack through the erosion of the MFN principle, the pertinent questions of the 1990s and beyond will focus on the basic principles of commercial diplomacy. Should the GATT's system of multilateralism be abandoned? Is the growing trend toward preferential trading blocs and discriminatory trade restrictions a sign that bilateralism should be the guiding principle of trade policy? Does managed trade provide the best means of securing both world and national economic growth and welfare? These questions are all intimately related to the political economy of voluntary export restraint.

In order to examine these larger questions, a closer examination of the economic and political processes that motivate the use of induced export restraint is necessary. The political economy of VERs and related devices involves the study of not only price, market share and welfare cost effects, but also political and legal institutions. The scope of study encompasses not only the importing countries, which are the usual focus of trade policy analysis, but also the exporting countries, particularly the LDCs, and third countries, which such arrangements affect in sometimes unexpected ways. The policy implications of export restraint analysis pertain not just to current optimal policy choices by governments but also to a larger systemic choice between trade regimes, which will ultimately affect the stability of the framework for future international trade relations. The study therefore turns to a more detailed analysis of the market effects and institutional framework of VERs, which will reveal something of their paradoxical nature: their attractiveness as a policy device and their tendency to perpetuate conflict.

Notes

1. For a discussion of the ideology of economic nationalism and its relationship with protectionism, see Gilpin (1987 chap. 2 and 5).

2. Pomfret (1988 chap. 2 and 3), contains a historical discussion of discriminatory commercial policies.

3. For a discussion of the significance of the 1934 trade act for U.S. trade policy, see Kelley (1963 cha. 2) and Haggard (1988). Aggarwal (1985) provides a detailed account of the systemic impact of the series of textile VERs beginning in 1955.

4. The Uruguay Round negotiations attempted to phase out the MFA by the early twenty-first century (see chap. 8), implying a continuation of managed trade in this sector for several years, at least. Steel VER arrangements were terminated by the United States and the EC in 1992, but unfair trade petitions were filed by domestic producers in these countries shortly thereafter, placing a return to open trade in doubt. See the further discussion in this chapter and in chapter 6.

5. The GATT had compiled detailed lists of export restraint arrangements on a periodic basis in its *Review of Developments in the Trading System* (see, for example, GATT 1987). These listings had become controversial in that governments of importing or exporting countries often did not acknowledge the existence of such measures, especially the less formal means of restraint and industry-to-industry arrangements. The GATT discontinued these comprehensive listings in 1989, and the 1990 GATT report cited in the text limited its discussion of existing export restraint measures to a tally of otherwise unspecified measures. Information on export restraint in the subsequent *Trade Policy Review* studies, compiled in table 1, were subject to more direct and thorough review by the respective contracting parties, and may therefore reflect a more limited—and less controversial—scope of export restraint activity. Aside from the expiration of some export restraint measures in the meantime, this factor may account for the smaller tally of VER arrangements contained in the *Trade Policy Review* series.

6. The protectionist effects of unfair trade law measures are often difficult to verify. In addition to formal duties and terminations based on price or quantity undertakings, cases may be withdrawn unilaterally by petitioners. Collusive international agreements to restrain trade may result. See chapters 4 and 5 for a more detailed discussion.

7. For an opposing view, see Yoffie (1983). Chapter 7 examines this argument in more detail.

CHAPTER 2

The Political Economy of Export
Restraint Agreements

The increasing popularity of VER agreements is due to the specific incentive structures established by the existing set of political and legal constraints imposed on governments in their trade relations. These constraints, as explained in chapter 1, discourage the use of tariffs and import quotas to restrict trade. Yet despite their attractiveness as an alternative to traditional global import controls, tariffs, and import quotas, VERs differ from them in three essential respects. First the VER restricts trade by artificially limiting supply rather than demand, as is the case with import restrictions (Takacs 1978). Furthermore, it is a discriminatory device insofar as export restraint is selective, which contrasts with the global application of general tariffs and quotas. Finally, it is a bilaterally negotiated restriction on trade rather than a unilateral measure applied by the importing government. These differences suggest that the interests of governments, producers, and consumers defined by a VER are also likely to differ in many respects from those of traditional import controls. In addition, the method of policy formation and implementation departs significantly from that of direct import controls.

This chapter sets out to identify the economic and political incentive structures that govern the use of export restraint. The first section establishes the VER's most important market effects, contrasting them with those of an import-equivalent tariff. The following section traces the influence of the VER's market effects and methods of implementation on the political and economic interests of groups affected by the agreement. The section "VER Policy Pitfalls and Their Implications" discusses the problems that importing governments face in pursuing policies of induced export restraint and their implications for further VER policy development. The final section offers a summary and considers the outlook for policies of export restraint.

VERs, Import Shares, and the Terms of Trade

A VER is a bilateral agreement that provides for an exporting country to restrict deliveries of a specific good to an importing country to a certain quantitative level over a specified period of time. There is, to be sure, some variation in the form that such agreements take in current usage. In the United States, for example, bilateral restraint agreements that take place in accordance with provisions of section 201 (escape clause action) are referred to as orderly marketing agreements (OMAs). Although OMAs therefore represent a formal GATT-sanctioned trade restriction, they differ little from the ad hoc agreements negotiated under separate authority by the executive branch, usually called voluntary restraint agreements (VRAs) or trade pacts on a product-by-product basis. The degree of negotiation and formal agreement involved in export restraint can vary, however. In some cases, no actual negotiations are acknowledged and the trade restriction is officially explained as a spontaneous action of the exporter. This characteristic was more common when there were still questions as to the legality of trade restraint agreements in the United States under antitrust law, which has largely been resolved in most cases by legislation that specifically gives powers to the executive branch to negotiate such agreements. Export restraint is also possible without any negotiations or discussion at all. In these cases, some threat of direct protectionist action usually causes the exporter to exercise unilateral restraint, a case of pure trade intimidation by the importing country. The analysis of unilateral restraint of this type does not differ in principle from that of a formal bilateral agreement, although in the absence of an actual agreement on quantitative limits the predictability and length of the act of export restraint may be lessened.

Regardless of the form it takes, the VER restricts trade by artificially restricting supply. Figure 1 compares the effects of a VER with those of an import-equivalent tariff under an import-disruption scenario. Consider an importing country with initial import supply curves AA' and BB' from exporting countries A and B, respectively, summing horizontally to the total import supply curve BUW. Initial free trade equilibrium occurs at output Q_0 and price P_0, with A and B supplying Q_a and Q_b, respectively.

Suppose now that producers in country B introduce cost-saving measures, shifting their import supply schedule to B_0B_0'. This would represent, for example, increasing comparative advantage of a NIC or of an LDC in the import market of a more advanced industrialized country. Total import supply is now represented by B_0VZ, expanding imports of Q_1 at the lower price P_1. Producers in B increase deliveries to Q_b', while A's deliveries drop to Q_a'. However, protectionist pressure accompanies the surge in imports, demanding a return to the original import level. Trade authorities yield to the pressure, and must decide between two alternative policy instruments: a tariff on all imports or a VER agreement with the disruptive supplier B.

A tariff $(P_0 - P_2)/P_2$ on all imports reduces total imports to the original level Q_0 while raising the domestic price back to P_0. In this case, the tariff lowers the import price, thus improving the importing country's terms of trade, since the importing country enjoys some monopsony power (in the limiting case of infinitely elastic import supply, the import price would be unaffected).

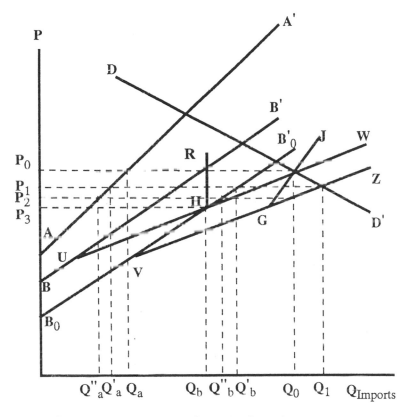

Fig. 1. VER vs. Tariff under an Import-Disruption Scenario

The resulting tariff brings total imports back to their original level by taxing suppliers in an equiproportionate manner, thus allowing B's expanded supply capability to determine its increased import share.

If on the other hand the importing country induces B to voluntarily restrain its exports, the same import level Q_0 and domestic price P_0 can be achieved, but with a different composition of import shares and a higher import price. The VER causes the exporting country's import supply curve to become vertical at the self-imposed limit. Thus country B's supply curve becomes B_0HR while country A's remains at AA'. The VER quota limit Q_b is set is in such a way that the sum of the two supply curves will pass through the point (Q_0, P_0), forming a new total import supply curve B_0VGJ. This construction requires that the target of induced restraint be that exporter or group of exporters whose price elasticity of supply is large enough to undercut the desired domestic price if it is not restrained.[1] Under the VER, country A regains its original import level Q_a while B must reduce its supply to the VER limit. It is clear that B's share in the import market has fallen when compared with either the free trade or tariff regimes, since $Q_b/Q_0 < Q_b'/Q_1$ and $Q_b/Q_0 < Q_b''/Q_0$.

The discriminatory impact of the VER on import shares can be traced to the differential supply responses it creates. The artificial restriction on B's import supply causes the premium on imports, and thereby on the import price, to rise (Takacs 1978). However, while B is restrained to supply Q_b at marginal resource cost P_3, A can move unrestrained along its supply curve until the full premium value of the imported good equals its marginal resource cost at (Q_a, P_0). The discriminatory effect is thus found in a divergence of the marginal resource cost of imports between the two suppliers: The rise in import price elicits increased supply from nonrestraining exporters, but not from participants in the VER. This phenomenon of import trade diversion is comparable to the differential supply response effect of a customs union and points to a decrease in world allocative efficiency as import supply from more efficient producers is reduced. The discriminatory operation of the VER and its efficiency effects also indicate the likely targets of any export restraint arrangement: cost-efficient, growing, and usually large foreign suppliers to a vulnerable domestic market.

The divergence between marginal resource costs of import supply also means, however, that the restraining exporters can sell their product at the higher import price and collect an economic rent on its reduced supply. In figure 1, the economic rent associated with country B's VER equals $(P_0 - P_3)Q_b$, while B loses $(1/2)(P_2 - P_3)(Q_b'' - Q_b)$. More important to the importing country is the fact that what would have been tariff revenues of $Q_0(P_0 - P_2)$ have been transferred to exporters in B in the amount[2] $Q_b(P_0 - P_2)$, and to exporters in A in the amount $(1/2)(Q_a - Q_a'')(P_0 - P_2) + Q_a''(P_0 - P_2)$, a gain in these suppliers' surplus, while the remaining $(1/2)(Q_a - Q_a'')(P_0 - P_2)$ is a deadweight loss.[3] The importing country thus suffers a deterioration in its terms of trade as a result of the VER agreement.

Political and Economic Interests

The analysis of the previous section revealed two significant differences in the market effects of a VER as compared with those of a global tariff (or global import quota): (1) the VER is discriminatory in that it lowers the import share of restraining suppliers, and (2) the VER causes a deterioration in the importing country's terms of trade, which leads to the creation of an economic rent transferred to the restraining exporters. A third crucial difference lies in the process by which the VER agreement is implemented. Unlike unilaterally imposed, openly administered tariffs, the VER is generally a negotiated trade restriction achieved by usually clandestine consultations and implied threats. In this regard, the agreement is not strictly speaking voluntary, since individual firms do not willingly restrict supply if market opportunities dictate otherwise. Genuinely voluntary export restraint implies the exercise of price-making power on international markets rather than negotiated agreements with foreign governments on export limits. In fact, a VER represents the successful effort of the importing country's government to induce export restraint as an alternative to unilateral import controls. Even the rent transfer to exporters resulting from the VER can only be obtained under an administrative system of collective action which, as will be shown below, is induced by the protectionist threats that surround the negotiations. In general, the threat of alternative action by the importing country stands behind the VER, although its severity and credibility may vary. The irony of the term voluntary in describing the agreement is thus reflected in the protectionist motives of the importing government and in its intention to ensure the exporters' adherence to the quota levels.

The distinguishing characteristics of voluntary export restraint offer some insight into its perceived advantages over tariffs and quotas as a protectionist device and provide a framework for understanding the political and economic interests involved in VER agreements. This section will examine the impact of these characteristics on the interests of trade authorities, exporting and import-competing producers, and import consumers.

Trade Authorities in the Importing Country

For trade authorities in the importing country, the principal advantage of a VER agreement stems from its ability to achieve protectionist ends at low political cost. Since the VER restricts trade on the exporting side, it allows trade authorities under protectionist pressure to circumvent GATT restrictions on quantitative (art. XI) and discriminatory (art. II, XIII) trade barriers. In addition, the VER provides an alternative to raising tariff levels, which are bound by GATT-sponsored trade negotiations.

Trade authorities also find political advantage in the discriminatory aspect of a VER agreement in that it allows the trade restriction to be targeted at disruptive suppliers. This tends to lower the cost of the restriction to the government of the importing country by isolating the potential retaliatory response of affected exporting countries. Imposing a global tariff in response to a surge in imports would risk retaliation from all supplying countries, whether or not they were a part of the disruptive surge in imports. The GATT's escape clause (art. XIX), for example, requires MFN treatment in any emergency trade restrictions taken, and is one reason that governments have gone outside the GATT to conclude discriminatory VER agreements.

The VER may also be superior to a GATT article XIX-based compensation scheme in terms of national economic welfare, although political factors are likely to be more important. Moore and Suranovic (1993) use a model of perfect competition to show, for example, that the VER is welfare superior to an equivalent[4] tariff compensation scheme when the reduction in the importing country's welfare due to the VER rent transfer is sufficiently small compared to the loss that would alternatively occur either from offsetting tariff reductions or from foreign protectionist retaliation. Notwithstanding the economic logic of such a strategy, government officials are probably more concerned with the political liabilities of article XIX, since the accompanying tariff concessions or foreign retaliation would raise the hackles of other domestic special interest groups among import-competing and exporting producers. Political economy considerations suggest that this factor, in which VERs have the advantage of isolating the disruptive source of exports and offering direct compensation through the quota transfer, will dominate the process of policy choice.

The terms-of-trade and discriminatory effects combined with the negotiated aspect of the VER contribute to a further political advantage for policymakers: the ease of VER negotiation and implementation. While direct import restrictions such as tariffs and quotas must be implemented through legislative means, as in the United States, or highly visible administrative means, as in the European Community (EC), a VER can be negotiated in secret, unhindered by open political processes and public scrutiny. Since clandestine VER negotiations are not subject to the open political debate that accompanies traditional protectionist proposals, the trade-restricting agreement can generally be concluded in a short period of time. An expeditious settlement is also aided by the rent transfer that the importing country's government can offer to exporters. The speed of VER implementation is important to government officials whose policy time-horizon reaches only the next round of elections, thereby dictating a need to satisfy protectionist demands quickly. In addition, the low political profile of VER negotiations also lowers the political risk associated with it, since potential political opponents will be less aware of their content and since, in the end, trade authorities in the importing country can always point to the exporter as the source of the restriction.

Import-Competing Producers

For import-competing producers, the VER arrangement offers traditional protectionist benefits: the ability to raise prices and expand output if producers are price-taking firms (the case of domestic monopoly or oligopoly, in which a VER leads to decreased domestic output, will be discussed in the next section). Beyond that, the most attractive aspect of the VER for this group is that it sets quantitative limits on trade (See Deardorff 1987, 1989). This is especially true for industries where domestic producers are lagging behind world efficiency standards, thereby leaving the domestic market open to import disruption. Whereas a tariff cannot maintain a stable domestic price under given demand conditions when the world price is falling, quantitative restrictions can. In addition, the discriminatory aspect of the VER fits well into the probable protectionist strategy of domestic producers fighting an increase in import competition. By identifying specific exporters as the source of the import surge, domestic firms can dramatize their plight as one of being victims of unfair or disruptive trade practices. The political advantage of a VER for import-competing producers in this context is that it focuses attention on exporters that have caused the trade disruption, thereby heightening protectionist sentiment among policymakers.

Inasmuch as import-competing producers favor an assurance of airtight controls on imports, however, they will prefer direct import quotas to any system of voluntary trade restraint. From their viewpoint, exporters cannot be trusted to restrain shipments in the face of profitable export opportunities. Suspicions of clandestine transshipments via third countries in past VER agreements, such as the one on steel trade between the United States and Japan from 1969 to 1974, increased general skepticism regarding the effectiveness of VERs as a protectionist device. The section "VER Policy Pitfalls and their Implications" will discuss problems of enforcement in more detail. Still, direct import quotas, as noted above, represent a drastic and politically costly measure that import-competing producers cannot always expect to obtain. The quantitative, discriminatory qualities of the VER thus make it an attractive alternative for protectionist lobbies to pursue.

VERs as Facilitating Devices

While perfectly competitive domestic firms will increase output when protected by a VER agreement, as shown in figure 1, it is useful to constrast this outcome with those of a domestic monopoly or oligopoly, or an international oligopoly. In such cases, VER quotas can facilitate price-making power. Consider, for example, a dominant firm, price leadership model including a single domestic firm with price-making power and two exporting countries A and B, whose exporters are price takers in the domestic import market, as illustrated in the two-panel graph in figure 2. Panel (a) shows the joint supply curve of imports BUW as the horizontal sum of AA and BB. Total domestic demand is shown as DD'. Panel (b) shows the domestic firm's marginal cost curve mc, as well as its residual demand curve dd and marginal revenue curve mr, constructed as the horizontal difference between domestic demand DD and import supply BUW. In the absence of trade restrictions, the domestic firm maximizes profits by setting price and quantity (P_0, Q_0) for the entire domestic market, while foreign suppliers A and B follow the price leader and deliver Q_a and Q_b, respectively.

Now consider a VER quota on the principal foreign supplier B alone, set at B's original freetrade import level Q_b. Total import supply is now represented by $BUGJ$. Residual demand for the domestic firm pivots around R to become $d'Rd$, and the relevant segment of the new marginal revenue curve is mr'. Under the VER agreement, the domestic firm now sets its profit-maximizing price and quantity at (P_1, Q_1). Imports from B are subject to the VER quota limit Q_b,

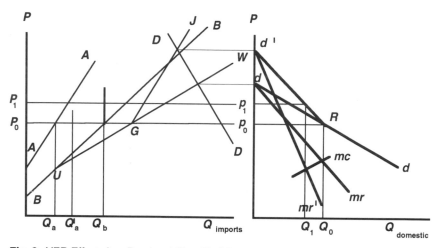

Fig. 2. VER Effects in a Dominant Firm Model

while imports from *A* expand to Q_a'. The welfare effects for the two foreign suppliers are comparable to those described in figure 1. However, even though the VER quota is set at *B*'s free-trade import level, the VER in this case has clearly enhanced the domestic firm's price-making power by eliminating the ability of its main foreign rivals in *B* from responding to price increases. Such reductions in domestic output as the result of a VER agreement have been observed in the U.S. automobile industry after the Japanese VER agreements of 1981-85, for example (see Pomfret 1989a). In the case illustrated in figure 2, the VER has facilitated domestic price-making power, whereby foreign suppliers passively respond to the domestic price leader.

The analysis of figure 2 is really an extension of Bhagwati's model of the effects of a quota in the presence of domestic monopoly (Bhagwati 1965; see also Pomfret 1989b). However, including the differential supply responses of restrained and unrestrained exporters under a VER arrangement reveals the impact of the structure of the VER on the interests of the domestic firm. For example, in figure 2 the price leader's market power is based directly on the market share and the price elasticity of supply of the foreign firms.[5] Its ability to raise prices will therefore be enhanced by a VER agreement that 1) sets smaller quota levels in general and 2) makes sure that major exporters are included. The latter criterion is critical, since surges in supply from nonrestrained exporters will clearly undermine the domestic firm's price-making power. If protectionist pressure from the domestic industry persists, it is likely that exporters from *A* and other potential foreign suppliers will become targets of VER negotiations.

Other models of firm interaction show how such quotas can lead to joint price increases between foreign and domestic competitors in an international oligopoly. Krishna (1985), for example, uses a Bertrand price strategy model to show that the typical result of a VER imposed on a foreign producer in a duopolistic market is to raise the prices and profits of both firms. This outcome is not dependent on collusion between the firms, but results from the pricing opportunities introduced by the competition-reducing VER quota. The profit implications of this anticompetitive effect suggest that both domestic and foreign firms in an oligopolistic market would prefer VERs over import-equivalent tariffs.[6]

Trade Authorities and Exporters in the Restraining Country

While import-competing producers can be expected to favor the VER purely for its protectionist qualities, it is noteworthy that this particular form of protectionism often finds acceptance—even favor—in governments and among producers in the exporting countries. For trade authorities in the exporting country, this is especially true if the implementation of protectionist policies in the importing country is considered inevitable. Under such conditions, trade authorities will seek to minimize the expected cost of trade restraint to the exporting country (Bhagwati and Srinivasan 1976). A negotiated VER, in which both trading partners have a hand in determining the extent of the trade restriction, is more attractive to the exporting country than a unilateral import quota, under which the exporters' interests will have reduced influence.[7] In considering voluntary export restraint, trade authorities in the exporting country thus make a judgment as to the probability of more severe protectionist measures, along with the economic and political costs associated with such alternatives. For policymakers in both countries, one of the biggest political advantages of a VER is that it reduces the uncertainty of bilateral trade relations, a topic to be pursued further in chapter 4.

The advantages of a VER to existing exporting firms derive from the quantitative limit it places on export supply, which calls for competition-reducing measures in the export market and for the creation of monopoly rents. In order to implement export restraint, the government in most cases forms (or allow the formation of) an export cartel. Such an arrangement tends to favor the established firms in the industry by introducing a forum through which the export market is to be organized. The cartel provides the possibility for existing firms to capture guaranteed export market shares and to keep potential newcomers from entering the export market. Although profits for some firms may thereby be constrained, this is compensated by a reduction in the variance of profit levels as long as the VER limit is operational, and thus in the risk associated with fluctuating market conditions.[8] Whether or not these competition-reducing effects will come about will depend on the administration and distribution of export licenses and quotas.

The manner in which voluntary restraint is achieved will also determine who receives the quota profits that result from the increased export price of the good. In figure 1, the total scarcity rent associated with country B's supply of the good under a VER is equal to $(P_0 - P_3)Q_b$. The rent could be captured by the exporting country's government if export licenses were competitively auctioned off for their premium value. The free issuing of the licenses would transfer the rent to whoever managed to obtain them.

Murray, Schmidt, and Walter (1978) have investigated the theoretical possibility that a VER could lead to even more restrictive behavior on the part of exporters. If the licenses are tradable and if the net import demand curve faced by the restraining country is of sufficiently low elasticity, an incentive will be created for a single exporter or group of exporters to obtain all the export licenses, with the intention of restricting supply below the VER level in order to maximize monopoly profits. The formation of such an exporters' cartel is illustrated in figure 3. The importing country has an import demand curve DD' while the two foreign countries A and B have import supply schedules AA' and BB', respectively, summing to BJT. As in figure 1, a VER on B alone fixes Q_b' such that total imports Q_0 are equal to those alternatively set by a global tariff $(P_0 - P_1)/P_1$. Country B's VER import share Q_b'/Q_0 is smaller than its tariff share Q_b/Q_0.

Now consider the residual import demand curve RD' faced by country B (derived by subtracting quantities AA' from DD' horizontally). If a monopolist acquires all export licenses, or if exporters collude, then supply can profitably be restricted to Q_b^*, where B's marginal revenue curve MM' intersects its marginal cost curve BB'. The import price rises to P^*, further deteriorating the importing country's terms of trade. Imports drop to Q_c, and B's import share drops further to Q_b/Q_c. This drop is immediately evident from the fact that A's share clearly increases from Q_a'/Q_0 to Q_a^*/Q_c. This analysis shows that three conditions must be present in order for a VER to lead to the monopoly solution: (1) the VER must be set at a higher level than that given by the point of intersection between the restraining exporters' marginal revenue and marginal cost curves; (2) export licenses must be tradable or otherwise open to concentrated acquisition by firms; and (3) an export monopoly or collusive agreement among exporters must exist. It is worth noting that, if exporters are already organized as a cartel, it will not make any difference whether there is a VER agreement or not (as long as it is set above Q_b in figure 3); exporters will seek the monopoly solution (Q_b^*, P^*) regardless. Yet an important implication of the supply-restricting nature of a VER is that it requires state-sponsored collusive activity, with cartel discipline maintained by the administrative powers of the government. Once such a forum is created, the possibility of even more collusive behavior emerges.

Exporters in Third Countries

The shortfall in export supply caused by the VER also benefits exporters not participating in the agreement. Figures 1, 2, and 3 show that the increase in

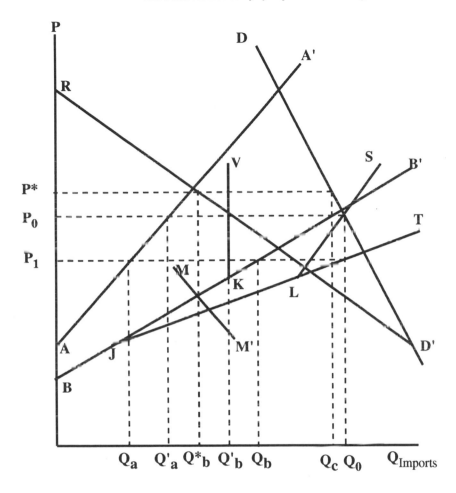

Fig. 3. VER Effects under an Exporter Monopoly

export price due to the VER allows nonrestraining exporters to increase deliveries to the importing country, expanding their import market share. They are free riders on the increase in export price caused by the selective VER. While these producers are ostensibly excluded from negotiations on the VER, their interests clearly lie in encouraging such selective export restraint as long as such agreements do not imply even stricter VER limits on their own exports in the future. In heavily concentrated or cartelized industries—a trend in itself promoted by VER agreements—a motive is further created to collude on an international scale, as (for example) potential VER candidates could offer to adjust their negotiated export limit to favor nonparticipating countries in exchange for market shares elsewhere.

Import Consumers

Like any other trade restriction, the VER imposes the greatest burden on consumers in the importing country, since they must pay the higher domestic price for the good (both imported and domestically produced) that results from its scarcity premium. Yet insofar as consumers would have benefited from tariff revenues had such a device been alternatively used to restrict imports, the former can be said to bear a double burden as a result of the VER. In other words, consumers pay twice for the VER: once in the form of higher domestic prices and again in the form of foregone tariff revenues.

It is important in this context to recall that the VER's rent transfer lies at the root of its perceived political advantages since it allows trade authorities in the importing country to secure exporter cooperation. Consumers in general, however, are conveniently excluded from the policy-making process of VERs, which are negotiated by administrative officials away from public view (see Finger, Hall, and Nelson 1982). Since a VER involves a deliberate effort by trade authorities to worsen the country's terms of trade, its political viability hinges upon restricted access by the public and others who lose from the trade restriction (for example, domestic firms that use the importable good in the production of another final good) to the negotiating process.

"Rebound" Countries

The VER agreement causes restraining exporters to redirect export supply towards other importing countries where markets are still open. The resulting trade diversion in exports is a result of the discriminatory nature of the VER. Its main impact is felt by import-competing producers in the "rebound" country and by governments that must deal with the probable protectionist fallout. Pressure for trade restrictions will stem from increased imports and price competition as the restraining exporters seek unprotected markets in which to sell the good. Import-competing producers and trade policy officials in the rebound country are thus likely to oppose the selective VER agreement that creates a new trade problem for them. In this manner protection, usually in the form of VERs or other discriminatory measures such as trade law enforcement, is likely to spread as restricted exports continually rebound toward unprotected markets.

The first stage of export trade diversion due to a selective VER agreement is shown in figure 4. The export-restraining country is assumed to comprise individual exporters in competition supplying two importing countries, A and B. Exporters have a total export supply schedule of SS' and face demand schedules $D_a D_a'$ and $D_b D_b'$ in the two import markets, summing horizontally to the total export demand schedule $D_t D_t'$. This configuration of demand schedules yields residual export supply curves $S_a S_a'$ and $S_b S_b'$ for the two respective import markets. Initially, exporters deliver quantities Q_a and Q_b to A and B, respectively, at the common export price P_0.

Suppose now that country A induces the exporting country to conclude a VER agreement, setting a limit of Q_v deliveries to that country. The restriction on export supply to A raises the export price for that country alone to P_a. However, the limit on deliveries to A causes a rotation of that part of the residual export supply curve for B lying below P_a. The new segment of the export supply curve for country B is RS_h' and is constructed by shifting the relevant portion of SS' to the left by the amount of the VER quota limit Q_v. The more restrictive the VER quota imposed by A against the exporter, the greater will be the rotation of the residual export supply curve for B and the surge in diverted exports toward that unprotected market. In figure 4, B now imports Q_r at price P_b.

The initial surge of diverted exports to B is likely to alarm import-competing producers there. The VER between the exporter and another country has increased imports and in this case (at least temporarily) lowered the domestic price of the good. Producers of the good in B are thus likely to oppose selective VER agreements involving exporters that are also in competition with them. The government in B will also oppose these VERs, since they ultimately put policymakers under protectionist pressure, which in turn endangers B's trade relations. Yet, like consumers in the country that induces export restraint, producers and governments of third countries are typically excluded from representation in the VER negotiations.

To be sure, the import price divergence on international markets caused by the VER cannot persist indefinitely unless the two import markets in A and B are somehow isolated. As long as the VER on trade to A is not universal and world export supply conditions permit, price arbitrage would tend to encourage the shifting of export supply toward the more lucrative market in A. However, further protectionist repercussions are likely to bring about a proliferation of trade-restricting devices in both importing countries before international market adjustment proceeds very far. The imposition of discriminatory trade restraints by country B against the exporting country would reduce its imports, raise the domestic price of the importable good and shift disruptive exports toward any remaining unprotected markets. Country A, on the other hand, may have to impose further restrictions on imports in order to avoid attracting exports from unrestrained suppliers. In this manner, VER-induced rebound protectionism can produce a daisy chain of escalating discriminatory quantitative agreements with all exporters of the good, or else an internationally coordinated cartel, as has been the case in textiles, apparel, and steel products.

It is useful to note, finally, that countries may induce export restraint and trade diversion through policies other than formal VER arrangements. Trade law enforcement and threats of administrative and legislated protection may have the same chilling effect on trade as an outright trade barrier, as will be shown in chapter 4. In order to avoid threatened unilateral trade law or other

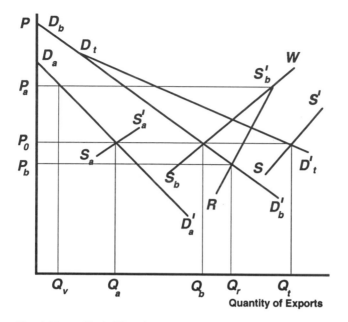

Fig. 4. Export Trade Diversion under a VER

trade-restricting actions, the exporting country may unilaterally withdraw from the politically volatile market. At the same time, the mere anticipation of trade diversion may spark preemptive trade restricting actions or threats in third countries. The speed with which rebound protectionism occurs is thus likely to increase as governments gain experience in the market dynamics of VERs. After the United States concluded its 1981 automobile VER with Japan, for example, the swift response of Canada and the EC countries in introducing and adjusting, respectively, their own VERs with Japan is a case in point. Especially in politically sensitive goods, an initial VER agreement concluded by a major importing country will spark a rapid policy response among other major importing countries in the era of VER commercial diplomacy.

VER Policy Pitfalls and Their Implications

The analysis of the preceding section points to the many political advantages of a VER agreement: All parties involved in setting the export limit apparently stand to gain while potential opponents of the VER are systematically excluded from the negotiating process. Yet those VER qualities favoring political expediency also bear the seeds of its most serious shortcomings as a policy instrument. The two major problems are (1) the value escalation effect and (2) the difficulty of enforcement in the absence of a network of VER agreements covering all actual and potential suppliers.

Value Escalation

The need for a framework of enforcement measures points to the general problem of "leakage" that often plagues VER agreements. Bergsten (1975) has noted that carelessness in defining VER coverage can create loopholes for exporters to exploit. The lack of exactness in coverage of a VER, for example, may allow differentiated products to be exported in different categories such that no true restraint is actually practiced. A similar problem occurs when a VER quota category covers a broad range of products of differing quality and value. Within the restraining export industry, firms typically find it profitable to shift sales towards higher-valued subgroups of goods, a phenomenon whose empirical evidence will be examined in more detail in chapter 3. One important result of this analysis is that the exporter's shifting of shipments toward higher value added products tends also to cause the price of the lower value product to rise relative to the price of the higher-value product within the quota category. The resulting surge in imports among the higher value-added categories may then renew the protectionist cycle.

The theoretical foundations of quota-induced product upgrading were developed by Falvey (1979), Rodriguez (1979), and Santoni and Van Cott (1980). An intuitive explanation of product upgrading under a VER constraint runs as follows. In the absence of trade restrictions a multiproduct exporter will adjust shipments in such a way as to ensure that the marginal profit from the last item shipped in each category is equal to zero. When an export quota restrains total deliveries, the exporter will cut back deliveries in each category such that marginal profits of goods covered by the quota are still equal, but now take on a positive value. Thus the exporter will make each successive cutback in that product category where foregone profits are lowest.[9] The more rapidly marginal profits for a particular category rise as cutbacks occur, the less the cutback will be in that category in order to maximize profits under the quota. Since cutbacks of the high-cost item typically reduce profits more rapidly per unit than those of the low-cost item, the proportion of high-cost to low-cost items within the quota category will generally rise as a result of the VER.

Figure 5 illustrates the exporter's product mix adjustment to a VER quota. Marginal profit is measured in the upper two quadrants for high-cost good 1 and for low-cost good 2. In the absence of trade restraints initial equilibrium quantities are Q_1 and Q_2, where the respective $m\Pi$ functions intersect the quantity axis. The free trade product ratio is represented in quadrant IV by the slope of the line segment OS.

Suppose now that a binding VER is introduced, such that $Q_1 + Q_2 \leq \overline{Q}$, as represented by the line segment RR. If cutbacks were made proportionally, the new quantities Q_1' and Q_2' (determined by the intersection of line segments OS and RR at point S') would result in a divergence between marginal profits for the two goods. Specifically, $m\Pi_1 > m\Pi_2$, indicating that the production ratio $Q_1/$

Q_2 is too low. The exporter thus has an incentive to reallocate restricted output towards the good whose mP curve has the lower elasticity until marginal profits for the two goods are again equal.

Figure 5 indicates that, under a binding VER, profit maximization requires finding a common (positive) level of marginal profits l, whereby the coordinate of the associated equilibrium quantities Q_1^* and Q_2^* falls along the line segment RR. A rotation in the product ratio line from OS toward the lower Q_1 axis indicates that the VER has caused product upgrading. The change in the product ratio will depend upon the relative cutbacks required in Q_1 and Q_2, as described above. These cutbacks will depend, in turn, upon the slope and position of the $m\Pi$ curves, that is to say, upon the configuration of relative marginal production costs and price elasticities of demand between the two goods.[10] In addition, changes in income will have an impact on product upgrading to the extent that income elasticities ε_i are nonzero. Specifically, if an increase in income shifts demand more toward the high-cost good, product upgrading will be enhanced.[11]

A number of policy implications follow directly from a consideration of VER-induced product upgrading. Certainly, policymakers can expect more upgrading to occur as price and income elasticities of demand diverge between products within a quota category. Their anticipation of (or reaction to) product upgrading will play an important role in determining the quota structure of VER arrangements. To the extent that product upgrading by exporters in response to a VER agreement leads to surges in imports that damage the interests of domestic producers, it creates a strong incentive for policymakers to define quota categories narrowly in order to minimize upgrading opportunities. Export restraint arrangements in steel, textiles, and apparel have followed this pattern. These industries produce a wide spectrum of differentiated goods, ranging from standardized commodity items to highly specialized grades. In the early VER arrangements, exporters often took advantage of the broadly defined quotas by shifting deliveries to higher value-added goods within the quota categories, renewing protectionist pressure among import-competing producers of these goods. Predictably, the response of governments administering the VERs was to tighten and subdivide the quota categories in order to prevent product upgrading from disrupting the arrangement.

Perhaps the greatest danger of such situations for commercial policy is that they can lead to the progressive micromanagement of the market by cadres of government bureaucrats, creating an interest group for trade protection within the government (an issue for trade policy reform that is addressed in chap. 9). In addition, the detailed administration of the quota system in textiles and steel has helped to create virtual cartels in the export trade of these goods.

In cases where product upgrading represents a much smaller threat to domestic producers, on the other hand, VER quotas may be left open. There is evidence, for example, that U.S. government officials anticipated the upgrading phenomenon in the proposed VER arrangment with Japan on automobile trade of the early 1980s (Savage and Horlick 1985). In this instance, trade officials apparently concluded that upgrading would only play to U.S. automakers' comparative advantage in producing larger, higher-cost models. Similarly, the VER arrangement negotiated by the United States in nonrubber footwear left quotas defined broadly enough to allow considerable upgrading, possibly reflecting the perception that the import problem lay only in the abundance of cheaper types of foreign shoes. Yet the opportunity for upgrading may actually encourage foreign producers to invest resources in the production and design of higher-cost goods within quota categories, contributing to their ability to compete in these products in the future.

The impact of income changes on upgrading also has important implications for the structure of VER agreements, especially in highly cyclical industries. Since income increases tend to amplify product upgrading, a VER imposed at the end of cyclical downturn will typically lead to more upgrading than one imposed at the start of a downturn. Highly cyclical demand conditions may therefore motivate governments to negotiate more detailed, narrowly defined VER quota categories as a hedge against disruptive product mix changes (upgrading or downgrading) over the business cycle. This concern may be particularly relevant in long-standing agreements that have crossed business cycles, such as the detailed VER quotas in steel. The political necessity of more detailed VER quotas is diminished, on the other hand, when income changes shift the product mix in the "right" direction, as was apparently the case with the boom and associated product upgrading in the U.S. automobile market under the VER agreement of the early 1980s.

Unrestrained Exports, Transshipments, and Quota Hopping

Weaknesses of structure and discipline in the export cartel are another source of leakage. The cartel may, for example, not succeed in bringing all exporters into its fold. However, even if the cartel is indeed successful in raising the export price, the incentive is still created for firms to cheat on their cartel quota allotment. Induced export restraint is thus more likely to be effective, the more the export industry is either concentrated or already used to cartel discipline.

A different problem arises when firms in restraining countries surreptitiously exceed their export quota limit by means of transshipments via nonrestraining countries. Prime candidates for this form of cheating are goods with no distinguishable marks of origin. Transshipments could be illustrated in figure 1 by a "mysterious" rightward shift in *A*'s import supply curve after a VER is set on *B*'s supply. In the absence of additional import controls, prevention of VER evasion through transshipment schemes requires comprehensive monitoring of import volume by country and meticulous inspection of certificates of origin against fraud. Even then, firms in the restraining country may

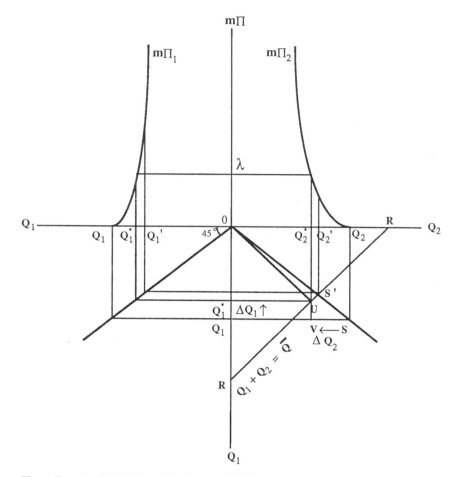

Fig. 5. Exporter Product Mix Adjustment under VER

find it possible to avoid the VER restriction by means of direct foreign investment in a nonrestraining country, a strategy that was apparently pursued by
Japanese manufactures in shifting color television production to South Korea
and Taiwan after an export restraint agreement with the United States, for example. In these cases of quota hopping, VERs are plagued by the *porous protection* effect (i.e., they cannot "hold water"), a phenomenon that would occur
most readily in industries where technology and investment are internationally
mobile (Bhagwati 1986).

A related source of the erosion of the VER protectionist effects lies in the
amount of total export supply not covered by the VER. It was shown earlier
that the shortage of export supply caused by the VER raises the export price for
all suppliers. Other exporting countries unfettered by VER limits provide the

channels for transshipment schemes described above. Yet the problems of nonuniversal VERs run even deeper. Even if enforcement against transshipment is strong and trade authorities determine that a selective VER agreement with the major supplier or suppliers) will achieve the desired protective effect in the short run, the ensuing rise in the relative export price to the importing country will invite additional export supply. This is shown in figure 4 by the premium import price P_a established by the selective VER agreement, which is likely to have the effect of bringing new entrants into the export market, shifting existing world export supplies toward the more profitable VER-protected market. International market adjustment will thus tend to erode the VER-induced price rise and increase imports into the protected market.

International trade policy repercussions could further erode the initial protective effects of the VER. As noted earlier, the VER tends to divert export trade toward other import markets, subjecting trade authorities there to protectionist pressures. In this context it is likely that this third country will impose discriminatory trade restrictions of its own (VER, country-specific import quota, antidumping measures, etc.) against the disruptive exporters. As access to other import markets is cut off, a further incentive is created for exporters to cheat on all of the VER agreements. Repercussions in trade relations may also redound to the disadvantage of the importing country that first induced export restraint if the victims of export trade diversion link the import disruption in their domestic markets with the original VER agreement and retaliate with trade sanctions.

Policy Consequences of Failed VERS

In view of the various channels of leakage and supply response from unrestrained exporters leading to an erosion of the VER agreement's protective effects, trade authorities must decide whether to scrap the VER approach if it is not working or take steps to tighten the mechanism that induces export restraint. The nature of VER shortcomings suggests two general solutions to the problem, both of which point to a broadening and deepening of protectionist intervention and its proliferation worldwide.

One possible approach addresses the difficulties raised by the selectivity of VER agreements. The logical policy response is to extend the VERs to cover all exporters supplying the country's import market. This type of global orderly marketing agreement would strive to seal the import market effectively from clandestine transshipments and rebounding diverted exports. All actual and potential sources and channels of disruptive supply would have to be covered by VER quotas.

The use of a global VER arrangement only heightens, however, a second problem: VER compliance. How can trade authorities in the importing country best enforce the exporters' adherence to a voluntary quota limit, especially when renegade firms are able to circumvent cartel-determined allotments? The threat of more severe protectionist measures may be effective for awhile (i.e., until exporters perceive it as a bluff), but such threats ultimately depend on the ability of trade authorities in the exporting country to maintain cartel discipline and effectively monitor total exports. A more effective means of inducing compliance would be to establish an automatic tripwire whenever VER limits are violated. From 1979 to 1985 the EC, for example, established a basic price system (BPS), subjecting steel imports to antidumping investigations if their price fell below a predetermined basic level. The basic prices were calculated on average costs and presumably represent the lowest fair price an exporter could charge without violating antidumping laws. However, the BPS was suspended for those exporters participating in (and adhering to) a VER agreement. Since basic price levels were set by the EC trade authority and were subject to administrative discretion, steel suppliers faced the nearly certain fate of antidumping duties if VER limits are violated. In general, using antidumping law as a VER backup device may therefore allow the importing country to artificially maintain a premium import price.

It is noteworthy that such a system of basic prices is, in itself, another method of inducing voluntary export restraint, since it forces exporters to follow minimum pricing guidelines and thereby limit their deliveries. While it does not set quantitative limits on import supply, it does provide an alternative to policymakers in search of unilateral technical-track measures to induce export restraint. The United States used a similar system of trigger prices to control steel imports from 1978 to 1981. Although the manipulation of antidumping law as a means of inducing or enforcing voluntary export restraint may not be equally applicable to all types of goods, its development in this direction is limited only by the imagination of trade authorities under protectionist pressure. The nature of these and other tools of inducing export restraint will be the subject of chapter 4.

Summary

At a time of increased international constraints on trade policy and renewed protectionist pressures, the VER agreement represents an attempt by governments to retain the power to implement trade restrictions. Because it is designed to circumvent GATT restrictions on the nature and magnitude of import controls, the VER agreement differs significantly from traditional instruments of trade restriction, both in the parameters of its implementation and in its impact on import shares and the terms of trade. These distinguishing features contribute to the unusual alignment of interests that marks the political economy of voluntary export restraint. The terms-of-trade effect allows the government to secure exporter participation by means of a rent transfer. The discriminatory effect allows the government of the importing country to target disruptive suppliers and isolate potential protectionist retaliation. The administrative nature of VER agreements permits a low political profile to be kept and promotes prompt implementation. The rent transfer and negotiated trade levels also appeal to exporters and trade authorities in the restraining country seeking to minimize the costs of (and maximize the profits from) protectionism. In fact, VERs tend to serve the interests of all participants in the agreement, while the main losers, consumers in the importing country, are excluded from the policy-making process. Low-income consumers, in particular, appear to suffer disproportionate welfare losses from VER protection.

The pattern of VER use established so far indicates that its initial implementation is usually an improvised response to import disruption. A lessening of import pressure points to a quick abandonment of the agreement. Only if the surge in imports (and protectionist pressure) continues will trade authorities be forced to deal with the inevitable problems of VER enforcement that lead to increasingly sophisticated systems of induced export restraint, including the use of more detailed product coverage and antidumping backup devices. The spread of crisis market conditions implied by selective voluntary restraint also points to the proliferation of such agreements worldwide. The most likely candidates for extended VER agreements are those national industries undergoing structural decline whose foreign competitors can be easily cartelized, such as steel, automobiles, and shipbuilding. With other protectionist paths blocked, the VER emerges as the most efficacious means of protecting politically sensitive crisis industries.

However, beyond its implications for the world economy as an instrument of protectionism per se, the major significance of the VER lies in its impact on the conduct of commercial diplomacy in general. As noted earlier, the use of VER agreements could therefore unravel many of the gains of postwar trade liberalization. The following chapters set out to document the ability of such agreements to disrupt trade patterns, trade relations, and the very system of multilateral commerce. The study turns now to an examination of the empirical evidence of the cost of export restraint and its ability to distort trade patterns and perpetuate trade disputes.

Notes

1. Dinopoulos and Kreinin (1989) use a three-country model to show that if the supply response from the nonrestrained country is large enough, it may deprive the VER-restrained country of a portion of the rents and in some cases even leave it worse off as a result of the VER agreement. This theoretical possibility is diminished by the incentives of the government to target the major suppliers for VER quotas. However, new entry into the market, spurred by the VER-induced premium, may erode the rents of the original targeted countries.

2. This transfer of rents assumes a competitive market structure on the exporting and importing side. If importing facilities are monopolized, however, the quota rents would accrue to the monopoly importer. See Bergsten, et al. (1987, 22).

3. If prices do not rise sufficiently to capture the scarcity premium associated with the VER, calculation of its economic cost requires an evaluation of the quantity rationing that results. See Brenton and Winters (1993).

4. One simple criterion for equivalence is tariff-revenue neutrality. That is, under GATT article XIX compensation, a VER set to be import-equivalent to a particular tariff level would be offset by a reduction in other tariffs such that the net tariff revenue effect would be zero. See Moore and Suranovic (1993, 449–50).

5. The price elasticity of demand for the domestic price leader can be expressed as: $\eta_d = (\eta/S_d) + [(Q_f/q_d)\varepsilon_f]$, in which η_d is the price elasticity of the domestic price leader, η is market price elasticity, S_d is the domestic firm's share of total market sales, Q_f represents total foreign sales in the market, q_d is the domestic firm's output and ε_f is the price elasticity of supply of the foreign firms. The VER quota will reduce η_d, and hence increase the domestic firm's price-making power, to the extent that it reduces Q_f, increases S_d and q_d, and minimizes ε_f.

6. See Krugman (1989) for a survey of trade protection models under imperfect competition, and a useful summary and graphical presentation of Krishna's model.

7. See Hillman and Ursprung (1988), who incorporate foreign interests and lobbying activities into a model of trade policy choice.

8. Li (1991), for example, provides evidence that the fluctuation in Hong Kong's textile exports was much greater under conditions of unrestricted trade than under the subsequent VER protection regimes.

9. Falvey (1979) uses a model featuring an export monopolist producing two goods with low and high costs C_1 and C_2, respectively, to identify the VER-induced percentage change in price for the two goods as:

$$(P_1^* - P_1)/P_1 = (C_2/C_1)([P_2^* - P_2]/P_2)$$

in which P_i and P_i^* represent the unrestricted and VER-induced prices for the two goods, respectively. Since $(C_2/C_1) < 1$, the percentage increase in the high-cost product is less than the percentage change in the low-cost product. Thus, typically, the proportion Q_1/Q_2 will increase as a result of the VER.

10. Formally, the proportional change in the ratio of high-cost to low-cost deliveries is: $Q_1 - Q_2 = (\eta_{11} - \eta_{21})P_1 + (\eta_{12} - \eta_{22})P_2$. Thus, the upgrading effect could theoretically be reversed under certain own-price and cross-elasticity conditions. However, both theoretical considerations and empirical observations suggest that this perverse outcome is unlikely. See Falvey (1979, 1106–8).

11. In a simple model with no cross-price effects, for example, ceteris paribus, $\varepsilon_1 > \varepsilon_2 > 0$ is sufficient to cause further upgrading when income rises if $\eta_2/\eta_1 > (C_2+\lambda)/(C_1+\lambda)$. See Jones (1992).

CHAPTER 3

Empirical Evidence of the Effects
of VER Agreements

The peculiarities of VER agreements examined in chapter 2 suggest that an evaluation of their likely market effects as an exercise in public policy analysis should focus on the empirical evidence of welfare and income distribution effects, as well as value escalation and trade diversion effects. An examination of the impact of VERs on general welfare in the importing country, for example, can indicate their costs to the economy as compared with equivalent tariffs. In this regard, the rent transfer to targeted exporters may represent a significant portion of the economic cost. Unexpected income distribution effects may be contained not only in the choice of product protected, but also in value escalation effects and labor market adjustments.

The international market effects of VERs also provide evidence of their usefulness as an instrument of trade policy. The effectiveness of export restraint agreements in settling a trade dispute resulting from surges of imports, for example, will depend on the degree to which they can contain the disruptive imports and remove protectionist pressure. To the governments of countries experiencing severe import competition and protectionist pressure, the attractiveness of VERs and similar discriminatory trade policy instruments lies in their perceived ability to isolate the source of the import problem and to reduce the imports quickly. The discussion in chapter 2 of VER pitfalls suggested, however, that export restraint agreements typically cause markets to adjust in such a way as to vitiate their protective effect, or to create new protectionist problems elsewhere through (1) value escalation, (2) import surges from unrestrained exporters, and (3) the diversion of restrained exports toward unprotected markets. These market effects are likely to rekindle protectionist sentiment and renew trade disputes, increasing the likelihood of a proliferation of protection and a tightening of the trade restrictions.

This chapter will present empirical evidence of the cost of VER agreements and of the trade effects of VER-induced upgrading and trade diversion with an eye toward their applications in policy analysis. This information will provide the basis for considering their impact on the evolution of export restraint agreements.

TABLE 2. Distribution of Costs and Benefits from Special Protection

Case	Annual Consumer Losses Total (Mill.$)	Per job saved ($)	Annual Producer Gains Total (Mill.$)	Annual Welfare Costs of Restraints Gain to Foreigners (mill.$)	Tariff Revenue (mill.$)	Efficiency loss (mill.$)
Textiles & Apparel, Phase I	9,400	22,000	8,700	negligible	1,158	1,100
Textiles & Apparel, Phase II	20,000	37,000	18,000	350	2,143	3,100
Textiles & Apparel, Phase III	27,000	42,000	22,000	1,800	2,535	4,850
Carbon steel, Phase I	1,970	240,000	1,330	330	290	50
Carbon steel, Phase II	4,350	620,000	2,770	930	556	120
Carbon steel, Phase III	6,800	750,000	3,800	2,000	560	330
Specialty steel	520	1 million	420	50	32	30
Nonrubber footwear	700	55,000	250	220	262	16
Color TVs	420	420,000	190	140	77	7
Autos	5,800	105,000	2,600	2,200	790	200

Source: Hufbauer, Berliner, and Elliott, 1986. Reprinted by permission. Copyright © 1986 Institute for International Economics. All rights reserved.

Estimates of the Economic Cost of VERs

All forms of trade protection will typically carry an economic welfare cost to the importing country through higher domestic prices, decreased consumption and increased domestic production of the protected good, foreign retaliation, dynamic and X-inefficiency losses (productive efficiency losses due to the weakened incentive structure that accompanies reduced competition), rent seeking among domestic recipients of the benefits of protection, possibly reduced competition in market structure, and administrative costs. Export restraint agreements carry the additional welfare cost that comes from the fact that they give the exporter control over the trade restriction, thereby lowering the importing country's terms of trade and transferring consumer welfare to the exporting country, as described in chapter 2 and shown in figure 1. In addition, the political economy of VERs, as well as the associated value escalation effect, tends to make this trade policy tool more regressive in terms of income distribution than traditional trade restrictions.

Net Welfare Effects of VER Protection

Table 2 tabulates annual welfare effects compiled by Hufbauer, Berliner, and Elliott (1986) for the United States of selected export restraint arrangements concluded with foreign suppliers. The estimates are presented under the assumption that imported goods are imperfect substitutes for the domestically produced import substitutes. In most cases, export restraint transferred significant amounts of welfare from domestic consumers to foreign producers, especially in the cases of VERs in automobiles (1981–84), steel (1982 to present), and textiles and apparel (1982–86) concluded by the United States. Efficiency costs have been particularly high in textiles and apparel, indicating a very high level of protection and a major deterioration in the world competitiveness of that industry in the United States. In every case, the annual consumer cost per job saved or maintained in the industry by virtue of the protection granted has exceeded the annual wages per worker. In other words, if the purpose of protection is to protect the incomes of workers, then it would be less costly for the country to permit free trade and compensate laid-off workers at the full value of their foregone earnings through a subsidy financed by general taxation or by a phase-out tariff or quota auction (Bergsten et al. 1987). This consideration suggests the possible benefits of converting export restraint agreements into import-equivalent import tariffs, to be discussed in chapter 8.

Table 3 shows the estimates of the economic cost of protectionist policies in steel, textiles and apparel, and automobiles to the United States, using a computable general equilibrium (CGE) trade model (Tarr 1989). In contrast to the partial equilibrium studies cited above, the CGE estimates incorporate the

TABLE 3. Welfare Gains to the U.S. from Removing Quantitative Restraints on Textiles and Apparel, Automobiles and Steel: Central Elasticity Case (in billions of 1984 U.S. dollars)

	Remove QRs	Keep QRs but Capture Rents from Foreigners	Remove All Tariffs After QRs Removed
All Three Sectors	20.90	14.21	0.94
Textiles/ Apparel	13.06	7.07	
Automobiles	6.90	6.20	
Steel	0.91	0.78	

Note: gains are the value of the Hicksian eqiuvalent variation (see Tarr, 1989, chapter 3)

Source: Estimates from U.S. General Equilbrium Trade Model (Tarr 1989).

effects of VER agreements as they filter through the economy of the importing country. Thus any VER-induced terms-of-trade effects, for example, will have not only a primary impact on the protected import-competing industry, but also a secondary impact on other exporting and import-competing industries in the importing country. Exchange rate, wage rate, and price effects will also spread throughout the economy because of the market distortion introduced by the VER. In principle, CGE estimates of the cost of protection can be expected to be lower than comparable partial equilibrium estimates because of the failure of the latter in taking account of exchange rate and balance-of-payments effects of trade policies (see ibid., 9–4). However, the results of table 3 are in fact higher than many comparable partial equilibrium estimates, due largely to the more detailed background studies used for determining the price effects of VERs, which resulted in higher estimates of quota-induced price premia (ibid, 9–5). Thus the net gains to the United States from removing textile and apparel quotas (incorporating consumer, producer, rent transfer, and economic efficiency effects across the U.S. economy) would be about $13 billion (in 1984 dollars) annually. Net U.S. annual gains from liberalizing VER-constrained trade in automobiles and steel are estimated at about $7 billion and $1 billion, respectively.

The cost-of-protection estimates for VERs are significant because they suggest the extent to which gray-area negotiated trade restrictions have eroded GATT-sponsored tariff reductions and other liberalization measures since World War II. For example, the price increases experienced in the United States due to VERs alone are estimated to be 23 percent for imported autos, 7 percent for steel and more than 40 percent for textiles and apparel (Tarr 1989). Not only have such protectionist policies negated the benefits of negotiated tariff reductions in these products, but they have also hidden their costs in the nontransparent market effects of discriminatory quantitative restrictions. The political economy of VERs described in chapter 2 suggests that demands for massive protection from high-profile, politically powerful domestic industries can be accommodated with a minimum of public backlash through such devices.

VER agreements have also inflicted extensive economic damage on European countries. Smith and Venables (1991) estimate an annual net welfare cost to the EC countries of approximately 4.7 billion ECU (European Currency Units at 1989 prices, equal to about $ 7.7 billion) from automobile export restraint agreements with Japan, a figure that represents about 3 percent of base automobile consumption. Their calculations are based on the existence of individual national VER agreements with Japan among EC member countries, which are being consolidated into an EC-wide residual quota under the Single European Act trade policy reforms. However, the consolidation of national VER quotas will, according to this study, not change the overall welfare cost of automobile export restraint to the EC, but rather redistribute the welfare and anticompetitive effects. EC countries that previously had the most restrictive automobile trade policies, such as France, Italy, Spain, and Portugal, are expected to experience welfare gains, while countries that previously had more open markets, such as Germany and most of the rest of the EC, will suffer welfare losses under the new VER regime.[1]

VER-induced welfare losses to Europe are also significant in the textile-apparel, footwear, and consumer electronics sectors. Hamilton (1986b) estimates that the rent income transferred through clothing VERs from EC and European Free Trade Area (EFTA) countries to Hong Kong alone averaged $131 million annually from 1981 to 1983, representing approximately 10.5 percent of value added in Hong Kong's wearing apparel industry. Winters and Brenton (1991) calculate the annual consumption cost to the United Kingdom alone of VERs and quotas on footwear (deadweight loss plus external transfers) to be £68.98 million (approximately $114 million) in 1986 and a net cumulative social cost to the U.K. from 1977 to 1986 of £568 million ($937 million). At the same time, these trade restrictions saved at most approximately 2 percent of jobs (1064 workers) in the U.K. footwear industry. Greenaway and Hindley (1986), also focusing on VER agreements affecting the United Kingdom, calculate the annual consumer cost per job (at 1983 prices and dollar exchange rates) saved in that country to be £80,000 ($120,000) for video cassette recorders; between £13,250 and £31,500 ($19,875 and $47,250) for automobiles; £13,000 ($19,500) for woven trousers, shirts and blouses, and £7,500 ($11,250) for leather footwear. In each case, the cost per job saved exceeds average annual wages in the respective industries. The authors also note (ibid., 54) that the VER agreement in video cassette recorders was costing EC buyers of this product £6 to transfer each £1 to the local producers Philips and Grundig, the remaining £5 going to Japanese producers as a quota rent.

Using CGE techniques, Jones, Nguyen, and Whalley (1990) estimate the worldwide effects of removing textile and clothing VERs and quotas against developing countries. Based on 1983 data, the major developed countries—the United States, EC and Canada—would experience large annual welfare gains, approximately $8.4 billion collectively. For developing countries, the outcome would be mixed: the loss of quota rents would cause welfare in the major established exporting countries in the MFA, such as Hong Kong, Macau, and Thailand, to decline, while smaller and lower-income developing countries that have been locked out of MFA quota shares, would benefit. This configuration of developing country interests in existing VER arrangements will play a major role in the discussion of chapter 7.

The general message to trade policymakers from the empirical evidence regarding the cost of VER agreements is clear. Export restraint agreements involve a large social cost to the importing country, due particularly to the massive transfers of VER quota rents to exporters. The net social cost per job saved is usually well above the level of existing wages, and continues to accumulate as long as the restriction is in place. In contrast, the adjustment cost of removing VER barriers, while politically painful, would be temporary and could be addressed by retraining programs and other trade adjustment assistance, preferably reinforced by incentives to encourage the adjustment process. The empirical studies of the cost of VERs also imply a potentially large rent-seeking cost linked with lobbying efforts to internalize the gains from protection, not only among domestic import-competing producers, but also among exporting countries with established VER quota shares and accompanying rent transfers. This coalition for protection among domestic and foreign firms tends to harm competition in the affected industries and threatens the trading system as a whole.

Export Restraint and Income Distribution

Insofar as the political economy of export restraint tends to focus trade restrictions on low-cost imports that threaten established domestic industries in competitive decline on world markets, the costs of protection are foisted disproportionately upon lower-income groups. This can be seen in the type of goods that are subject to export restraint: low-cost Japanese automobiles, textiles and apparel from developing countries, footwear from Korea and Taiwan, etc. For lower-income groups, purchases of these items represent a greater percentage of income than for higher-income groups, and the impact of price increases on their welfare is correspondingly larger. The losses tend in fact to be so large that they more than offset any gains, on a national scale, that lower-income workers in the protected industry receive through unemployment avoidance.

Cline (1987) estimated the income distribution effects of textile and apparel protection in the United States by identifying the gains and losses to each of five income groups, defined by quintile ranking (table 4). The benefits of protection are by Cline's calculations concentrated in the small numbers of workers in the third and fourth quintiles whose jobs are saved, and among owners of the protected firms whose profits rise, assumed to be in the highest quintile. The transfer to producers has in fact the most regressive effect on income distribution, far outweighing any benefits to lower-income groups of income maintenance. The losses take the form of higher prices to consumers in each group, estimated, on average, to be $250 per year, each year. As a percentage of income, the greatest losses are concentrated in the lowest-income group, which suffers a 3.64 percent drop in income. Relative losses become lower as income rises, and the highest-income group actually benefits from protection, gaining 0.32 percent of its income.

It is highly likely that similar results would obtain in other industries protected by export restraint arrangements, and there may be even greater regressivity in automobiles and steel, where protected jobs fall in higher-income groups. This cost-benefit analysis also confirms the theoretical expectation that the benefits of protection are concentrated among a small group of workers and owners of corporations, while the cost of protection is spread widely among all consumers of the good, with the net result of a large welfare loss for the country as a whole.

Furthermore, the value escalation effect of export restraint will tend to exacerbate the regressive effect of protection on income distribution through product upgrading. As indicated in chapter 2, quantitative export restraint will generally cause exporters to shift their export deliveries toward higher-value items, a prediction confirmed by most empirical work (see the following section). The theory also implies that the price of lower-value items within the quota category will rise by a greater percentage than the price of higher-value items. Thus, the small, stripped-down models of Japanese imports will be relatively scarcer, and their prices will rise by a relatively greater amount, than the higher-value models. The implication for income distribution is clear: lower-income groups suffer more from the trade restriction than higher-income groups, not only because the automobile purchase represents a higher portion of their income, but because the availability of lower-price models is diminished and their price has risen by a greater-than-average percentage. Boorstein and Feenstra (1991), for example, have estimated the welfare cost to consumers of steel of VER-induced quality changes to be about 1% of U.S. import expenditures on steel from 1970 to 1973. Their estimates suggest that the welfare cost of quality upgrading in steel is similar in magnitude to estimates of the conventional measures of VER-induced deadweight loss, and they argue that it should in fact be added to deadweight loss and quota rent transfers in calculating the net welfare loss of VER agreements to the importing country.

TABLE 4. Income Distributional Effects of Textile and Apparel Protection (by quintile of consumer units)

	Income Group					
	Lowest	21–40%	41–60%	61–80%	81–100%	Total
Income Range ($)	0–7,582	7,583–14,232	14,233–24,197	24,280–35,623	> 35,623	all
Average income ($)	3,577	10,828	19,297	30,370	58,639	24,578
Percentage share in:						
Income	2.9	8.8	15.7	24.7	47.8	100.0
Expenditure	10.3	12.5	17.2	23.1	37.0	100.0
Apparel expend.	10.1	11.1	16.3	21.0	41.4	100.0
Effects of protection						
Consumer cost	–2,057	–2,260	–3,319	–4,276	–8,431	–20,344
Unemployment avoidance	0	110	157	0	0	267
Transfers to	0	0	0	0	9,519	9,519
Gov't. transfer	105	319	568	895	1,732	3,621
Net effects	–1,1951	–1,831	–2,590	–3,374	2,835	–6,907
As percentage of income						
Consumer cost	–3.84	–1.39	–1.15	–0.94	–9.96	–1.11
Unemployment avoidance	0	0.07	0.05	0	0	0.01
Transfer to producers, retailers	0	0	0	0	0	0.52
Gov't. transfer	0.20	0.20	0.20	0.20	0.20	0.20
Net effects	–3.64	–1.13	–0.90	–0.74	0.32	–0.37

Source: Cline 1987, table 8.1 and U.S. Department of Labor (1986). Copyright © 1987 Institute for International Economics. All rights reserved.

Empirical Evidence of Value Escalation

Textiles and Footwear

One way to measure the degree of value escalation is to examine the export mix in terms of value-added categories for countries subject to a restraint agreement. A study by the U.S. International Trade Commission (1986, 1–5), for example, presents evidence that the multi-fiber arrangements have caused an upward shift in the stages of processing (indicating an increase in value added per unit) among restrained exporters of textiles and apparel. Imports of yarn (lowest stage of processing) have actually declined from 1972, the first MFA year, to 1985 from 1.9 billion square yards equivalent (SYE) to 1.25 billion SYE. Output from the next stage of processing, fabric, has risen from 1.7 billion to 2.4 billion; next highest is apparel, 2.2 billion to 5.0 billion; and finally made-up textiles (carpets, etc.), 0.4 to 1.1 billion. Growth rates for each category are, respectively, –3.2 persent, 2.8 percent, 6.5 percent, and 8.1 percent, indicating a pattern of value upgrading.

Cline (1987, 174-178) partially confirms these results by calculating the unit values of imports from restrained countries under the MFA. Textile import unit values in the United States were declining sharply from the mid-1960s to the early 1970s (a result of technological innovations, including the development of synthetic fibers, that reduced production costs). This trend was reversed after the implementation of MFA I in 1972, however. Unit values continued to increase until the early 1980s, when lower oil costs, a recession in the United States, and the subsequent rise in the value of the U.S. dollar appeared to suppress unit import values. For apparel, the evidence of upgrading is stronger. From 1971 to 1973, real import unit values of apparel to the United States rose by 22 percent, and after the recession of 1974-1975, rose again by 23 percentto a peark in 1978. Thus the MFA, at least in its early years, appears to haved caused a shift in the unit value of imports, as predicted by the theory.

The problem with measuring unit values, however, is that it cannot systematically isolate the effect of export restraint agreements on quality upgrading. Unit values can decline, as Cline's data shows, in periods when input costs are decreasing, and when recessions decrease demand for the product, lowering prices. In addition, if unit values are measured in U.S. dollars, an appreciation of the currency (which occurred from the early to mid-1980s) would tend to decrease the unit values in terms of that currency. A more accurate approach to analyzing value escalation therefore appears to lie in identifying product categories defined by quality or value, and seeing if shifts in the categories can be linked with the existence of an export restraint agreement.

Aw and Roberts (1986) took a step in this direction by applying an indexing method to identify shifts in the export mix of nonrubber footwear during the VER agreements imposed by the United States on the Republic of Korea and Taiwan from 1977 to 1981. By using Tornqvist index numbers, part of a technique developed by Diewert (1976), they were able to take changes in the unit value of imports of footwear and isolate pure price changes from price changes due to upgrading into higher-value categories. Thus, under a VER agreement, at least part of the price change should be due to upgrading, and the upgrading effect should be more prominent during VER years.

The results of the study by Aw and Roberts indicate that upgrading within the three major quota categories (leather, plastic, and fiber uppers) was indeed more prominent during the VER years 1977–81 than it was on average over the period 1974–82, and also showed that pure price increases for all footwear imports increased by a greater amount during the VER years. Both the upgrading and the price hikes are consistent with the theoretical expectations of the model presented in chapter 2. The results are also consistent with the study done by Pearson (1983), which showed that the unit value of imports from the restrained suppliers Taiwan and the Republic of Korea increased by 118 percent from 1976 to 1980, compared with the more modest unit value increase of 29 percent from unrestrained foreign suppliers over the period.

In view of the structure of the model, it is, however, necessary to recognize the limits of the Tornqvist number analysis. First of all, it cannot statistically identify individual sources of price and quality changes (such as VERs, demand changes, etc.) but only break the price change down into its two constituent parts. In addition, the degree of observable quality changes relies heavily upon the degree of disaggregation of the data into quality groupings. If quality upgrading took place within a product grouping, for example, any resulting price increase would be improperly included as a part of the pure price increase rather than as a quality change. In addition, price data may not always reflect final consumer costs, which could understate prices elevated by VER premia or understate prices during a sharp decline in demand.

Automobile Export Value Escalation

The automobile export restraint agreement concluded by the United States with Japan from 1981 to 1984 provides another opportunity to observe the value escalation effect. The automobile VER agreement is of particular interest in studying value escalation because there were no subdivisions within the general export quota, allowing all affected exporters to adjust quality content and shift export deliveries freely in response to the quota constraint. Figure 6 shows the striking increase in the unit value of Japanese automobile deliveries to the United States compared to the trend in overall U.S. new car prices since the beginning of the VER agreement in 1981. Theoretical and empirical studies have subsequently attempted to identify the sources of value escalation and to separate quality changes from price changes attributable to VER arrangements.

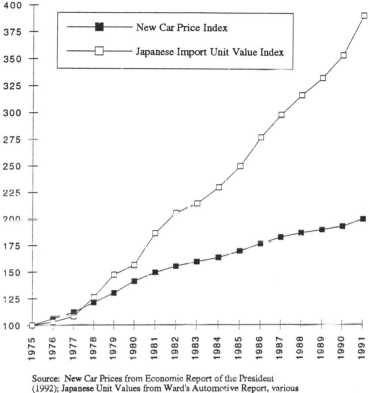

Source: New Car Prices from Economic Report of the President
(1992); Japanese Unit Values from Ward's Automotive Report, various
issues.

Fig. 6. Index of U.S. Average New Car Prices and Japanese Auto Import Values, 1975–1991

The complicated forms that automobile value escalation may take reveal some of the problems involved in identifying the phenomenon. When facing a VER limitation on export sales, automobile manufacturers have two basic means of upgrading their product mix. First, they can increase the delivery of additional equipment or features on existing models. Automatic transmission, air conditioning, power steering, and higher-quality radio units are examples of factory-installed equipment that manufacturers can add to enhance the value of existing models. In addition, firms can upgrade their entire product offerings, creating new designs and improved performance. In many cases, the first type of upgrading also takes place within the framework of the second, as new models typically contain more factory-installed equipment than existing models.

One approach to the measurement of VER-induced value escalation is to examine price changes of automobiles from one year to the next, and then to distinguish between price changes due to quality changes alone from those that could be linked to the scarcity premium of the trade restriction. Collyns and Dunaway (1987) estimated the general effect of the quotas on the quality component of all domestic and all foreign automobiles by comparing actual transaction prices with the consumer price index for new domestic and foreign models. Feenstra (1985) focused on the quality component of Japanese imports in a regression analysis of automobile prices from 1980 to 1982. He used base prices of various models as his dependent variable, and examined the changes in standard equipment (air conditioning, automatic transmission, etc.) as measures of quality adjustment as a possible source of the price change, as well as a dummy variable for the effect of the VER agreement in 1981 and 1982. His results showed an average price increase of Japanese automobile imports of 19.8 percent from 1980 to 1981, of which 6 percent could be linked to quality improvements. After correcting for general inflationary effects, he concluded that Japanese automobile prices relative to U.S. prices increased by 8.4 percent, of which 5.3 percent was attributable to quality improvements and the remaining 3.1 percent represented a scarcity premium for which the consumer was not compensated.

The results of the value escalation analysis point to broader questions regarding the impact of VER agreements on consumers and trade policy. Quality upgrading may be a way of compensating consumers for the higher prices that accompany VER agreements, as implied by Feenstra (1985), but the literature has only recently begun to address the loss to consumers from the reduced choice and associated distortions caused by the trade restriction (see Boorstein and Feenstra 1991). If the automobile VRA added features and equipment that consumers did not value at the price they were charged—in a market with reduced opportunities to bid down the price of these features—then improved quality cannot be said to fully compensate (all) consumers for the corresponding increase in price. To illustrate the point, one need only consider the hypothetical example of a government regulation restricting import buyers to purchases of models like Mercedes or Rolls Royces. Apart from the effect of such a regulation on prices, all consumers who would not otherwise have purchased the required model will suffer an economic loss from reduced choice. Market adjustment to the resulting vacuum at the lower end of the market will eventually draw in imports from other sources not immediately threatened with VER-type constraints. This phenomenon was apparent in U.S. automobile imports of Hyundais from the Republic of Korea and Yugos from Yugoslavia, and in the shift in the source of low-value footwear imports during the VER agreement from Korea and Taiwan to nonrestraining exporters (Pearson 1983, 40). Quality upgrading thus implies an eventual market response of import surges of low-value items within categories subject to export restraint from countries not covered by the export restraint agreement, but in the meantime, consumers will suffer a loss in welfare due to reduced choice.[2]

Finally, the value escalation phenomenon lends further evidence in favor of eliminating VER agreements as policy instruments in trade disputes. Aside from the damage done to consumer welfare, they tend to refocus import competition on higher-value products and encourage lower-value replacement imports to come in from unrestrained suppliers. This market response tends to recycle the protectionist process as domestic producers demand more trade restrictions against the new foreign suppliers. The automobile VER, for example, has intensified import competition in the higher-value models, leading to renewed calls for protection by U.S. automakers.[3] Alternatively, frustrated policymakers may try to tighten the VER product coverage and expand the number of countries covered by export restraints, but this strategy only leads to the further economic and political disasters of an international export cartel, blueprints for which are provided by the networks of steel and textile trade restrictions that have been negotiated since the 1960s. Far from suggesting that quotas be more strictly defined under a VER agreement, the study of value escalation points to the need for a return to GATT principles barring quantitative restrictions and trade discrimination.

Empirical Evidence of Trade Diversion

VER Effects on Import Share

Traditional policy instruments of import control, as explained in chapter 2, can be expected to reduce the total import volume without altering import patterns in terms of supplying countries' market shares. Thus, global tariffs and quotas reduce imports in an equiproportionate manner. Formally, the market share of a given country in a given import market can be expressed in terms of relative price advantage and market structure:

$$M_i = f(p_i / p_w, n) \tag{1}$$

where M_i is the import share of country i, p_i is its import price, p_w is the weighted import price of all suppliers, and n is number of market participants, whereby the first partial derivatives of the two arguments are less than zero.

The implementation of discriminatory export restraint agreements will distort the pattern of import market shares. Specifically, the theory predicts that the market share of exporters targeted by restraint-inducing policies will decrease. The economic reason for the market-share shift is that unrestricted suppliers are allowed to move up their supply curves in response to the induced price increase, while restrained countries are not. As shown in the previous section and in chapter 2, value escalation among restrained exporters will tend to magnify the trade diversion effect, to the extent that it causes the price of the homogeneous good represented in equation (1) to rise even further due to the differential price effects of quality upgrading. Furthermore, if other countries impose discriminatory export restrictions against a foreign supplier, then that supplier's import share will tend to increase in those importing countries that have not also increased trade restrictions in the same manner. These market-share effects represent the essence of the trade diversion phenomenon associated with discriminatory export restraint.

Hamilton (1985) has identified the export restraint agreement as a sort of perverse customs union in which the importing country moves from free trade with all trading partners to the creation of a free trade "club" that includes all trading partners except the ones targeted for export restraint. Since the most efficient, lowest-cost producers are typically the ones subject to export restraint, world economic efficiency declines. Hamilton goes on to show how export restraint agreements in textiles, clothing, and footwear imposed by EFTA and EEC countries (particularly Sweden) caused the source of imports to shift toward partner countries and away from countries subject to VER agreements. Pearson (1983) notes that the nonrubber footwear VER imposed by the United States on Taiwan and the Republic of Korea was followed by an immediate increase in the import market share of unrestrained exporters.

Steel Import Market Shares and Export Restraint

Steel, traditionally one of the most heavily protected industries in the world economy, provides a good opportunity to observe the market-share effects of various policies of induced export restraint in the United States and the EC. This was especially true until the late 1970s and early 1980s, when both the United States and the EC effectively cartelized the world steel export market and import market shares of most steel-exporting countries were locked into managed trade pacts. It is important to remember, however, that the discriminatory impact of export restraint continues even when all suppliers are subject to restraint, since the most efficient and growing exporters' shares are typically suppressed below the levels that an open market would create. Among exporters, the beneficiaries of such a system are generally the established, large industrialized countries with the requisite economic and political power to negotiate favorable export quotas.

The United States concluded export restraint agreements with Japan and the EC in 1968 and renewed them in 1972. These agreements covered steel imports to the United States from 1969 to 1974. As negotiated market-sharing arrangements, they attempted to stabilize imports by freezing import market shares of the participants. A number of factors make it difficult, however, to calculate with precision the effect of the agreements on trade patterns. Such factors include the apparent nonparticipation of some EC and Japanese firms in the quota program, the lack of specific product coverage, and an apparent demand resurgence in the United States during the period when the agreements were in force.

Still, the first two years of the VERs did appear to decrease imports and to effect at least a temporary shift in import patterns. As table 5 indicates, 1969 exhibited a sharp drop in imports, but the brunt of the reduction was borne by EC producers, since Japan had exceeded its quota limit by 9 percent while the EC had stayed 10 percent below its limit. This composition of imports, favoring Japan, was repeated in 1970. Considering the trend in Japan's increasing cost-efficiency and increased U.S. market penetration during the 1960s, this pattern was probably similar to that which would have resulted under nondiscriminatory import controls.

However, market shares reversed during the second VER agreement (1972–74), with EC producers increasing their market share at the expense of Japanese producers. The most obvious component of this shift was the addition of the United Kingdom to the European VER, which automatically increased the quota for that region. Yet more subtle factors were also at work. While market conditions in the United States from 1972 to 1974 reduced import demand to the point where the VER quotas were not filled anyway, Japanese producers had already acknowledged the protectionist trend in U.S. steel import policy. They therefore turned their attention to other markets during these three years (see the discussion of trade diversion in the following section). Given their increasing competitive advantage on world markets, Japanese steelmakers had more alternative markets to cultivate than their EC counterparts, notably those in east Asia, Oceana, and the EC itself. In short, the relative market opportunities in the United States for the Japanese were directly reduced by the riskiness of increased import penetration associated with the protectionist surge in the United States. Only after the VER agreements were discontinued in 1974 did Japanese exporters refocus their attention on the U.S. market.

Since 1975, a number of policy devices designed or used to induce export restraint have appeared, including direct VER agreements, trigger price mechanism (TPM), basic price system (effectively establishing floor import prices for steel), and antidumping and countervailing duty petitions. In the United States, antidumping petitions aimed at Japan emerged as the primary means of steel import restriction in 1977 with the *Gilmore* case. The enforcement of the fair trade laws through private suits and the TPM (a violation of which triggered an antidumping investigation) was geared to limit imports on a product-by-product basis.

The analysis of chapter 2 suggests that, aside from relative price and the number of import suppliers, possible trade intimidation effects affecting market share in equation (1) might include variables representing the impact of the TPM and BPS, threatened protectionist legislation, and antidumping petitions. A regression equation can therefore be used to estimate these effects (see Jones

TABLE 5. U.S. Imports of Steel Mill Products by Region of Origin, 1961–80 (thousand net tons)

	Japan(%)		EEC(%)		Other(%)		Total	
1961	597	(18.9)	1,952	(61.7)	614	(19.4)	3,162	(100)
1962	1,072	(26.1)	2,087	(50.9)	941	(23.0)	4,100	(100)
1963	1,808	(33.2)	2,246	(41.2)	1,398	(25.6)	5,452	(100)
1964	2,446	(38.0)	2,585	(40.1)	1,408	(21.9)	6,439	(100)
1965	4,418	(42.6)	4,191	(40.4)	1,774	(17.0)	10,283	(100)
1966	4,851	(45.1)	3,841	(35.7)	2,061	(19.2)	10,753	(100)
1967	4,468	(39.0)	4,842	(42.3)	2,145	(18.7)	11,455	(100)
1968	7,294	(40.6)	7,097	(39.5)	3,569	(19.9)	17,960	(100)
1969	6,253	(44.6)	5,199	(37.0)	2,582	(18.4)	14,034	(100)
1970	5,935	(44.4)	4,573	(34.2)	2,865	(21.4)	13,364	(100)
1971	6,908	(37.7)	7,174	(39.2)	4,240	(23.1)	18,322	(100
1972	6,440	(36.4)	7,779	(44.0)[a]	3,462	(19.6)	17,681	(100)
1973	5,637	(37.2)	6,519	(43.0)	3,003	(19.8)	15,150	(100)
1974	6,159	(38.6)	6,424	(40.2)	3,387	(21.1)	15,970	(100)
1975	5,844	(48.6)	4,118	(34.3)	2,050	(17.1)	12,012	(100)
1976	7,984	(55.9)	3,188	(22.3)	3,113	(21.8)	14,285	(100)
1977	7,820	(40.5)	6,833	(35.4)	4,654	(24.1)	19,307	(100)
1978	6,487	(30.7)	7,563	(35.3)	7,185	(34.0)	21,135	(100)
1979	6,336	(36.2)	5,405	(30.9)	5,777	(32.9)	17,518	(100)
1980	6,007	(38.8)	3,887	(25.1)	5,601	(36.1)	15,495	(100)

Source: American iron and Steel Institute (annual), various issues.

[a] From 1972 includes the United Kingdom, which joined the European VRA with the United States in that year.

1981). The model sets up the change in Japanese market share in the U.S. import market as the dependent variable and estimates the effects of a linear combination of the following explanatory variables: (1) *DP*, the percentage change in relative import price; (2) *DP2*, the change in relative import price assuming *no* trade-intimidating policies are in effect[4]; (3) *DN*, the absolute change in the number of suppliers to the U.S. import market (supplying 1 percent or more of the import market); (4) *TPM*, a dummy variable for a change in the status of the TPM; (5) *PL*, a dummy variable indicating a change in the status of trade-diverting legislation (i.e., directed principally against Japan); (6) *DUMP*, a dummy variable indicating a change in the status of U.S. antidumping suits against Japanese firms; and (7) DIV, a dummy variable indicating a change in the status of trade-diverting policies against Japan in a non-U.S. import market. The expected sign of coefficients for variables 1 through 6 is negative, while variable 7 has an expected positive effect on import market share.

Data for the regression represented semiannual imports from Japan of six steel products from 1974 to 1980: carbon steel plate, galvanized sheet, cold-rolled sheet, structural shapes, standard welded pipe, and stainless steel round wire. A six-month lag in reported import prices was used. The results of the regression are represented in the following equation (*t*-statistics in parentheses):

$$\text{DMSH} = 0.476 + 0.6791\ DP - 1.1102\ DP2 - 1.6440\ DN-$$
$$\quad\ \ (0.41)\quad (1.34)\qquad\ (-1.94)\qquad\ (-2.48)$$

$$4.879\ TPM - 10.377\ PL - 6.856\ DUMP + 7.496\ DIV \qquad\qquad (2)$$
$$(-1.45)\qquad (-2.15)\qquad (-2.14)\qquad\quad (2.09)$$

$$R\text{-sq(adj)} = .378 \quad \text{d.f} = 64 \quad \text{SER} = 8.157 \quad D\text{-}W = 2.41$$

While changes in relative price in general appear to have no significant impact on market share, the negative value for *DP2*, with just below 5 percent significance, supports the idea that a 1 percent change in Japan's relative import price will decrease its market share by 1.11 percent, assuming that no trade diverting action is being taken against it. An antidumping investigation has a strongly negative and significant impact on market share, while the introduction of the TPM had a lower and statistically insignificant effect. The sequence of protectionist policy developments indicates that the *Gilmore* and subsequent anti-dumping suits had the greatest impact on Japanese import market shares, while the later implementation of the TPM seemed to reinforce the lower share levels that had already been established. The greatest impact on import shares, however, is found in the protectionist threat of import quota legislation, which caused the import share to drop 10.377 percentage points. The implementation of the VER between Japan and the EEC in 1975, captured in the variable *DIV*, caused an increase of 7.496 percentage points in the Japanese U.S. import share, while an increase of one foreign supplier to the U.S. market resulted in a drop of 1.644 percentage points.

A similar regression was run using Japanese import share in the EC as the dependent variable. The results were generally insignificant, although a VER agreement concluded in 1975 limiting Japanese deliveries to the EC appears to have had the expected negative effect on Japan's EC market share. By the late 1970s, however, the EC had embarked upon a policy of concluding export restraint agreements with all major suppliers of steel to its market. Thus, the poor results do not necessarily conflict with the theoretical basis of the model, since a universal orderly marketing arrangement does not always lead to measurable trade diversion in a comparative statics framework. In general, the trade diversion effects will be most evident if the export restraint arrangement is less than universal, although as was noted above, such trade restrictions typically stunt the growth of what would otherwise be rapidly growing exports from countries with increasing comparative advantage in the product.

Diversion of Japanese Exports to Third Countries

In addition to predicting a drop in import market shares as a result of a trade-diverting policy or action in the importing country, the hypothesis of this study also predicts that exports from the supplying country will subsequently be diverted to other countries. Table 6 lists Japanese export shares by country and/or area of destination for two steel product groups, light sections and plates and sheets, which cover most of the steel categories treated in the regression analysis for both the U.S. and the EC import markets.

The trends in export destination revealed in table 6 suggest that policies of export restraint divert the destination of exports as well as the source of imports. Japanese exports of steel plates and sheets, for example, shifted away from the EC and toward the United States in 1976, the year of the VER agreement with the EC. By 1977, however, trade-diverting actions and threats in both the United States and the EC caused Japanese export trade to shift to other countries, especially in the Oceana/Far East region. In the case of light sections exports from Japan, the data are obscured by the inclusion of heavy sections, but U.S. and EC import data show that Japanese deliveries to the EC dropped while those to the United States increased in 1976. Japanese exports of this product to the United States were also high in 1977, but declined in both the United States and the EC in 1978 and 1979, shifting again largely to the Oceana/Far East region.

These patterns of export trade diversion are important in understanding steel trade policy developments in the United States and the EC. The refocusing of diverted Japanese exports to the United States in the wake of the 1975 VER agreement contributed heavily to the subsequent policy crisis in the United States in 1977. Antidumping investigation and the announcement of the TPM in the United States in 1977 in turn caused the EC to threaten, and then to take, preemptive action to prevent Japanese import disruption.

As the steel crisis continued into the 1980s, the anticipation of trade-diverting effects became a matter of increasing concern for U.S. and EC trade officials. When the United States concluded a detailed steel VER agreement with the EC in 1982, trade opportunities for nonrestraining exporters, bolstered by the appreciation of the U.S. dollar, increased. Imports from these countries surged for the next two years, setting the stage for a renewal of the policy crisis in 1984. The ensuing VER negotiations established a nearly global network of

TABLE 6. Japanese Steel Exports by Country of Destination, 1963-82
(thousand metric tons)

Year	Total	U.S.	%	EC	(%)[a]	Far East	(%)
1963	5,283	1,544	(20.2)	464	(8.8)	1,825	(34.5)
1964	6,539	2,352	(35.8)	298	(4.6)	2,139	(32.7)
1965	9,746	4,122	(42.3)	160	(1.6)	2,502	(25.7)
1966	9,478	4,416	(46.6)	268	(2.8)	2,851	(32.7)
1967	8,707	4,094	(47.0)	181	(2.1)	2,852	(32.7)
1968	12,774	6,617	(51.8)	210	(1.6)	3,609	(28.3)
1969	15,548	5,272	(33.9)	947	(6.1)	4,710	(30.3)
1970	17,589	5,580	(31.7)	950	(5.4)	5,314	(30.2)
1971	23,194	5,787	(25.0)	1,653	(7.1)	6,819	(29.4)
1972	20,992	5,658	(27.0)	1,116	(5.3)	6,666	(31.9)
1973	24,805	4,696	(18.9)	1,282	(5.2)	9,629	(38.8)
1974	32,220	5,791	(18.0)	1,054	(3.3)	10,869	(33.7)
1975	28,942	5,126	(17.7)	1,573	(5.4)	8,778	(30.3)
1976	36,016	6,800	(18.9)	1,467	(4.1)	10,722	(29.8)
1977	33,628	7,016	(20.9)	1,265	(3.8)	12,235	(36.4)
1978	30,925	5,614	(18.2)	623	(2.0)	14,068	(45.5)
1979	30,697	5,799	(18.9)	720	(2.3)	13,306	(43.3)
1980	29,705	4,883	(16.4)	616	(2.1)	12,959	(43.6)
1981	28,455	5,920	(20.8)	198	(0.7)	11,458	(40.3)
1982	28,635	3,913	(13.7)	260	(0.9)	12,020	(42.0)

Source: United Nations (annual), various issues.

[a] From 1973. the figures for the European Community include those of the United Kingdom, Denmark, and the Republic of Ireland.

steel export quotas on trade to the United States. The EC, which had already begun to establish a similar network of comprehensive VER arrangements with its suppliers in 1978, tightened the trade restrictions during the next six years. The only way to avoid trade diversion from nonrestraining countries in this case was to make the trade restriction as global and airtight as possible.

Conclusion

The high social cost of VERs, combined with their tendency to induce quality upgrading and a diversion of exports to unprotected third markets, point to their most important drawbacks as an instrument of trade policy. The largest element of lost social welfare in the basic analysis of the cost of VERs is the quota rent transfer to the exporter, implying that tariffs could provide equivalent protection at greatly reduced cost. Export restraint arrangements typically cause value escalation and trade diversion, creating a porosity effect that allows exporters to use various channels (other products, other markets) to avoid the full impact of the trade restriction. The common result is that the disruptive imports are refocused on other products or markets, or begin to come from different sources. These effects, which stem in general from the discriminatory and quantitative nature of export restraint, tend to create new protectionist pressures, either in the upgraded product, in a third market not previously subject to import surges, or against suppliers not restrained by the trade restriction.

Value escalation will tend to appear whenever there is room in the quota categories to shift exports to higher-value products. If imports continue to be a problem in the general or upgraded product categories, new VER negotiations will often create more detailed quota categories in an attempt to stop this process. In addition, the original VER arrangement may have to be expanded to include other exporters who are drawn into the market by the vacuum at the lower end of the market created by upgrading. In general, the attractiveness of a market protected by a limited VER arrangement virtually assures some diversion of the source of imports from restraining to nonrestraining countries, and the importing country will often find that expansion of the number of countries covered by export restraint is required in order to maintain the protective effect. These factors have defined the progressive tightening of VER arrangements in steel, textiles, and apparel, in particular.

Trade diversion by shipments of restraining countries to open third markets also tends to renew the protectionist cycle and has the potential for causing serious trade conflict. A surge in imports that can be linked with an export restraint agreement elsewhere not only increases the likelihood of the spread of protectionism to other countries, but may also increase tensions between the two importing countries. This was the case with the United States and the EC in steel trade in the 1970s. A resolution of such conflicts often involves a globalization of the export restraint agreements into a comprehensive export cartel, the results of which may be a further reduction in competition, a raising of prices, and an increase in the welfare cost of protection.

Notes

1. The consolidated VER arrangement between the EC and Japan received an exemption from the general VER phaseout proposal in the safeguards negotiations of the Uruguay Round. See chapter 8.

2. The work of Boorstein and Feenstra (1991) suggests that a greater degree of quality upgrading may imply a greater potential for such welfare losses. Given the degree of VER-induced upgrading observed in automobiles, as well as the large expenditures on automobile imports, the absolute level of consumer losses due to upgrading are likely to be correspondingly large in this sector.

3. The breathing space granted to U.S. automobile manufacturers from the VER apparently did not lead to the degree of increased U.S. competitiveness that Detroit claimed would be possible from modernization, productivity increases, and research and development. See Crandall (1984). In the meantime, efforts at imposing unilateral protection or inducing further Japanese export restraint have focused on minivans (see USITC 1992).

4. This variable takes on a zero value when the *DUMP* or *TPM* dummy variables are equal to one, and assumes the value of *DP* when the *DUMP* and *TPM* variables are both equal to zero. The inclusion of *DP2* reflects the expectation that trade-intimidating devices will dominate changes in import market share and that changes in relative price have the power to predict changes in import market share only in the absence of such devices.

CHAPTER 4

U.S. Policy Instruments of Induced Export Restraint

The study so far has shown that the use of voluntary export restraint has arisen in the postwar period as a result of the progressive decline of tariffs and import quotas as instruments of trade policy. These traditional tools of trade policy restrict trade by artificially reducing import demand, that is, by taxing or placing quantitative restrictions on foreign goods as they pass through the importing country's borders. A government thereby exercises direct control over import levels and prices, since it controls the source of the trade restrictions. However, GATT restrictions on the use of traditional import barriers, as well as tariff binding under GATT-sponsored trade negotiations, have caused governments to turn to new protectionist devices, including VERs.

Yet export restraint agreements can best be understood as part of a system of trade-restrictive policies, often described as the safeguards complex, that has developed under U.S. trade policy to accommodate persistent protectionist demands (see Schott 1990, 18–25). The system, moreover, relies generally on the principle of induced export restraint against specific suppliers as the means of trade control. Consider, first of all, the means of direct import restriction provided by U.S. trade legislation (table 7). Antidumping and countervailing duty law, as well as sections 406 (directed at nonmarket economy imports) and 301, provide legal avenues to selectively restrict imports based on unfair, disruptive or unreasonable trade practices. Because they are selective and involve numerous self-defined administrative controls, procedures, and criteria for determining "guilt," however, they provide a framework for encouraging export restraint among targeted suppliers, as will be shown in this and the following chapter. Sections 201 and 232, on the other hand, provide for import restrictions on goods that are fairly traded, but nonetheless cause serious injury or threaten national security, respectively. These trade law measures have proven difficult for the U.S. government to apply, due to the GATT restrictions on their use and the threat of retaliation, but they, too, have provided a framework for identifying troublesome sources of imports and encouraging export restraint agreements. Not shown in table 7 is the broad power of Congress to regulate imports through directly legislated protectionist measures, which often provides a convenient threat of unilateral action designed to bring targeted exporters to the negotiating table.

TABLE 7. Summary of Major U.S. Trade Remedy Laws

Statute	Cause of Action	Administrative Authority	Form of remedy
Antidumping law, TitleVII, Tariff Act of 1930	Import sales at LTFV resulting in material injury	Commerce (dumping margin); ITC (injury)	AD duties
Countervailing Duty Law	Import sales benefiting from foreign subsidies	Commerce (subsidy level); ITC (injury)	CV duties
Sec. 201, Escape Clause, Trade Act of 1974	Increased imports a substantial cause of serious injury	ITC recommends; President (final decision)	Tariffs, TRQ, QRs, OMAs, AA
Sec. 406, Trade Act of 1974	Increased imports from NMEs a significant cause of material injury	ITC recommends; President (final decision)	Tariffs, TRQ, QRs, OMAs, AA
Sec. 301, Trade Act of 1974	Violation of U.S. rights under a trade agreement, any foreign act "unjustifiable, unreasonable, or discriminatory & burdens or restricts U.S.commerce"	USTR	Suspension/ withdrawal of trade benefits, import restrictions
Sec. 232, Trade Expansion Act of 1962	Imports threatening national security	Commerce recommends; President (final decision)	Presidential discretion

Source: U.S. Congress (1984).
Legend: AA=adjustment assistance; AD=Antidumping; CV=countervailing; ITC=International Trade Commission; LTFV=less than fair value; NME=non-market economy; OMA=orderly marketing agreement; QRs=quantitative restriction; TRQs=tariff rate quota.

Protection from import competition is therefore now achieved primarily through selective actions based on either legal enforcement against so-called unfair trade practices, executive action mandated by specific trade laws, or the trade-intimidating effects of threatened protectionist legislation. The result of the use of these legal and political measures is typically one of the many of forms of induced export restraint, either a formal accord among governments on voluntary export restraint, an agreement on prices of quantities to terminate an unfair trade investigation, or partial or total withdrawal from the market based on pure trade intimidation. In contrast to traditional import barriers, these trade-restricting devices use administrative procedures, threats, bluffs, and negotiations to induce specific exporters to restrict deliveries to the import market.

This chapter sets out to examine the new structure of U.S. trade policy and sets forth two propositions: first, that most new import barriers are now based on a system of induced export restraint, from antidumping actions to negotiated VER agreements; and secondly that the higher the political profile of the trade dispute, the more formal will be the type of export restraint instrument used, a phenomenon described as *structural escalation*. The chapter pursues an analysis of the various export restraint-inducing mechanisms of negotiated export limitations, trade law enforcement, and threatened protectionist legislation. There follows an investigation of the process of policy choice in the importing country, leading to a discussion of some of the implications of the present system for trade law and trade relations in the future.

The Instruments of Induced Export Restraint

The Levels of Structure in Export Restraint

In order to analyze the phenomenon of induced export restraint, it is useful to divide the instruments of restraint into three categories: structured, semistructured, and unstructured. Structured export restraint restricts trade through explicitly negotiated, quantitative limits on exports and therefore has a specific, predictable impact on trade. In contrast, unstructured export restraint occurs when trade law actions or threats of protectionist legislation cause the exporter to reduce deliveries unilaterally, with no explicit agreement on price or quantity limits. In between lies semistructured export restraint, which is based on implicit agreements on import pricing behavior, but not on export quantities, and is most often found in price undertakings used to terminate antidumping cases.

While structured restraint is based on an agreement among the parties in a trade dispute, unstructured restraint is based on the perceptions of the exporter alone to the threat of trade restrictions; its trade effects are therefore much less predictable. The following analysis will show that higher levels of structure can offer greater assurances of trade restriction-induced rents to both exporters and domestic producers, a factor that pushes the policy choice toward negotiated export restraint in cases where the political influence of the protection-seeking firm or industry is strong. Political constraints on the use of negotiated trade restrictions, on the other hand, tend to move the policy choice toward less structured devices.

Negotiated Export Restraint Agreements

In U.S. trade policy, structured export restraint takes three forms. The orderly marketing agreement (OMA) is a bilaterally negotiated arrangement limiting deliveries of specific goods to the United States from one or more foreign countries. The legal basis for such agreements was established in the escape clause provisions of the Trade Expansion Act of 1962 and are consistent with article XIX of the GATT; they must therefore conform to the GATT rules on applicability, injury determination, and nondiscrimination. Industries that have received such protection include specialty steel, color television sets and nonrubber footwear.

A similar means of structured export restraint is available through provisions of the antidumping (AD) and countervailing duty (CVD) laws, which allow the president to authorize an export limitation arrangement in order to terminate an unfair trade practice investigation. A negotiated quantitative export restraint agreement of this sort was used in the steel pact of 1982 with the EC, which limited EC exports in several specific steel products. The president received further powers to negotiate bilateral quotas in steel in the Trade and Tariff Act of 1984 and in the Omnibus Trade and Competitiveness Act of 1988.

Finally, the VER agreement represents a means of structured export restraint outside normal GATT rules. Although VER agreements are negotiated bilaterally, their format is technically one of a unilateral declaration of intent by the exporting country to limit its deliveries of particular products to the United States over a specified period of time. Trade officials have used VER agreements when the legal basis for GATT-consistent export restraint arrangements described above has been absent. The VER agreement on steel exports from the EEC and Japan from 1969 to 1974 and the agreement limiting Japanese automobile exports from 1981 to 1985 are two examples of this type of structured export restraint. The multilateral system of textile trade quotas, administered under the MFA, also falls into this category, although it exists as a formally recognized exception to GATT rules.

Structured export restraint is designed to restrict trade by causing the exporter's supply of the designated product to the importing country to become price inelastic at the negotiated quantitative limit, as described in chapter 2. In essence, control over the trade restriction is turned over to the exporter, as opposed to the case of tariffs and import quotas, which give the direct trade-restricting authority to the importing country. Under traditional trade controls, the resulting scarcity premium could be captured by the importing country in the form of tariff revenues or quota license profits. The terms of trade of the importing country would not suffer under these circumstances, and could in fact improve if the importing country were large enough to exercise price-making power on the world market of the traded good. Negotiated export restraint, in contrast, awards the scarcity premium to the exporter, who, as the source of the trade control, has the power to raise the export price as the self-imposed limit causes export supply to become scarce.

The transfer of quota profits to the exporter represents the principal positive incentive for exporters to participate in the trade restriction. In addition, the VER agreement will normally require the formation of an export cartel, which usually benefits existing firms, restricts new market entry, and may lead to even greater rents.

The possibility of unilateral protectionist action by the importing country may, however, provide an even more compelling reason for exporters to conclude a structured restraint agreement. As indicated earlier, by unilaterally imposing trade restrictions the importing country could reduce total imports to the same level while depriving foreign producers of the quota profits given them by the export restraint agreement.[1] Furthermore, without negotiations the levels of protection could be much higher. Other alternatives to structured export restraint may include equally or more damaging antidumping or countervailing duty investigations or more exotic legislated protectionist measures, such as discriminatory import quotas or domestic content rules. The threat of these alternative measures is in fact what is most often used to bring exporters to the negotiating table. Voluntary export restraint is in this regard not voluntary at all; export restraint is induced by various threats, with an economic rent included as enticement.

Unfair Trade Law and Export Restraint

Structured agreements represent the most direct and systematic way of inducing export restraint, since they are designed to cause the exporter's supply curve to become vertical at a specific quantitative level. However, any actions taken by an importing country that cause exporters to restrict deliveries by manipulating their export supply curves can be regarded as means of inducing export restraint. In fact, the unstructured export restraint mechanisms of trade law enforcement, which restrict trade through intimidation effects, provide both a model for the use of discriminatory protectionist measures and a set of incentives for the exporters to conclude structured export restraint agreements.

Antidumping Investigations

Among the unstructured means of inducing export restraint, the application of AD laws is the most significant. Dumping, classically defined, is a form of price discrimination: the selling of a product at a lower price abroad than in the home market. Economic theory predicts such behavior when the two markets can be separated and isolated and the exporting firm has some price-making power in the home market. In order to establish a case of injurious dumping the law requires first of all that a gap be shown to exist between the fair value and the actual (lower) selling price. In addition, there must be proof that the dumped imports themselves have caused or are likely to cause injury to the domestic industry producing a like product. If the investigation shows that these criteria are met, the AD duty on imports of the unfairly traded good is assessed in the amount of the gap between the fair value price and the actual selling price.

This analysis shows that, theoretically, enforcement of AD laws represents a means of import reduction, not induced export restraint. However, the administration of the law and the accompanying investigation tend to cause—and in part seem *designed* to cause—the exporter to adjust the price or quantity of the good in order to avoid a final determination of dumping or the collection of duties. Unlike normal import tariff duties, AD duties are assessed on a contingency basis, that is, when the exporter sells at prices below the legal fair value price.[2] The exporter can then avoid the duty by raising his price to the fair value level. Such price adjustment and the resulting export restraint are in fact the typical results of an affirmative AD duty order.

Yet the upward shift in supply by those found guilty of less than fair value (LTFV) sales does not represent the only means by which these laws induce export restraint. The uncertainties of the investigation itself, plus provisions for a preliminary determination of dumping, tend to reduce the level of exports from countries named in a AD petition, even if no final determination of dumping is made.[3] The outcome of the investigation is dependent to a large extent on the discretionary application of alternative definitions of fair value price, selling price, scope of the investigation period, etc., which involve technical and legal aspects of U.S. law that are likely to be unfamiliar to the foreign exporters (Caine 1981). Hemmendinger and Barringer (1981) have also noted that the short amount of time allotted the exporter to prepare his case, the less stringent standards for a preliminary (as opposed to a final) determination of injury, and a bias toward exaggerated dumping margins increase the probability of an affirmative preliminary determination of injury and substantial dumping margins. It is here that the most important export restraint-inducing mechanism comes into play. An affirmative preliminary finding subjects any further imports to eventual AD duties should a final affirmative determination be made. In the meantime, the exporter must post a bond or other security in the amount of the preliminary dumping margin on subsequent imports. Although a final conviction (i.e., postive determination of injurious dumping) is by no means certain, and the margins are in any case likely to be much smaller in the end, the situation provides a compelling incentive for the exporter to raise the selling price, restraining exports (Hemmendinger and Barringer 1981). Furthermore, until definitive AD duties have been assessed, the indeterminate liability of the importer will hamper his business, further reducing trade (Caine 1981). Aside from the incentives provided by AD determinations, both preliminary and final, to restrain exports, the investigation itself contains numerous trade-intimidating elements. To be sure, the specific circumstances of the case are crucial in determining the exporter's behavior. An exporter may be convinced, for example, that the case will be decided in his favor and will therefore secure his position in the import market and discourage further legal harassment by his local competitors. In this instance, the exporter may not be intimidated by the investigation. However, AD procedures impose considerable costs and risks upon the exporter, often making it desirable for him to avoid or cut short the investigation. The most significant factors include:

1. *Legal Costs.* Fees incurred by a litigant in a full-length AD case are typically in the range of $500,000, according to a 1992 estimate.[4] While the domestic petitioner must also bear such expenses, it is noteworthy that the cost of the investigation per unit of sales in the U.S. market is likely to be much higher for the foreign exporter than for the domestic petitioner (Finger 1981).

2. *Possibility of Extended Litigation.* Both the preliminary and the final decisions on AD and other administrative actions are subject to judicial review. The exporter may therefore face seemingly endless litigation as a result of an AD suit, sometimes casting doubt upon his access to the import market for years (Caine 1981).

3. *Risk of Disclosure of Confidential Submissions.* The investigation often requires foreign firms to submit confidential information, which can be released under a protective order to representatives of interested parties. Because of the difficulty of detection, this provision makes possible illegal disclosures damaging to the exporter (Patenode 1980).

4. *Stigma of Unfair Trade.* Most exporters and their importing agents are concerned about being identified as unfair traders. If the exporter always knew his guilt or innocence under the AD laws from the outset, this factor would not intimidate the innocent exporter. However, the obscurity of much of the technical cost and pricing criteria used often leave the final outcome of the investigation in doubt.

5. *Use of Best Information Available* (BIA). If the foreign firm does not respond adequately to the Commerce Department questionnaire regarding cost, price, and quantity information, the U.S. investigating team is entitled to substitute alternative estimates, usually supplied by the domestic firms that filed the petition, in calculating dumping margins.[5]

Barshefsky and Cunningham (1981) have in addition observed the *in terrorem* effects of the mere filing of an AD petition, leading to immediate price increases by the exporter or total withdrawal from the import market.[6] Once an investigation has begun, and especially after a preliminary determination of dumping has been made, exporters are often eager to terminate the investigation. The AD statute allows the investigation to be terminated if exporters agree to either (1) cease all exports within six months or (2) adjust their prices upward, by formal agreement, to eliminate the dumping margin. Alternatively, a withdrawal of the AD petition by the domestic industry terminates the investigation, which suggests that unilateral export-restraining behavior by foreign suppliers can achieve the same result as a formal price/withdrawal assurance.[7] Finally, a structured quantitative agreement can be negotiated as a quid pro quo for a termination of the investigation. This possibility is limited to cases of high political visibility and sensitivity, such as the steel AD cases, which were terminated in this manner in 1982.

The incentive structure of AD law enforcement can be summarized as follows. Unlike structured restraint agreements, which restrict exports by direct negotiation, AD law depends primarily on intimidation to induce export restraint. The power of formal trade restriction through AD law lies with trade authorities in the importing country, and the uncertainties of the investigation place future access of the exporter to the importing market in question. In this context, the ad hoc response of unstructured restraint prevents the exporter from gaining the rents that typically accompany a coordinated export quota with assured market access. If some form of trade restriction is inevitable, the exporter therefore prefers a more structured export restraint agreement, where the rules of market access are clear. The facts of the case, as well as its perceptions of the legal and perhaps political environment, will determine the exporter's response to the investigation and the importing country's policy choice.

Countervailing Duty Investigation

The CVD statute is designed to protect against export subsidies by foreign governments. A CVD investigation seeks first to establish whether or not a good imported into the United States has received a subsidy. In most, but not all, cases a successful CVD petition must in addition show that the subsidy has caused or is likely to cause injury to the domestic industry producing a like product.[8] If the investigation is affirmative on both points, a per-unit subsidy is calculated and an equivalent duty assessed on each unit. A CVD investigation, unlike an AD inquiry, focuses on the amount of the subsidy itself rather than on a fair value selling price. CVDs are thus designed only to offset the per-unit amount of the subsidy.[9]

If the duty is actually assessed, it represents a direct import control. However, the incentive structure of the CVD statute tends to promote mechanisms of export restraint, as was the case with AD law. The distinguishing feature of export restraint under the CVD law is that the foreign government, rather than the firm or industry, must take actions in order to avoid the CVD. The CVD investigation will be terminated, for example, if the foreign government agrees to eliminate the subsidy or to impose an export tax on the good equal to the per-unit level of subsidization (Practicing Law Institute 1983). Both of these actions represent semistructured export restraint, since they establish an implicit agreement on pricing behavior.

Alternatively, a more formal structured export restraint agreement will also terminate the investigation. This solution may be particularly appealing to countries whose industrial policies conflict with U.S. CVD laws. A negotiated export restraint agreement allows the foreign government to prevent duties from being assessed and thereby avoids the onus of an unfair trade conviction. At the same time, an export restraint agreement may even be welcomed by industrial planners in the foreign country, since it allows continued subsidization and introduces a framework for calculating market access. These motives figured prominently in the EC's negotiation of structured export restraint in exchange for a termination of CVD cases against steel imports in 1982, for example. The more politically sensitive and centrally planned is the exporting industry in the foreign country, the greater is the incentive for the foreign government to conclude a structured export restraint agreement to terminate a CVD investigation.

The Unfair Trade Law Paradigm
The foregoing examination indicates that AD and CVD laws bear a remarkable resemblance to the highly structured VER devices insofar as both types of trade actions identify specific exporters guilty of harming domestic producers' interest. Trade law provides a legitimate, GATT-sanctioned model of discrimination in restricting trade. While most trade policy actions under the GATT are subject to the most-favored-nation clause (i.e., nondiscrimination), this requirement is suspended when dealing with unfair trade, where the importing country can identify a specific country's producers violating antidumping or countervailing duty law. The only added requirement, as noted earlier, is that proof of injury be shown. By extension, a political determination of injury due to the import competition of specific exporters with domestic producers provides a basis for negotiating a discriminatory structured export restraint agreement. In addition, the vague application of the term unfair trade in public debate over trade policy emphasizes the fluidity between trade law and ad hoc protectionist policies in the eyes of policymakers. A protectionist campaign benefits greatly from a determination (by either legal or political means) that specific foreign exporters are responsible for the poor performance of domestic firms. The unfair trade laws have provided the designers of structured export restraint agreements with the politically expedient model of selectivity in restricting trade. As noted in chapter 2, the GATT's acceptance of the necessity of unfair trade laws as a means of achieving a political consensus favoring general trade liberalization established the paradigm of discrimination. Within this framework, trade law enforcement, as well as threats of escape clause and legislated protection, provide incentives to induce unstructured export restraint and encourage structured restraint against specific disruptive suppliers to the domestic market.

The Means of Political Pressure

The Escape Clause

Escape clause protection also plays an important role in the incentive structure of export restraint, although it is a more openly political device than AD and CVD law and enforcement. While AD and CVD investigations deal with unfair import competition, escape clause legislation provides industries with the means to petition for temporary emergency protection that can last a maximum of eight years, including an extension.[10] Escape clause protection is based on a determination that increases in imports (whether fairly or unfairly traded) have injured an import-competing domestic industry. After a positive determination of injury by the U.S. International Trade Commission (USITC), the president may decide to aid the domestic industry through trade adjustment assistance or through tariffs, import quotas, or OMAs. However, the president may also refuse to grant protection despite the ITC's determination of injury if he decides that such relief is not in the national economic interest. Congress may override the president's decision if it differs from the ITC's recommendation, although it has not occurred at this writing.

The export restraint-inducing effects of escape clause investigations themselves tend to be weaker than those of unfair trade investigations, for three basic reasons. First, the former do not carry the stigma of unfair trade attached to the latter. Second, and more important, is the fact that the injury standard used in escape clause investigations is much more difficult to satisfy. Finally, even if there is a positive determination of injury, the president may refuse to grant protection, as has often been the case. These factors make the escape clause a much less credible threat of trade restriction than AD and CVD investigations.

Yet escape clause legislation contains its own distinctive incentive structure that may encourage export restraint. A number of scenarios are possible. Insofar as the injury investigation and subsequent presidential decision may be prejudiced against the exporter should high levels of imports continue, the exporter may be motivated to restrain deliveries once it becomes known that a petition will be filed. If the USITC recommends protection, this strategy is of particular significance in view of the politicized atmosphere in which the final presidential decision takes place. If the level of imports under investigation can be portrayed by the domestic industry as politically unacceptable, a concerted protectionist campaign may be able to exploit the issue and create increased pressure for protection. Even if the president rejects an ITC recommendation for protection, the ITC's determination of injury may serve as a basis for further protectionist action, as was the case in the 1981 automobile VER and the steel export pacts of 1984.

On the other hand, the investigation could conceivably lead to an immediate increase in deliveries from the exporter. Since escape clause protection is only implemented after the presidential decision, an incentive is created for the exporter to speed up deliveries before the trade restrictions come into effect. Export restraint may indeed follow for the three- to eight-year period of the escape clause relief, but the exporter may then reenter the market knowing that the domestic industry is enjoined from further escape clause petitions for two years.

The great financial expense of an escape clause investigation (estimated to be a minimum of $500,000 for a successful petition) may also seriously drain the legal and lobbying funds of a small domestic industry. If the domestic industry is denied escape clause protection, foreign exporters with a deep pocket may then be in a position to wage a price war, increasing their market share. Once the escape clause proceedings reach the stage of a presidential decision, the clause's intimidating effect on exporters depends heavily on the size, financial resources, lobbying power, and political influence of the domestic industry behind the escape clause petition.

Yet the foreign exporters, backed by their governments, have political weapons of their own that may reduce the ability of the escape clause to induce export restraint. If the president decides to grant protection, the GATT entitles the affected exporting countries to some form of compensation, through either reduced tariffs in other areas or a negotiated agreement on the quantitative OMA that presumably raises export prices and effects a transfer to the exporters. If an agreement on compensation is not reached in a GATT forum, the exporting country often retaliates against the importing country with trade restrictions of its own, as the EC did in response to the 1983 OMA on specialty steel. These policy constraints in fact play a large role in discouraging the president from granting escape clause protection, especially when the exporter is a country or group of countries with credible retaliatory power. The evidence suggests that the intimidating effects of the escape clause are strongest on countries with little political influence or bargaining power. This is why escape clause OMAs have been used most often with Japan, the Republic of Korea, and Taiwan, countries with large trade surpluses and little retaliatory power.

In the end, an escape clause investigation will create incentives for the foreign suppliers to negotiate a structured export restraint agreement if the foreigners stand to derive greater benefits through the associated rent transfers and guaranteed market access than through unrestricted trade. The existence of retaliatory power greatly increases the foreign government's bargaining power and can play a large role in a presidential denial of escape clause relief. Structured export restraint induced by an escape clause investigation may take the form of an OMA negotiated directly as a result of an affirmative determination, or it may result indirectly from the protectionist pressure generated by the investigation, even if formal escape clause relief is rejected.

Threats of Legislated Protection

Threatened congressional action against imports often represents the most direct means of political pressure on foreign exporters to conclude a structured export restraint agreement. Protectionist legislative proposals are, if anything, more threatening to exporters than trade law enforcement because of the wide discretionary powers of Congress in regulating trade. Among the protectionist weapons available to Congress are those most detrimental to exporter interests, such as unilateral (and possibly discriminatory) import quotas and exotic devices like the proposed domestic content rules for automobiles. The threat of domestic content rules in the Japanese automobile case, for example, continues to induce export restraint, despite the Reagan administration's decision to end the structured VER agreement in 1985.

Yet it is not merely the power of Congress that can induce export restraint, but also the political process that is used to mobilize that power. Influence on congressional policy-making is strongest among industries with extensive lobbying power and high political visibility, such as steel, automobiles, and textiles. Increased import penetration in politically sensitive markets often provides the impetus for a broad-based protectionist campaign. The promulgation of proposed trade-restricting legislation and the accompanying public debate signals the exporter that current import levels are politically unacceptable and indicates the type of restriction and probable stakes involved should the legislation be implemented. The exporter (or the government of the exporting country) will then have some basis for assessing the chances export restraint will have in forestalling the legislation and comparing the welfare effects of export restraint with those of legislated import restrictions (Bhagwati and Srinivasan 1976). Threatened protectionist legislation may therefore induce unilateral, unstructured export restraint, or it may lead directly to negotiated structured export restraint.

The credibility of the legislative threat will determine its potential ability to induce export restraint. In this regard, the retaliatory power of the targeted exporter will tend to diminish the credibility of the threat, as was the case in escape clause investigations. In addition, many proposed legislative trade restrictions are GATT-illegal and would involve serious political costs to the U.S. government if they became law. Nonetheless, from a negotiating point of view, U.S. trade officials may find such renegade congressional action useful as a convenient bluff in bringing recalcitrant exporters to the negotiating table. Thus, the congressional threat of domestic automobile content legislation allowed U.S. trade negotiators to posture as the "good cop" in offering Japanese automakers a VER to forestall action by the "bad cop" Congress. Proposed legislative action in any case indicates that the trade dispute has passed a political threshold that is likely to require diplomatic attention.

Section 301 Investigations

Section 301 of U.S. trade law, contained in chapter 1 of Title II of the Trade and Tariff Act of 1974, as amended, allows the U.S. government to retaliate against foreign government practices that are, in the words of the statute, unjustifiable or unreasonable. The first category refers to foreign government policies or actions that violate U.S. international rights under the GATT or other formal agreements; the second refers to foreign policies, acts, or practices that, while not in violation of U.S. legal rights, are nonetheless deemed unfair or inequitable.[11] The law then allows retaliation against the offending countries if the practice in question is not removed. Legislative amendments to the original provisions have imposed strict timetables for foreign compliance to U.S. demands in cases where violations have been officially identified, and have also increased the likelihood of retaliatory action.[12]

Section 301 provides the United States Trade Representative (USTR) with an effective means of bringing foreign exporters to the negotiating table. While its purpose has principally been to serve U.S. exporter interests in opening foreign markets, it has also served as a source of leverage in getting foreign countries to suppliers to conclude VER agreements. For example, section 301 petitions were filed against several countries in 1981 claiming violations of the GATT Subsidies Code regarding support of their domestic stainless steel industries, a case that eventually led to an OMA under section 201 in 1983 (USITC 1984, 370–71). Another petition was filed against Korea in 1983 over that country's steel import restrictions, which allegedly diverted Japanese exports toward the United States (*ibid*, 372), and the threat of renewed petitions on this basis was used to convince Korea to join the steel VER program in 1984.[13] The threat of a section 301 petition was also used in negotiating an agreement with Japan in 1986 regarding semiconductor pricing, which led to a minimum pricing arrangement similar to price undertakings used to terminate antidumping cases (USITC 1987, 4–26).

Summary: A Taxonomy of Induced Export Restraint

Table 8 summarizes the restraint-inducing mechanisms of the six major policy instruments of export restraint. What distinguishes structured from unstructured and semistructured restraint emerges most clearly in a comparison of specific incentives. Structured restraint allows exporters not only to gain an economic rent, but also to avoid facing all other types of protectionist measures. The political economy of induced export restraint thus suggests that exporting countries tend to prefer high-structured to lower-structured restraint when the net benefits of negotiated export restraint exceed the costs imposed by the alternative trade restriction. Strictly speaking, such a consideration involves comparing the discounted present value of the rent transfer and value of guaranteed market access with the similarly calculated financial and economic costs of alternative trade law, executive actions, and legislated trade restrictions.

An additional consideration for the exporting firms or country involves the consequences of an unresolved trade dispute. While structured export restraint usually settles the dispute for a specified time period and provides the opportunity for renegotiation, unstructured restraint contains no such assurances. Without a more specific agreement, in other words, foreign exporters have no guarantee that their stopgap, unstructured export restraint will prevent protectionism from reemerging, perhaps in more virulent form. Semistructured export restraint falls between the two poles. It may temporarily defuse a trade dispute by establishing acceptable import pricing behavior, but it may not be able to forestall further administrative action or litigation. In summary, unstructured or even semistructured restraint may not appreciably reduce the risk of future trade restrictions; structured restraint in contrast is designed to reduce that risk.

Policy Choice

While exporters tend to favor structured restraint in facing trade-restricting actions in the importing country, the conclusion of a negotiated agreement on structured restraint requires that interested parties in the importing country also prefer it as a policy alternative. The following section sets out to show that the cooperative, rigid qualities of structured export restraint tend to satisfy the goals of domestic industries seeking protection. Policymakers in the importing country, on the other hand, are generally reluctant to pursue a negotiated, structured export restraint agreement unless pushed into it by strong political considerations. Once some form of high-profile, political-track trade action becomes necessary, however, policymakers tend to favor structured export restraint as the most expedient policy tool of trade restriction.

Interests of Protection-Seeking Industries

Bhagwati (1982) and others have examined protectionism as a form of rent seeking. If the goal of protection-seeking industries is to maximize the expected value of rents accruing from trade restriction, induced export restraint provides the most reliable framework for current protectionist rent-seeking strategy. Among the available avenues of trade restriction described at the beginning of this chapter, protection via unfair trade laws depends largely on the satisfaction of specific legal criteria. Protection through escape clause or section 301 action is also based on legal criteria, but in addition requires meeting political criteria in order to obtain an affirmative decision by the president. Other forms of executive action, for example through national security considerations encompassed by section 232 actions, are rarely used because of the

TABLE 8. A Taxonomy of Induced Export Restraint

Device	Type	Method of Restraint	Principal Catalyst	Specific Incentives
1. Negotiated quantitative export restraint	Structured	Negotiated quantitative restriction	General protectionist threat	a. Gain rent b. Avoid devices 2, 3, 4, 5, or 6
2. Antidumping investigation	Semistructured/ unstructured (structured if quantitative agreement results)	Price adjustment or ad hoc (unless negotiated quantitative)	a. Fair value price b. Administrative uncertainty	a. Avoid unfair trade label b. Avoid duty (if assessed) c. Pursue quantitative agreement
3. Countervailing duty investigation	Usually semi-structured (structured if quantitative agreement) quantitative)	a. Eliminate subsidy b. Offsetting export tax (unless negotiated	Subsidy determination	a. Avoid unfair trade label b. Avoid CVD duty c. pursue quantitative agreement
4. Escape clause investigation	Unstructured (structured if OMA results)	Ad hoc quantitative (unless OMA)	a. Administrative political uncertainty b. Forum for OMA negotiation	a. Avoid import restriction b. Pursue OMA option
5. Threat of protectionist legislation	Unstructured	Ad hoc quantitative	Legislative uncertainty	Avoid import restriction
6. Section 301	Unstructured negotiated agreement)	Ad hoc quantitative (unless negotiated agreement)	Scope of executive discretion	a. Avoid import restriction b. Avoid implicit unfair trade label

dangerous precedent they may set and the foreign retaliation they may trigger. Legislated and negotiated restrictions are largely political actions, subject to whatever constraints the GATT or an ideological commitment to open trade may impose. Typically, large, politically influential industries with established lobbies in Washington simultaneously pursue some combination of legal, legislative, and executive avenues in an effort to build protectionist momentum, a strategy used successfully by the steel and automobile industries, for example. An affirmative determination in an unfair trade practice or escape clause investigation not only provides the opportunity for immediate protection, but also strengthens its case for subsequent legislative or administrative protection, and may also impose pressure on the exporter to conclude a structured restraint agreement. Even an investigation ending in a negative determination can benefit the industry by presenting its case and exhausting the administrative option, strengthening its case for legislated or negotiated protection. For industries without effective political influence in Congress, on the other hand, receiving protection will depend entirely on the administrative channels of relief.

The previous section has already emphasized the possibility that industries vigorously pursuing relief from import competition can, through administrative and political processes alone, achieve a certain degree of protection by inducing semistructured and unstructured export restraint. Such restraint may in fact satisfy the industry's protectionist demands, and for most industries, such protection is the most that they can expect to receive within the constraints of limited lobbying budgets and political influence. However, the degree of such protection cannot reach the level achieved by more direct actions such as import quotas. Ironically, the same elements of threatened protection and trade law investigations that induce unstructured export restraint can also frustrate the designs of protection-seeking industries. Domestic producers prefer specific, predictable means of protection to the uncertain and often fragile methods of trade intimidation represented by semistructured and unstructured export restraint. Threats of unilateral action and the daunting legal processes of AD and CVD investigations described earlier can only induce lasting export restraint as long as they are perceived by exporters as credible precursors to more definitive action. Time and experience erode the intimidating effect if the petitions do not lead to final affirmative decisions and the bluff becomes less credible. Even semistructured restraint induced, for example, by a final determination of unfair trade is based on narrowly defined market conditions, product lines, and pricing data and can only induce export restraint within a limited time period. Changes in cost and demand conditions may embolden exporters to try new strategies of import penetration, especially after they have gained some experience with the legal process.

Industries and firms with the political power to pursue protectionist goals past the level of semistructured and unstructured export restraint therefore face a narrow range of attainable means of further trade restriction. While lobbying for unilateral import quotas may continue to act as a convenient bluff, the attainment of such protection, through either legislation or an escape clause action, is unlikely. The next best and strategically most efficient alternative is a structured export restraint arrangement, which, like an import quota, achieves a rigid, quantitative trade restriction. Even though export restraint may lead to exporter strategies to circumvent the restriction, such as product upgrading, transshipping and quota hopping, as described in chapter 2, such an agreement still establishes a framework for further negotiations and tightening later. Exporter participation in structured export restraint requires, however, the existence of credible protectionist threats. For this reason, the conclusion of a negotiated export restraint arrangement is often the result of the simultaneous pursuit of legislative and administrative channels of protection, which applies pressure on both domestic policymakers and foreign exporters to settle the trade dispute by negotiating quantitative restrictions. In this manner, protectionist pressure by politically influential industries within the current framework of policy constraints may work toward the eventual conclusion of negotiated export restraint arrangements if external factors also goad trade officials to take action.

Interests of Trade Policymakers

For trade policy officials, the system of induced export restraint provides a framework for resolving and avoiding disputes associated with international trade. The choice of policy within this framework depends on (1) the level of domestic political pressure for protection, (2) international constraints on protectionist action, and (3) the expected domestic demonstration effect of granting protection.

Clearly, if domestic protectionist sentiment is strong and the potential for international protectionist retaliation is high, negotiated export restraint represents the safest course of action. Aside from granting quota protection to domestic producers, export restraint negotiated by the executive branch forestalls dangerous unilateral action by Congress and potentially embarrassing AD or CVD decisions that link foreign exporters and governments with unfair trade practices. At the same time the agreement is discriminatory and can thereby focus the trade restriction on the disruptive supplier. Cooperation by foreign exporters is reinforced by the rent transfer that occurs. Finally, the export restraint negotiations remove the trade restriction from public scrutiny and protracted legal and legislative processes. They can therefore be negotiated with relative speed and efficiency. As the analysis in chapter 2 showed, their main political advantage is that, while all direct participants gain from the agreement, the main losers, domestic consumers, are excluded from direct involvement in the negotiations.

Yet the potential economic damage to the importing country, as well as the extensive efforts involved in coordinating such negotiations, will limit the government's use of structured export restraint devices. Political action by the government demands requisite political cause: in this case, a substantial level of political influence of the domestic industry and the potential for damage to trade relations should alternative protectionist measures be used. Finger, Hall and Nelson (1982) have noted that, in matters of administrative discretion, decision makers may turn down one request for protection if this action thereby discourages several more from even applying for protection, a principle that may indeed be true at all levels of administrative protectionist action. The recent popularity of public choice and rent-seeking models of decisionmaking often underestimate this factor in the conduct of trade policy. Government officials tend to avoid conflict whenever possible, and conflict is inevitable when circumstances or incentives encourage petitions for trade protection. For executive branch officials in particular, entertaining unlimited requests for negotiated trade restrictions not only guarantees that there will be a long line of lobbyists outside their door, most of whom will be disappointed at the eventual outcome of their cases, but also ensures that foreign governments will engage in counterthreats and often bitter negotiations. The political price of negotiating trade restrictions is, in other words, usually prohibitively high.

For this reason, there must be a strong political force—both internal and external—behind the trade dispute before government officials pursue negotiated export restraint. The principal external forces that motivate such negotiated trade restrictions include GATT trade talks and major threats of trade wars. The history of VER usage by the United States outside GATT rules suggests, indeed, that a broad, overriding trade issue is necessary to motivate government efforts to negotiate such trade restrictions. For example, the first use of a VER arrangement on Japanese textiles in 1937 was motivated primarily by the larger interests of implementing reciprocal trade legislation. The textile industry, which had historically received heavy tariff protection, was in a position to block broader trade liberalization measures if Japanese imports were not curbed. It was therefore politically necessary to go outside the traditional import tariff-quota framework by negotiating a VER, from the U.S. government's perspective, in order to facilitate trade liberalization in general. When export restraints against Japanese textiles were reintroduced in 1957, the broader issue was the functioning of the GATT system, as described in chapter 1. The politically sensitive textile industry could have prevented the otherwise normal participation of Japan in the new postwar trading system in the absence of such an arrangement. Fealty to this political consideration of textiles as a special case was later enshrined and institutionalized in the much more comprehensive MFA.

GATT trade negotiations have also stood behind major VER negotiations, especially in textiles and steel. Brandis (1982) has documented the textile industry's ability to force the negotiation of export restraint agreements in the context of the Kennedy and Tokyo rounds of trade negotiations. Steel trade also threatened the Kennedy and Tokyo rounds in 1968 and 1979, respectively. In 1968, the United States concluded a formal VER agreement on steel exports with Japan and Europe, and in 1979, the United States negotiated a similar but informal agreement with Japan. Both agreements were instrumental in allowing a successful completion of the trade negotiations.

Finally, the threat of a major trade war can push trade officials to negotiate VERs. The steel and automobile industries provide the best examples of this phenomenon. Both are highly cyclical industries with an equally high political profile linked to their perceived strategic importance in the national economy. These characteristics apply equally to the counterpart industries in Japan, Europe, and elsewhere. International disputes over trade in these industries have proven to be explosive enough to threaten trade relations in general, and set the stage for VER negotiations on automobiles with the Japanese in 1981, on steel with the EC in 1982, and on steel with all supplying countries in 1984.

In general, making special protectionist provisions for a politically sensitive industry can be described as a nesting strategy (Aggarwal 1985) that allows other areas of trade relations to proceed unimpeded by protectionism. In order to make a liberal trading order possible, according to this strategy, some protectionist concessions are necessary. This view has merit to the extent that trade relations inevitably involve compromise, so that the two steps forward of overall trade liberalization may be contingent upon taking one step backward by protecting a politically sensitive industry. However, the record of negotiated export restraint reveals serious dangers to the trading system when the protection becomes institutionalized, a topic that will be discussed further in chapter 8.

In contrast to the gray area VER measures taken outside the GATT, the government's resort to structured export restraint through escape clause or other executive measures depends largely on circumstances that will allow it to implement them without major retaliation. As noted earlier, the president must decide whether the proposed trade restriction is in the national interest. Aside from purely domestic economic and political considerations, this means also that the possibility of foreign retaliation plays a large role in the presidential decision. Ultimately, once the president decides that overall domestic economic interests are served by the escape clause trade restriction, final presidential approval is shaped by GATT strictures and the threat of retaliation. Requirements for compensation, nondiscrimination, and a strict adherence to the injury test, as well as the possibility of GATT review, restrict the freedom of governments to use the escape clause freely. As noted earlier, it is safest from the point of view of commercial diplomacy to use the escape clause against countries with little retaliatory power, although the investigation itself may eventually lead to a VER arrangement outside the GATT, even if escape clause relief is denied. The Japanese automobile VER of 1981 and the network of steel VERs of 1984 are examples of this phenomenon.

In practice, positive escape clause determinations and presidential approval are most likely when a domestic industry can clearly document the link between its declining fortunes and imports from countries without the power to retaliate—usually, non-European countries. In cases that meet all the proper criteria, the president may then decide to restrict imports through negotiated OMAs, although tariffs and global import quotas may also be used. Yoffie (1988) has noted that the structure of escape clause tariffs, for example, may have the same discriminatory effect as a formal quantitative export restraint agreement, as shown in the 1982 motorcycle case, which was targeted primarily against Japanese imports. However, recent escape clause protection has typically involved OMAs against Japan, the Republic of Korea, and Taiwan in products such as color television sets, nonrubber footwear, and specialty steel (see table 9).

The Policy Filter

The foregoing account suggests that the process of governmental policy choice in trade disputes involves a policy filter that assigns cases (a) to either the technical-administrative or to the political track and (b) within the political track to either GATT-sanctioned channels or to gray area measures. At the first level of policy filtering it is useful to distinguish between requests for protection according to their political profile. If the policymakers' goal is to limit special protectionist action to those cases in which political pressure is strongest, then the two levels of trade regulation—the technical track and the political track—can be assigned to the appropriate cases. In those cases where the political profile of the case is sufficiently low, protectionist pressures can be conveniently relegated to the technical-legal track, where the final determination of action is made at a safe distance from high-level decision making. This is consistent with the original design of trade law as a safety valve for protectionist pressure.

In cases of high political profile, protectionist pressure may enter the policy-making structure through trade law channels, through congressional pressure, or through direct appeals for executive action. If domestic or international politics threaten to ignite a major trade dispute, then the case enters the political track, and high-level trade officials must choose between policy tools within or outside the GATT framework. A review of U.S. trade policy experience suggests strongly that policymakers will resort to negotiating VERs outside the GATT only when both the domestic and the international political stakes are high.

Regardless of the type of trade dispute, the structure of policy incentives and constraints tends to engage the use of induced export restraint as the most

TABLE 9. Major Instances of Negotiated Export Restraint in U.S. Trade Policy

Type/Coverage	Enforcement Period	Exporters	Negotiating Authority	Concurrent or Prior Protectionist Activity
1. VER-textiles	1937–39	Japan	Executive	Possible congressional blockage of general trade liberalization
2. VRA-steel	1968–74	EC, Japan	Executive	Threatened quota legislation (1967); CVD petition (1968)
3. MFA-textiles	1974– present[a]	Most textiles exporters	Executive	Threatened protectionist legislation; several previous restraint agreements
4. OMA- specialty steel	1976–79	Japan[b]	Escape clause	Threatened quota legislation
5. OMA-color televisions	1977–82	Japan, Taiwan, Korea[c]	Escape clause	Antidumping determination (1970); escape clause determination (1971)
6. OMA nonrubber footwear	1977–81	Taiwan, Korea	Escape clause	Escape clause (presidential denial, 1976); Escape Clause (no action, 1970)
7. VRA steel mill products	1982–85	EC	CVD statute	Several antidumping/CVD determinations (1982); threatened quota legislation; see also 2
8. VRA-autos	1981–85[d]	Japan	Executive	Escape clause (negative determination, 1980); threatened domestic content legislation
9. VRA-steel mill products	1985–92	All major suppliers	Executive	Escape clause (negative determination, 1984)
10. Export restraint- machine tools	1986–91	Japan, Taiwan	Sec. 232	Threatened quota legislation
11. Semiconductors	1986–present	Japan	AD statute	AD duties; possible congressional action; unilateral trade sanctions; threat of sec.301

[a] The MFA is scheduled to be terminated ten years after entry into force of the Uruguay Round agreement.
[b] Other suppliers were subject to a global import quota.
[c] The Japanese OMA covered the period 1977–80. The OMA with Taiwan and Korea covered the period 1979–82.
[d] Bilateral agreement expired 1985; unilateral export restraint continues.

politically expedient means of resolution, from unfair trade cases to high-profile VERs. In contrast to the confrontational nature of unilateral import controls, induced restraint allows the exporter to reduce market participation and avoid direct trade conflict and import controls. The flexibility of the system in dealing with disputes of varying political profiles is shown by the use of increasing structural levels of export restraint as the profile increases. In this manner, the system of export restraint exhibits structural escalation as the trade dispute becomes more politically charged.

Patterns of Induced Export Restraint

Table 9 illustrates the use of structured export restraint in U.S. trade policy and its link with semistructured and unstructured export restraint. Protection through negotiated export restraint is in fact quite rare; these eleven cases are but a handful compared to the hundreds of applications or pleas for protection since 1968 in Congress or under U.S. trade laws. Two important patterns among these few cases help to explain the phenomenon. First, all the industries eventually receiving such protection had previously or simultaneously pursued other protectionist possibilities, either through the trade laws or congressional lobbying. This pattern supports the idea presented earlier that such devices of unstructured export restraint apply pressure on both exporters and government officials to seek a negotiated settlement. The other important pattern lies in the choice between GATT-consistent escape clause relief and gray area VERs. In this regard, the importance of the industries for international trade relations in general is crucial. Steel, automobiles, and textiles and apparel all represent large, highly visible industries with strong industry lobbying organizations and union organizations. Refusal to grant protection in these cases could compromise broader trade policy goals, and unilateral recourse to escape clause measures is either unsupportable by the rules or would risk damaging foreign retaliation. Major government-to-government negotiations on discriminatory marketsharing therefore become politically necessary.

The affirmative escape clause cases, in contrast, typically involve onetime protectionist "fixes" for cases in which the injury test is clearly met and the number of disruptive exporters is both small and incapable of major retaliation. The machine tools VER agreement, negotiated under the national security provisions of article 232, also falls into this category. It is noteworthy, however, that these negotiations failed to bring West Germany and Switzerland into the agreement, even after the threat of unilateral action by the U.S. government. The semiconductor arrangement with Japan, which is unusual in that it was negotiated as a major government-to-government price-floor agreement, also officially falls within the GATT framework, although a 1988 GATT panel forced Japan to modify its regulation of price reporting by exporting firms (USITC 1990, 110). As a semistructured export restraint agreement, it cannot provide assurances to protection-seeking firms in the United States about the quantitative level of trade, nor can it guarantee to Japanese exporters U.S. market access. As shown in the use of other, structurally lower export restraint devices, the future of trade in this area will depend on the ability of the U.S. import-competing industry to adjust or, alternatively, for the issue to lose its political bite. The failure of semistructured export restraint to resolve the issue would create strong pressures toward structural escalation in the form of a more rigid VER and demands for other so-called "results-oriented" trade arrangements.[14]

Most of the industries that have received protection through structured export restraint have suffered chronic adjustment problems and have persisted in their protection-seeking strategies over extended periods of time. The textile industry first received such protection in 1937 and has received continuous VER protection from import competition since 1955. The U.S. steel industry has conducted numerous campaigns for various forms of protection since 1967. The color television industry, which won a protracted AD suit against Japan filed in 1968, filed a petition for additional relief under the escape clause in 1971, which was rejected. Only after a second escape clause petition in 1976 did the industry receive OMA protection. Similarly, the nonrubber footwear industry persisted in its appeals for protection, and finally received OMA protection after a third escape clause investigation. The existence of persistent protectionist agitation over a long period of time thus also appears to contribute to the ultimate use of structured export restraint.

Summary

Devices of induced export restraint have penetrated the structure of U.S. trade policy from the level of technical-track measures against unfair trade to the major negotiated VER agreements. Unstructured export restraint occurs through an ad hoc retreat from the export market by foreign suppliers intimidated by threats of unilateral trade actions or restrictions by the importing government. Semistructured restraint typically involves a reduction in export supply through an establishment of fair value prices. Structured export restraint involves quantitative or market-sharing arrangements, usually achieved through detailed negotiations. It represents an attempt to forge a politically cooperative equilibrium between governments in cases where protectionist pressure is high, broader international trade policy goals are at stake, and constraints against the use of traditional import controls are binding.

Perhaps the greatest danger from the trend toward induced export restraint is its ability to restrict trade through the intimidating effects of opaque trade laws and threats. Faced with the choice between the uncertainties of a legal or legislative process perceived to favor domestic industries and an agreement to raise prices or restrict imports, many foreign exporters will rationally choose the latter. Even if the protectionist or trade law action is likely to be rejected, the uncertainties of continued protectionist activity may provide a strong incentive for the exporter to adjust prices or quantities in an effort to eliminate the harassment.

Since political and GATT restraints limit the number of cases that can result in formal quantitative export restraint agreements, there is considerable political pressure on legislators, in particular, to direct protectionist pressures toward the technical track, which effects export restraint through more subtle means. The use of induced export restraint thus also threatens the integrity of the GATT and of national trade laws. The increasing use of AD, CVD, and escape clause investigations as a lever to force exporters to the export restraint negotiating table subverts the role of trade law in a system of open trade. The intended purpose of these measures within the GATT was to act as safety valves for protectionist pressures, not as a bludgeon to force the conclusion of quantitative trade restrictions. Recently, changes in procedural and substantive aspects of trade law investigations have reflected a progressive politicization of the legal process, with protectionist results. The time limits placed on decisions in unfair trade practice investigations by the Trade Agreements Act of 1979, for example, played a major role in the conclusion of the steel export restraint agreement with EEC producers in 1982.

Yet relief from import competition that occurs through administrative determinations based on technical criteria—or through the intimidating effects of the rules—is politically efficient in the sense that it absolves other policymakers of responsibility for having to make potentially difficult decisions. Changes in the trade laws themselves are therefore instrumental in establishing the institutional environment of induced export restraint. It is to this problem that the study now turns.

Notes

1. If the export restraint agreement is not universal, however, a global tariff may result in a higher level of exports than the VER limit. The restraining country's government may thus prefer the global tariff to a VER for domestic employment, or, depending on the comparative revenue effects, for balance-of-payments reasons.

2. Even a small final dumping margin exposes the importer to potentially large dumping duties. See Palmeter (1989, 190).

3. Dale (1980) notes that dumping findings normally apply to *all* companies' exports of the good from the country specified in the investigation, not just to companies guilty of dumping.

4. See Frum (1992). The estimate was made by Trade Arbed, importing agent for the Belgian firm Sidmar Steel, which was accused of dumping in the June 1992 unfair trade complaints filed by U.S. steel producers.

5. See the numerous contributions in Boltuck and Litan (1991) for a discussion of this and many other controversial aspects of U.S. trade law. Bovard (1991 chap. 5) provides details on some of the more egregious examples of the BIA rule in practice.

6. The same authors note that the opposite reaction is also possible: for example, an immediate surge in lower price deliveries by the exporter to beat a possible preliminary affirmative determination and its consequences. A similar phenomenon has been observed of Japanese steel deliveries in advance of enforcement of the trigger price mechanism. However, when a full AD inquiry is in progress, such import surges may prejudice the injury investigation against the exporter.

7. This provision could also encourage collusive activity. See Prusa (1992).

8. The injury provision does not apply in CVD cases against nonsignatories of the Multilateral Trade Negotiation Subsidies Code. See Hemmendinger and Barringer (1981).

9. Increases in the selling price could, however, reduce injury to the domestic industry to the point where the duties would be withdrawn.

10. See chapter 8 for a discussion of Uruguay Round negotiations on safeguard reforms.

11. Section 301 gives examples of unreasonable practices, including "conduct denying internationally recognized worker rights," "practices that deny fair and equitable market opportunities," and "export targeting." However, the definition of unreasonable remains open-ended. See Bhagwati (1990, 40) for a discussion and more details.

12. The most aggressive of the measures contained in the Omnibus Trade and Competitiveness Act of 1988 was the so-called super-301 provision, which required the USTR to identify priority practices and countries harming U.S. export interests and their impact on U.S. trade, and then imposed a strict timetable for their removal, under threat of mandatory retaliation (see Bhagwati 1990). The super-301 provision expired in 1990, but was under consideration for renewal under the Clinton administration in 1993.

13. The irony of this tactic is that the U.S. VER program created the same sort of trade diversion that was used to force reluctant exporters to the negotiating table. See Jones (1986).

14. By the time the semiconductor agreement was renegotiated in June 1991, for example, the emphasis had shifted from Japanese pricing practices toward a Japanese commitment to establish a 20 percent foreign import share in Japan's own domestic market (USITC 1992, 108). This development represents the next step from VERs toward more comprehensive trade management, to be discussed in chapter 8.

CHAPTER 5

Export Restraint through Trade L
Enforcement: The Impact of Cha
U.S. Trade Legislation

The previous chapter, in examining the means of inducing export restraint, identified unfair trade laws as potential devices for both trade intimidation on their
own and as catalysts for more formal, negotiated trade restrictions. To the extent that trade laws can be manipulated to reduce trade through direct or indirect means, one can expect that their usage, in terms of the number of petitions
for relief, will rise. This chapter begins with the observation that unfair trade
laws, once used rarely to combat mainly dumped or subsidized imports, have
increasingly become a major component of trade policy. Since the 1960s, when
the case load of unfair trade enforcement averaged twenty-five petitions per
year, trade litigation mushroomed in the 1980s, averaging over one hundred
cases per year (see fig. 7). Unfair trade cases have become "the usual first
choice for industries seeking protection from imports into the United States"
(Horlick and Oliver 1989, 1).

The analysis of chapter 4 suggested the political logic of this result. If
structural economic change or cyclical pressures on domestic industries are
accompanied by rising imports, protectionist demands will rise. In the absence
of circumstances conducive to structured VER and OMA quotas, firms are likely
to turn increasingly to unfair trade law enforcement as a channel of protection.
The effectiveness of the unfair trade laws in providing protection from imports
depends largely on the specific rules and procedures contained in the statutes
themselves, as shown in the description of export restraint-inducing aspects of
antidumping and countervailing duty law enforcement in chapter 4.

Recent studies in U.S. trade law enforcement have also identified the growing importance of the legal and political environment in the incentive structure
of filing an unfair trade law petition. Major trade law changes were enacted by
Congress in 1974, 1979, and 1988, introducing new provisions and procedures
that may have increased the willingness of firms to file for relief from import
competition through unfair trade statutes. If it is true that trade law is being
used increasingly as a channel of protectionism, then the implications for trade
relations and the world economy could be very grave. Even now, trade law
enforcement represents a major source of trade disruption and conflict. Finger
and Olechowski (1987) have shown that the phenomenon of trade law protec-

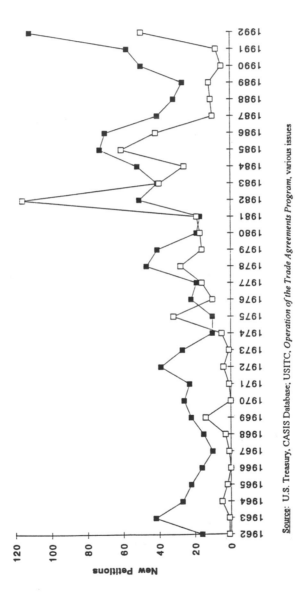

Source: U.S. Treasury, CASIS Database; USITC, *Operation of the Trade Agreements Program*, various issues

Figure 7. United States: New Unfair Trade Petitions, FY 1962-92

tionism has spread beyond the United States to other countries. Table 10 shows that the EC, Canada, and Australia also litigate significant numbers of trade law cases. EC enforcement of antidumping law has had protectionist and discriminatory trade effects (Messerlin 1989) where the discretionary application of rules and a bureaucratic preference for managed trade agreements to settle trade disputes have created a potent protectionist policy tool (see also McDermott 1988). The trend toward increased reliance on unfair trade laws as a means of restricting trade can also be seen in the proliferation of such measures to many other countries, especially in the developing world. In 1980, only eight countries had antidumping laws on the books; by 1992 this number had risen to forty-two (counting the EC as a whole as one), and unfair trade law enforcement has increased dramatically among developing countries since the late 1980s, as shown in table 10. While Robert Litan has described the United States as "the world's technological leader in dumping laws," it is becoming clear that such technology can spread, and U.S. firms are now increasingly being targeted for unfair trade petitions in their overseas operations (*Wall Street Journal*, 26 February 1993).

This chapter will focus on the trends in filings of unfair trade law petitions in the United States since 1962, with particular emphasis on the changes that have occurred as a result of trade legislation in 1974 and 1979. In addition, a regression analysis will test the effect of legislative changes on the incentive structure of choosing one type of trade law over another in pursuing relief from import competition.

Institutional Aspects of Unfair Trade Law

Unfair Trade Laws as Technical Track Protection

Finger, Hall, and Nelson (1982), in a seminal article, identified the increasingly protectionist use of U.S. trade laws, documenting different aspects of technical-track and political-track trade protection. Political-track protection, through such measures as escape clause measures or negotiated VER agreements, is granted on the basis of a highly visible, often politically charged decision by the U.S. president or other high-ranking officials entrusted with substantial discretionary authority.

Technical-track protection, in contrast, is granted on the basis of determinations of import pricing violations and injury tests by lower-level bureaucratic bodies: the U.S. International Trade Commission (USITC) and the International Trade Administration of the Department of Commerce. While political considerations may enter into the investigation, the outcome of each case depends in principle upon the application of detailed statutes and administrative guidelines, subject to judicial review. While each determination can thus be presented in principle as the result of an objective consideration of the facts of the

Table 10. Antidumping and Countervailing Duty Cases, FY1981–92

	1981	1982	1983	1984	1985	1986	1987	1988	1989	1990	1991	1992	TOTAL
Antidumping													
U.S.	17	51	41	52	73	70	41	32	27	50	58	112	624
EC	25	45	26	45	41	41	37	50	38	30	16	28	422
Australia	0	47	92	76	67	60	39	18	20	19	63	76	577
Canada	25	60	40	40	38	59	90	75	70	76	41	37	651
Other Developed[a]	3	2	0	3	0	2	5	12	12	10	9	21	79
Developing[b]	0	0	0	4	0	4	1	16	22	12	47	45	151
Total	70	205	199	220	219	236	213	203	189	197	234	319	2504
CVD													
U.S.	19	116	40	26	61	42	10	11	12	5	5	50	397
EC	0	1	3	1	0	0	0	0	0	0	0	0	5
Australia	0	0	9	3	5	3	2	0	2	7	10	11	52
Canada	3	0	2	4	2	7	6	3	4	4	0	2	37
Other Developed[c]	0	0	1	0	0	0	1	0	0	1	1	0	4
Developing[d]	0	65	29	12	7	12	0	0	0	0	3	14	142
TOTAL	22	182	84	46	75	64	19	14	18	17	19	77	637

Source: GATT Committee on Subsidies and Countervailing Measures, compiled in USITC, Operation of the Trade Agreements Program, various issues. U.S. case statistics compiled from CASIS database and USITC.

[a] Austria, Finland, Japan, New Zealand, Spain, Sweden;
[b] Brazil, Chile, Columbia, India, Mexico, Poland, Republic of Korea;
[c] Austria, Japan, New Zealand;
[d] Brazil filed one CVD case in FY1991 and 8 in FY1992, others are for Chile.

case, it is clear that the way the rules are written will heavily influence the outcome. As Finger and Murray (1990) have observed, the devil of the trade law is in the details. The legal rules and definitions regarding pricing violations "tend to be obscure, and the obfuscation they create allows the government to serve the advantaged interest group without being called to task by the disadvantaged" (Finger, Hall, and Nelson 1982, 454). Such an arrangement clearly provides a politically safe vehicle for trade protectionism.

Economic Aspects of Unfair Trade Law Enforcement

The legitimacy of unfair trade laws has always been questionable when subjected to economic analysis. The widespread notion that dumping and subsidization are in some sense unfair generally accepts the viewpoint of domestic import-competing producers, whose sales and profits may suffer because of the associated import competition. When taking the viewpoint of national economic welfare, in contrast, such unfair trade acts almost always benefit the importing country as a whole, since the gains of consumers from the lower prices and increased imports generally outweigh the losses of domestic producers. This proposition merely restates the general case for the gains from trade. In order to establish an economically valid case for restricting unfair trade, it is necessary to identify a market failure, whereby unrestricted trade damages national economic welfare.

The original economic motivation of AD laws, for example, was that the practice of dumping (a foreign producer charging a lower price in the international than in his home market) masked a predatory motive: to eliminate all competition in the targeted market in order to exploit the "captured" consumers through monopoly pricing. This scenario fits in only too well with the interests of domestic import-competing interests, and has through the long-standing enforcement and renewal of AD laws (recognized by the GATT as well) gained legitimacy over the years as a commercial policy tool.

Under U.S. trade law, the legal test for dumping determinations has two basic components: a test for LTFV pricing and a test for injury linked to the dumping. Similarly, a CVD investigation involves a test to establish a unit subsidy margin enjoyed by the foreign exporter, and a test (in most cases) for injury linked to the subsidized exports. The first component of a dumping investigation is to establish whether the foreign producers under investigation have violated pricing rules in selling their imports to the U.S. In the case of dumping, unfair pricing would involve either selling the product in the U.S. market at a cheaper price than in the foreign producers' home market (the price discrimination criterion) or, under certain circumstances, charging a price in the U.S. market that lies below the average cost of production (the cost-of-production criterion, introduced into U.S. law in the Trade Agreements Act of

1979). The difference between the fair value price and the dumping price is the dumping margin.

The predatory scenario described above suggests that a powerful foreign firm can use profits from its (presumably protected) home market monopoly to finance a price-cutting strategy to drive import-competing firms in the target market out of business. It is not clear that such a profit-maximizing strategy would always succeed in driving other firms out of business, since the foreign firm would usually need a deep pocket in order to finance the ruin of all its competitors, and an even deeper pocket to keep them from returning to the market when it raises the product's price. Proponents of antidumping laws contend that profits from the foreign firm's home market could help it to sustain losses in the export market (during cyclical downturns, for example), thereby giving it an advantage over its rivals. Yet if in fact the firm has the ability to implement this strategy successfully, the proper economic policy would be to remove the foreigner's ability to price discriminate. To the extent that dumping is made possible by trade barriers in the foreigner's market, for example, trade liberalizing measures would improve market efficiency and diminish the ability of foreign firms to finance predatory strategies.

Notwithstanding such economic considerations, antidumping laws make no effort to establish a predatory motive or strategy on the part of the foreign firm; the pricing investigation proceeds strictly on the basis of a calculation of LTFV pricing and an injury determination (Applebaum 1988). Thus we have, for example, the specter of steel exporters from the tiny island country of Trinidad and Tobago threatening U.S. steel producers with a predatory strategy of dumping. Clearly, the original economic basis of antidumping law—to protect an economy against threats of predatory pricing and monopolization—has long since been discarded.

This criticism is even more striking in the use of cost-of-production (COP) criteria, under which a foreign firm can be found guilty of dumping if the price it charges falls below average total cost. The investigation in this case would establish a constructed value of the firm's costs, including an 8 percent profit margin. COP criteria can be used if the foreign firm's home market sales or sales in a third country are deemed an inadequate basis for comparison (U.S. Congress 1989, 56). Pricing below average cost is, according to basic microeconomic analysis, the optimal pricing strategy when the demand drops below average cost but above the shutdown point. Domestic firms are, in addition, free to adjust their prices this way. The use of COP criteria has therefore made foreign firms more vulnerable to dumping allegations during cyclical downturns. In fact, in order to avoid dumping allegations, the foreign firm would typically have to raise prices during a market slump. There is in any case no economic basis for using COP criteria as evidence of predatory dumping, which would require some evidence that the foreign firm had the opportunity and means by which to monopolize the market. It is more instructive to consider the political purpose of this rule (and many others), which is to make it more likely for the investigation to reach a positive determination (See Boltuck and Litan 1991, chap. 2, 3, 6, and 8).

In a CVD case, the investigation of pricing violations seeks to establish a subsidy margin, which represents the unit value of subsidies enjoyed by the foreign firm. The economic case for levying countervailing duties is, as in the case of dumping, weak. The best economic argument for such intervention would again require some form of market failure, for example, a government-financed predatory strategy. The political legitimacy of the law depends heavily on the idea that domestic firms should not have to compete with foreign treasuries in an open market, even if net national economic welfare would benefit.

Nonetheless, rules for identifying subsidies tend to bias the determination toward a positive finding. For example, CVD guidelines require all state grants, bounties, and aids to the firm to be counted, but do not allow for offsetting negative subsidies to be subtracted from the total. Thus a government subsidy used to compensate firms for having to use domestically produced inputs, or for having to continue operations due to layoff restrictions, would be counted as a subsidy, even if the net effect of government intervention is not to change the firm's competitive position on international markets.

The injury test is the second component of the investigation. Under U.S. law, the USITC has the task of investigating the volume of imports, the effect of imports on prices, market penetration, instances of price underselling, sales lost to imports, etc., in order to determine whether the imports in question have in fact caused injury to the domestic firm or industry. Morkre and Kruth (1989, 82–83) note that there is no link made in the investigation between the size of the dumping margin and the injury it allegedly caused. Thus, whether the dumping margin is 100 percent or 0.75 percent will have no bearing on the determination of injury, even though the ability of a 0.75 percent dumping margin to cause measurable injury would logically be subject to extreme skepticism.

Nonetheless, Finger and Murray (1990, 20), in their investigation of AD and CVD cases, observe that LTFV pricing is found in the vast majority of cases, and that such a finding typically implies that the foreigner has gained comparative advantage in the product. Logit tests of LTFV investigations by Finger, Hall, and Nelson (1982) have given strong support to this hypothesis, showing that comparative advantage indicators are significant predictors of positive LTFV determinations. The outcome of a case therefore generally hinges on the injury test. Yet injury as measured by market penetration, sales lost to imports, etc., appears to correspond to the classic requirement of market-driven adjustment to foreign competition, leading to the gains from trade—if only the imports were in fact allowed in. In many cases, the increasingly aggressive nature of trade law enforcement appears to have redefined comparative advantage as an unfair trade practice (ibid., 465).

The long-standing legitimacy of antidumping and other trade laws and its recognition in the GATT have provided governments with the opportunity to push trade laws and their enforcement toward protectionist ends. It should be noted that for many years the major economic argument for antidumping and antisubsidy laws was that they provided a political safety valve for protectionist pressure, allowing injured domestic injuries to receive relief from import competition when import pricing violated fair pricing rules. This was the political price to be paid, so the argument went, for achieving the needed domestic coalition that would support trade liberalization. Despite the traditional economic objections to unfair trade laws, it could still be argued that as long as their use allowed the rest of the trading system to work smoothly, these laws served a useful economic purpose. In other words, the benefits of consistently enforced, transparent rules that generated a consensus for open trade created a net social benefit.

Yet the viability of the trade laws as an acceptable part of a system of rules depends on their integrity as a device to protect against practices commonly accepted as unfair. The progressive manipulation of trade laws for protectionist purposes threatens to undermine the trading system that such laws have traditionally supported.

The Changing Incentive Structure of U.S. Trade Law

The discussion in chapter 4 revealed that firms seeking relief from import competition through the trade laws must choose essentially between escape clause protection, in which no trade practice violation is alleged, and protection through unfair trade statutes. Government enforcement of the trade laws thus seeks first to screen applications for import relief based on whether or not an unfair trading practice is involved and, subsequently, to identify the link between the import competition and the alleged injury to the domestic industry.

Two elements of the screening and administrative process of the trade law enforcement are critical in determining which trade law remedy will be sought by a petitioning U.S. firm or industry. First, in seeking relief from imports the absence of a putative unfair trade practice means that the injury test will be more difficult to pass. Secondly, the political cost of restricting fairly traded imports is generally higher, particularly in terms of U.S. obligations under the GATT and of the danger of foreign retaliation.

As highlighted in the discussion in chapter 4, these considerations are dictated by the GATT itself, as well as by commercial policy practice. If a signatory to the GATT wishes to erect barriers to fairly traded imports, then it must fulfill very stringent requirements. The escape clause of the GATT requires, for example, that the imports in question "cause or threaten serious injury" (GATT art. XIX, 1b) before restrictions can be applied. As noted earlier, any escape clause action must furthermore apply globally, and not discriminate against individual exporters. The political logic of these provisions has rested on the fear that a widespread acceptance of barriers to fair trade could lead to the wholesale abandonment of the GATT rules in general. Similarly, import restrictions for national security reasons (treated in GATT art. XXI) are expected to be rare in peacetime; otherwise, there would be a danger that vaguely defined security criteria could be concocted to suit any internal protectionist demand. In the end, GATT requires its signatories to accept, in broad terms, the principle of comparative advantage in administering their trade policies. If all signatories at least acknowledge the legitimacy of market-driven trade patterns, an internally consistent system of rules governing trade practices is possible.

In this regard, the traditional approach to measuring domestic pressures for protection in the United States has been to document the efforts of lobbying groups to (1) force government officials to impose trade barriers unilaterally (as, for example, through legislated tariffs and quotas); (2) resist attempts to liberalize trade through multilateral trade negotiations; and (3) petition for escape clause protection. Presumably, industries, firms or their workers that petition for systematic protection from imports, pushing governments to the margin of GATT rules, are vulnerable to either a decline in international comparative advantage or to severe import surges over the business cycle. Unfair trade law enforcement would, in an ideal world of fidelity to GATT rules, be reserved for special cases of pricing and subsidy violations, not for cases of protecting declining domestic industries from import competition.

Takacs (1981) tested the link between macroeconomic indicators of protectionist pressure with the number of escape clause petitions from 1949 to 1979. Her results showed generally significant relationships between such explanatory variables as gross national product (GNP), unemployment, capacity utilization and import penetration, and the dependent variable of escape clause cases per year. In addition, Takacs found that the Trade Expansion Act of 1962, which increased the severity of the escape clause injury test, had a significantly negative impact on the number of petitions filed, while the Trade and Tariff Act of 1974, which loosened the injury criteria, had a significantly positive effect.

Despite the impact of the 1974 trade act, as well as subsequent changes encouraging escape clause use in the Trade Agreements Act of 1979, the escape clause continues to suffer from the major political drawbacks discussed above. A major problem with its use as a means of restricting imports is that it is exposed to an extremely high level of political scrutiny, particularly since the president is inevitably involved in a final application of escape clause protection. Not only do competing domestic interests have an opportunity to air their views, but foreign governments, cognizant of the president's final discretion in the matter, can threaten retaliation. The nondiscrimination requirement of the GATT in administering protection provides a further constraint. As Finger,

Hall, and Nelson (1982, 464) have put it, the final decision on escape clause protection occurs "at the razor's edge," with a built-in bias against its widespread use. In particular, the political cost of the escape clause will remain high as long as selectivity in its application is forbidden by the GATT.[1]

In the absence of selectivity, however, the escape clause has not provided a systematically reliable channel of relief from import competition. Increasingly, the attention of import-competing firms and Congress has focused on unfair trade laws as a means of restricting trade. The incentive structure of this trend is based on the political advantages of trade laws protecting against unfairly traded, as opposed to fairly traded imports:

1. Antidumping and countervailing duty laws have a long history of statutory legitimacy, and enjoy the imprimatur of the GATT;

2. The GATT provisions for antidumping and countervailing duty law are vague enough to provide legislative bodies with considerable discretion in defining rules, procedures, and administrative details, so that the law can be tilted toward the interests of domestic import-competing firms;

3. Once the legislation is in place, administration of the trade laws can proceed according to the new rules without further direct congressional involvement, so that protectionist pressure is diverted toward a legal process;

4. To the extent that the investigation results in a trade restriction, it can be defended as being driven by law and not by the craven spirits of protectionism.

Table 11 shows that, beginning with the 1974 trade act, Congress has progressively reduced the discretion of executive branch agencies in administering the AD and CVD laws, thereby making these trade laws a more reliable means of achieving protection from import competition. Prior to 1974, it was not uncommon for investigations to drag on for many years, particularly in cases whose outcome would provide difficulties or embarrassment for the sitting president. In subsequent trade legislation, Congress appears to have endeavored to close several remaining loopholes that had resulted in negative determinations, and to guarantee a more favorable environment for the interests of petitioners. Examples include the transferral of the dumping and subsidy margin investigations to the Commerce Department in the 1979 Trade Act, the requirement of cumulation in AD and CVD injury determinations in the Trade and Tariff Act of 1984, and exclusion of antidumping and countervailing duties from duty drawbacks in the Omnibus Trade and Competitiveness Act of 1988. Horlick (1990) considers the introduction of judicial review of AD and CVD cases in the 1979 trade act to be the most significant change in unfair trade law since 1945.

TABLE 11. Major Changes in U.S. Trade Laws since 1974

Trade Legislation of	AD	CVD
1974	Cost-of-production criteria; mandatory deadlines	Application to duty-free imports; mandatory deadlines; more limited executive discretion in administering CVD law
1979	Transfer unfair pricing to Commerce Department; tighten deadlines; introduce judicial review of cases	Transfer subsidy investigation to Commerce Department; tighten deadlines introduce judicial review of cases
1984	Cumulation of imports mandatory in injury investigations	Upstream subsidies subject to duties; cumulation of imports mandatory in investigations
1988	Third country dumping; anticircumvention measures; exclusion from duty drawback	Anti-circumvention measures; exclusion from duty drawback

Source: U.S. House of Representatives (1989); Baldwin (1985).

The Regression Study

Hypotheses to be Tested

The content of AD and CVD statutes suggests that the number of cases filed in a particular year will depend at least in part on macroeconomic and trade-related variables that one identifies with the injury test that must be passed in order to receive import protection. The structure of U.S. trade law suggests that the filing of unfair trade law cases has become increasingly subject to the influence of changes in trade statutes and protectionist strategies.

Institutional changes in unfair trade law enforcement therefore suggest three hypotheses associated with the number of AD and CVD petitions. First, trade legislation since 1974 appears to have increased the incentive of firms and other petitioning groups to file an unfair trade case. Under this hypothesis, unfair trade filings would be expected to rise systematically after the major new trade legislation of 1974, and again after the 1979 Trade Act.

Secondly, differential statutory changes in unfair trade laws may have altered the relative attractiveness of AD, as opposed to CVD petitions. If this proposition is true, then there will be a differential impact of the new trade laws on the number of AD and CVD cases filed.

Finally, the increased trade-restrictive potential of the unfair trade laws has led to strategic increases in petition filings for the purpose of forcing the conclusion of VER agreements, particularly in steel (the predominance of the steel industry in AD and CVD filings will be examined below). In those years when the steel industry is pursuing widespread VER agreements with foreign steel supporters, the number of petitions is therefore expected to rise.

Data Peculiarities and the Regression Model

In discussing the nature of the dependent variable it is important to understand how AD and CVD cases are counted. An escape clause petition (the subject of the study by Coughlin, Terza, and Khalifah 1989), can possibly cover several products and several foreign supplying countries in a single case filing. AD and CVD cases, in contrast, are filed on the basis of one product and one foreign supplying country per case. Thus, a single firm or petitioning group may file several AD or CVD cases at a time. Steel producers, for example, have often filed dozens of cases simultaneously, covering various steel products and several foreign supplying countries. In the context of the hypotheses described earlier, the general presumption is that the changes in the 1974 and 1979 trade legislation have expanded the number of foreign countries against which firms are motivated to file and the number of products in which they are likely to receive a favorable injury determination.

Another distinctive feature of the data is that unfair trade petition filings are concentrated among a few industries. Table 12 illustrates the distribution of cases by industry since 1980. Nearly half of all AD and CVD petitions during this period were filed by the steel industry, with another 13 percent filed by the chemical industry. The food, agricultural, forestry, electronics, textile, apparel, and nonferrous metals industries account for most of the remaining cases. The predominance of a small number of industries in unfair trade cases suggests that certain industry-specific explanatory variables may influence the number of cases.

The high concentration of case filings among a few industries is attributable to two major factors. First, the nature of unfair trade investigations, particularly the injury test, gives the best chances for positive determinations to industries producing homogeneous, usually intermediate goods. Pricing comparisons are most easily drawn and domestic injury is most easily established when goods are standardized. In addition, industry concentration appears to play a large role in case filings. Not only is it easier for concentrated groupings of firms to pursue a concerted, focused case-filing strategy and to muster the necessary resources (typically $500,000 or more per case) to finance the associated litigation; it is furthermore easier to internalize the costs and benefits of the action, and thereby to prevent nonparticipating firms from free riding. Feinberg and Hirsch (1989) examine these and other industry determinants of unfair trade petition filings. The highly concentrated U.S. integrated steel industry, with its dozens of categories of standardized products and a highly organized and active trade association based in Washington, D.C., thus exhibits the prototypical characteristics for filing large numbers of unfair trade cases, and is in fact well positioned to use the system in pursuing protectionist strategies.

The regression model to be tested includes macroeconomic, industry-specific, and dummy variables linked with legislative changes and VER strategies. Two specifications of the determinants of petition filings are tested:

$$\log(N_t) = a_0 + a_1 T74 + a_2 T79 + a_3 VER + a_4 \log(CAPACITY_t) + a_5 \log(XRATE_t) \tag{1}$$

$$\log(N_t) = a_0 + a_1 T74 + a_2 T79 + a_3 VER + a_4 \log(CAPACITY_t) + a_5 \log(IMPORTS_t) + a_6 \log(CHEMPROF_t) \tag{2}$$

in which:

N = Number of AD filings, CVD filings or AD + CVD filings in fiscal year t (1962-89);

$T74$ = Dummy variable for years in which the 1974 trade act was in effect (1975-79 inclusive);

$T79$ = Dummy variable for years in which the 1979 trade act is in effect (1979-89);

VER = Dummy variable for years in which the steel industry pursued a strategy to conclude VER agreements with large numbers of foreign steel suppliers (1982, 1984, 1985);

$CAPACITY$ = Capacity utilization in U.S. manufacturing in calendar year t;

$XRATE$ = Exchange rate index of the U.S. dollar (foreign currency units per dollar) in calendar year t;

$IMPORTS$ = Manufactures imports by the United States in calendar year t;

$CHEMPROF$ = Net profits (after taxes) in the U.S. chemicals industry in calendar year t.

The regression data are arrayed in such a way as to provide a six-month lag period for the macroeconomic and chemical profits variables to affect case filings. This lag structure is suggested by observations by U.S. Treasury officials of the typical delay between changes in important macroeconomic variables and case filings (U.S. Treasury 1975).

TABLE 12. Unfair Trade Law Petitions by Industry, FY 1980-1989

	AD	(%)	CVD	(%)	Total	(%)
Steel	190	(53)	163	(39)	353	(46)
Other Metals	12	(3)	27	(7)	39	(5)
Chemicals	31	(8)	70	(17)	101	(13)
Food, Agriculture, Forestry	47	(13)	22	(5)	69	(9)
Electronics, Batteries	6	(2)	31	(8)	37	(5)
Textile, Apparel	34	(10)	8	(2)	42	(5)
Other	36	(10)	92	(22)	128	(17)
TOTAL	356	(100)	413	(100)	769	(100)

Source: U.S. Treasury, CASIS Database

The expected sign of the dummy variables is positive. The first hypothesis implies that the coefficients for the two trade act dummies should be positive, with the 1979 trade act coefficient being greater than the corresponding coefficient for the 1974 trade act. In addition, the second hypothesis predicts that there may be a significant difference in the effect of the two trade acts on AD, as opposed to CVD, filings. Reference to the low number of CVD filings through the early 1970s and the political controversy generated by the extended investigations suggests, for example, that the 1974 trade act may have targeted CVD laws especially for reform measures. Otherwise, differential impacts of the trade acts on AD and CVD filings are difficult to predict before they take effect. The third hypothesis implies that the coefficient for the dummy for steel VRA campaigns will be positive. There were three years (1982, 1984, 1985) in which the steel industry specifically used a strategy of massive case filings in order to pressure reluctant foreign suppliers to agree to export restraint agreements; these spikes in unfair trade filings should be captured by this dummy variable.

The expected sign of the explanatory variables measuring capacity utilization and net profits in the chemical industry is negative, a prediction directly related to the injury test criteria for achieving a positive determination. The expected sign for the merchandise import variable is positive for the same reason. The sign for the exchange rate is more difficult to predict. Theoretically, an appreciation of the U.S. dollar will reduce the incidence of dumping, since the foreign firm's home price will then have a lower U.S. dollar value. However, the higher dollar value will also tend to increase imports, especially in those homogeneous (presumably price-sensitive) goods typical of unfair trade cases. Even if the chances of receiving a positive determination are reduced by the dollar appreciation, the number of filings may rise.

Regression Results

Tables 13-15 show the results of the regressions on the logarithm of the dependent variables AD + CVD filings, AD filings and CVD filings, respectively. In each table, two variants of the regression equation are tested, given by equations (1) and (2) in the previous section. In addition, the study compares the results of the three different estimation methods: ordinary least squares (OLS), Poisson regression, and negative binomial, a variant of the Poisson regression (see appendix to this chap.).

In general, the regressions yield results that support the hypotheses regarding the legal environment and the steel industry's protectionist strategy (to be described below). In addition, the results tend to support the hypothesis that the trade legislation of 1974 and 1979 increased the number of total case filings, and the coefficient for the 1979 trade act is consistently higher than that for the 1974 trade act. The associated trade law changes appear to contribute to progressively higher numbers of case filings overall. In variant #1, for example, the introduction of the 1974 trade act added between 0.4 and 0.6 to the logarithm of the number of total unfair trade filings. Using the negative binomial estimates for 1977, this information implies that 18 additional cases were filed in that year due to the legislation. The 1979 trade act adds approximately 0.8 to the logarithm of total cases; again using the negative binomial estimates, in 1983 the presence of the new trade legislation increased case filings by thirty-three.

Trade legislation appeared to have a differential impact on the two different types of unfair trade petition filings, however. The estimated effect of the 1974 trade act on AD filings is quite weak and statistically insignificant, while its impact on CVD filings is much stronger and consistently significant. Variant #1 shows that the 1974 trade act added 1.0 to 1.8 to the logarithm of CVD case filings, corresponding to an increase of thirteen cases in 1977 using the negative binomial results. The 1979 trade legislation, by comparison, appears to have significantly increased both AD and CVD filings, although the estimated relative impact on CVD cases is larger.

The dummy variable for steel VRA negotiation years is significant for total filings and CVD filings, with somewhat weaker results for AD filings. Variant #2 shows, for example, that steel industry's VRA campaign added an estimated seventy-two unfair trade filings in 1982, using the negative binomial estimates.

In a broader sense, the regression results tend to support the intuitive notion that the legal and political environment makes a difference in the number of unfair trade cases filed each year. Even in the negative binomial regressions, in which the significance levels of the corresponding dummy variables were generally lowest, a likelihood ratio test between the restricted (all dummy variables suppressed) and unrestricted regressions yielded results significant at the

TABLE 13. Estimation Results - Dependent Variables: Log(AD+CVD Filings)

	Variant 1			Variant 2		
	OLS	Poisson	Negative Binomial	OLS	Poisson	Negative Binomial
Intercept	-2.353	-0.9494	-2.36	2.6736*	3.071**	2.779
	(-0.598)	(-0.802)	(-0.37)	(2.00)	(-6.43)	(-0.683)
TA1974	0.5842**	0.4119**	0.5737**	0.4638	0.2786**	0.4894*
	(2.26)	(4.38)	(1.84)	(1.67)	(2.87)	(1.85)
TA1979	0.8368**	0.7810**	0.8000**	0.9036**	0.7683**	0.9606**
	(4.05)	(11.09)	(4.06)	(2.29)	(5.61)	(3.07)
STEELVRA	0.6872**	0.6712**	0.7392**	1.056**	0.9643**	1.070**
	(2.2)	(8.53)	(2.93)	(3.52)	(12.04)	(3.77)
LogCAPACITY	-0.3883**	-.03631**	-0.3505	-0.8684**	-0.7404**	-0.82
	(-2.07)	(-6.60)	(-.412)	(-2.93)	(-7.44)	(-0.909)
LogXRATE	1.523*	1.230**	1.506	(1.85)	(4.98)	(1.56)
LogMrchImp				1.186**	.9352**	1.36**
				(2.21)	(4.88)	(2.04)
LogChemProf				-1.03*	-0.8107**	-1.110*
				(-1.96)	(-4.21)	(-1.80)
α			.1017**			1.0E-01*
			(-2.11)			(1.88)
χ^2		173.27			173.33	
Adj R^2	0.616			0.623		
F-ratio	9.67				8.43	
DW	1.87				2.17	
Unrestr. Log-L	467.8	36.74		466.9	37.7	
Restr. Log-L				34.00		34.96

*Statistically significant at 10 percent level
**Statistically significant at 5 percent level

TABLE 14. Estimation Results - Dependent Variables: Log of AD Filings

	Variant 1			Variant 2		
	OLS	Poisson	Negative Binomial	OLS	Poisson	Negative Binomial
Intercept	-4.111	-4.263**	-3.861	2.549*	2.245**	2.327
	(-1.07)	(-2.80)	(-0.58)	(1.95)	(3.89)	(0.45)
TA1974	0.1607	0.174	0.2075	4.50E-02	4.60E-02	7.50E-02
	(0.637)	(1.42)	(0.865)	(0.17)	(0.357)	(0.348)
TA1979	0.5969**	0.5614**	0.5288**	0.7614**	0.7083**	0.6886**
	(2.96)	(6.7)	(2.12)	(1.98)	(4.09)	(2.52)
STEELVRA	0.3054	0.2455**	0.3048	0.7644**	0.7186**	0.7384**
	(1.00)	(2.34)	(0.652)	(2.62)	(6.57)	(1.92)
LogCAPACITY	0.4570**	0.4008**	-0.3872	-1.031**	-1.004**	-0.9692
	(-2.50)	(-5.68)	(-0.404)	(-3.56)	(-8.18)	(-0.87)
LogXRATE	1.928**	1.926**	1.828*			
	(2.40)	(6.07)	(-1.93)			
LogMrchImp				1.407**	1.464**	1.402**
				(2.68)	(6.33)	(2.52)
LogChemProf				-1.387**	-1.400**	-1.350**
				(-2.53)	(-5.79)	(-2.43)
α			1.828**			0.72E-01**
			(2.11)			(2.06)
χ^2		93.49			173.33	
Adj R^2	0.456					
F-ratio	5.53					
DW	1.77					
Unrestr. Log-L		152.5	23.7		156.72	26.24
Restricted Log-L		16.34				

* Statistically significant at 10 percent level
**Statistically significant at 5 percent level

TABLE 15. Estimation Results - Dependent Variables: Log of CVD Filings

	Variant 1			Variant 2		
	OLS	Poisson	Negative Binomial	OLS	Poisson	Negative Binomial
Intercept	-1.304	2.303	-3.256	3.541	2.529**	-0.1221
	(-0.16)	(-1.20)	(-0.18)	(0.13)	(2.85)	(-0.01)
TA1974	0.1837**	0.9520**	1.823**	1.389**	0.7909**	1.06**
	(3.40)	(6.26)	(2.80)	(2.38)	(5.44)	(2.35)
TA1979	1.965**	1.334**	1.904**	1.233	0.8799**	1.600
	(-4.54)	(-9.91)	(-3.43)	(1.49)	(3.98)	(1.57)
STEELVRA	1.294*	1.320**	1.250**	1.445**	1.301**	1.469**
	(1.98)	(10.43)	(1.99)	(2.29)	(10.74)	(2.14)
LogCAPACITY	-0.4076	-0.3738**	-0.3024	-0.6086	-0.2608	-0.738
	(-1.04)	(-4.17)	(-0.10)	(-0.98)	(-1.48)	(-0.27)
LogXRATE	0.8041	0.1842	1.188	(0.47)	(0.46)	(0.56)
LogMrchImp				0.6261	-0.1178	1.080
				(0.55)	(-0.33)	(0.77)
LogChemProf				3.80E-02	0.5134	-0.631
				(0.03)	(1.57)	(-0.44)
a			0.5554**			0.5585**
			(2.33)			(2.10)
c2		236.42			240.67	
Adj R2	0.658			0.662		
F-ratio	11.41			9.82		
DW	2.43			2.31		
Unrestr. Log-L		464.7	28.2		470.44	28.66

* Statistically significant at 10 percent level

**Statistically significant at 5 percent level

99 percent level. The hypothesis that legal and political factors are not a significant factor in explaining unfair trade case filings can therefore be rejected.

The coefficients for capacity utilization, merchandise imports, and net chemical industry profits had the expected signs but varied in their degrees of significance. The negative binomial estimation procedure, in particular, tended to diminish their statistical significance. However, merchandise imports and chemical industry profits maintain explanatory power at the 90 percent level or higher in the regressions of total unfair trade filings and of the AD filings. In other alternative specifications not shown, GNP, unemployment rates, steel import penetration levels, and nonferrous metals profits exhibited some explanatory power when replacing the variables actually used. The high correlation between certain sets of these explanatory variables suggests that they may be interchanged to some extent in explaining unfair trade filings, but no combination of them improved on the results shown in tables 13 to 15. Finally, the coefficient for the exchange rate was consistently positive, which contradicts the results of Feinberg (1989), but remained statistically significant at the 90 percent level only in the regression of AD filings. The results may be sensitive to the lag structure, and further testing would be required to establish a significant link between exchange rate movements and unfair trade filings in the context of this study.

An Alternative Hypothesis

The most common criticism of regression studies of trade law activity, as noted by Coughlin, Terza, and Khalifah (1989), is that the legislative (and political) dummy variables are endogenously determined. According to this argument, the number of filings in one period may affect the passage of trade law legislation in subsequent periods. Alternatively, unobserved variables that influence the number of filings may also influence the passage of new trade laws.

It is surely true that explanatory variables that influence unfair trade filings in any given year also influence congressional policymakers. Lawmakers tend to be responsive to industrial constituents, especially when jobs in high-profile industries are involved. In this context, the steel industry has allegedly had the greatest influence on the reform of unfair trade laws, although it is often difficult to trace specific sections of the law to specific industry lobbies.[2]

Even so, the main thrust of this argument is that the legislative and political dummies are *intertemporally* endogenous. The impact of filings on unobservables in earlier years may indeed affect the course of legislation in subsequent periods, but this consideration does not diminish the real impact that new provisions have on the incentive structure to file unfair trade cases once the new laws take effect. The best indication of this phenomenon is found in the fact that major legislative reforms have in fact changed the profile of trade law enforcement and the likelihood of positive determinations in many

TABLE 16. Profile of Antidumping Cases, 1980–86. Total Number of Investigations Initiated: 310

	Number	%
A. Final outcome of cases		
1. Investigations terminated: no dumping	19	6
2. Investigations terminated: no injury	92	30
3. Investigations terminated: petition withdrawal[a]	21	7
4. Investigations terminated on the basis of a pricing or quota undertaking or agreement[b]	79	25
Of which: (a) Government to government 72		
(b) Industry to industry[c] 0		
(c) Government to Industry 7		
(d) Other[d] 0		
5. Investigations dismissed by Commerce Dept. after initiation	3	1
6. Investigations which resulted in final dumping duties	96	31
Total	310	100
B. Investigations resulting in provisional dumping duties[e]	192	62
C. Breakdown of cases by product type		
1. Steel, iron, aluminum, copper and brass	190	61
2. Chemicals	35	11
3. Foods, animal feed, flowers	20	6
4. Electrical goods, batteries	14	5
5. Textiles	14	5
6. Other	37	12
Total	310	100

Source: Horlick (1990). Reprinted with permission.

Note: All determinations of investigations that resulted in termination or an antidumping order from 1 January 1980 to 30 December 1986, whether petition filed before or order made after the period. For the purposes of this table, an investigation is defined for an individual product or product from an individual country (i.e., multi-country investigations of the same product or product group are treated as separate investigations in respect of each country).

[a]For the purposes of this table, petition withdrawal refers to those antidumping cases terminated at the request of the petitioner for which the relevant Federal Register entry shows no indication that the motivation for withdrawal was a bilateral pricing or quota agreement. The number of investigations in this classification includes a single case where a petition was dismissed for containing conflicting information; four cases where the petition was withdrawn, but the investigation was reinitiated soon thereafter; a single case where the petition was dismissed because the petitioner lacked standing; and six cases later subsumed into steel sector VRAs.

[b]The Commerce Department infrequently suspends an investigation. When an agreement is reached or an arrangement is made which satisfies the local industry, the Commerce Department usually terminates its investigation. An agreement will frequently contain provision for the monitoring of imports, and an investigation may be reinitiated when this agreement is breached. The number of investigations in this classification includes seven terminations upon institution of the second steel trigger price mechanism and sixty-four terminations in other steel sector investigations due to VRAs.

cases. For example, nearly half of the AD investigations subsequent to the passage of the 1974 trade legislation have used the cost-of-production criteria in estimating pricing violations, and several cases have been subjected to judicial review as a result of the 1979 trade legislation (Horlick 1990).

Protectionist Effects of Terminated Cases

The nature of trade law investigations and procedures as examined in chapter 4 suggests that trade restrictions may result even if the investigation is terminated. In fact, many investigations are terminated or suspended on the basis of either a pricing arrangement, a quantitative agreement (such as a VER), the elimination of injurious imports, or a total withdrawal from the U.S. market, in accordance with provisions of U.S. AD and CVD law (U.S. Congress 1989). Finger and Murray (1990) identify 175 AD and CVD cases that were terminated on the basis of VER agreements, most of them in steel. Table 16 shows, furthermore, that while only 31 percent of AD cases from 1980–86 resulted in final AD duties, fully 61 percent of the investigations resulted in preliminary duties. Twenty-five percent were terminated on the basis of a pricing or quota arrangement, and another 7 percent were withdrawn for reasons that may or many not have involved informal trade restrictions (see table 16, nn. 2 and 4). Only 36 percent of the cases appear to have been terminated on the basis of either no injury or no LTFV pricing.

The use of unfair trade laws for the purpose of intimidation, or for leverage to negotiate a trade restriction, has thus become an established practice in steel trade. In addition, Messerlin (1989) has shown that AD laws in the EC typically have an intimidating effect on trade in goods under investigation, and appear to encourage the formation of soft cartels in the affected products, a topic to be discussed further in chapter 6. Indeed, the full impact of the AD and CVD laws on trade would require a detailed tabulation of the circumstances of case terminations, suspensions, and withdrawals, including an artful ability to read between the lines in the *Federal Register*. On the basis of the information in this chapter, it appears that the number of cases filed may give a more accu-

---

Table 16—continued

[c]It is possible that some petitions withdrawn without disclosure of a reason in the relevant Federal Register entry were the result of an undertaking offered and accepted between companies, notwithstanding the possible antitrust aspects of such price-fixing agreements under U.S. law.

[d]In four investigations, unilateral (as opposed to bilateral) quota undertaking by the foreign government or industry concerned led to withdrawal of petitions by the local industry (these cases have been entered under classification 4).

[e]Under 19 USC 1673b(d), the administering authority is required to suspend liquidation and order the posting of a cash deposit, bond, or other security for each entry of the goods determined to have been dumped after the preliminary investigation.

rate picture of the actual protection received (or effected) than the relatively small number of positive determinations.

Conclusion

This chapter has focused on the impact of changes in trade statutes on trade law petitions and outcomes. The results give support to the hypothesis that the trade acts of 1974 and 1979 progressively increased the number of unfair trade filings, and that the 1974 act favored CVD over AD filings. The differential effects suggest that the potential petitioner's choice of which trade statute to use in seeking protection from imports may rationally flow from the expected relative benefits to be received compared to the alternatives, especially as a result of statutory changes. An examination of the profile of AD cases in table 16 suggests, furthermore, that the benefits of filing a case may accrue to the petitioner through induced export restraint even if the investigation does not result in a positive determination. The progressive tightening of the rules to prevent foreign exporters from escaping a positive determination has undoubtedly increased the intimidation factor.

In a related matter, the study also provided evidence that the steel industry has used trade law filings as part of a broader protectionist strategy. The intimidating features of trade law investigations provide a useful means by which to bring foreign firms and governments to the bargaining table. The 1982 and 1984 VER steel negotiations were closely tied to alleged dumping and subsidization, leveraged by unfair trade filings.

The policy implications of these results are unsettling. To be sure, unfair trade laws have never made an objective measure of national economic welfare the determining factor in settling individual cases. Yet until the U.S. trade law sea change in 1974, these statutes had provided a generally acceptable safety valve for potential protectionist pressure driven by unfair pricing or subsidization practices, allowing the broader aims of the GATT to prevail. It now appears, however, that overt protectionist sentiment based on competitive decline and shifts in comparative advantage may be finding in the trade laws a channel by which to achieve discriminatory protection against their most efficient foreign rivals. As Finger, Hall, and Nelson (1982) have put it, the unfair trade laws have become the "poor (or small) man's" escape clause—without, it might be added, the requirement that the resulting protection be administered on an MFN basis. One way to address the problem of obfuscation that technical track measures create (and which reduce the political price of imposing trade restrictions) would be to include an economic impact test in any unfair trade investigation, a proposal to be discussed at length in chapter 9. An examination of Congress's purpose in making the unfair trade laws obscure, on the other hand, leads one to a pessimistic view of such prospects.

Clearly, the protectionist manipulation of trade laws provides the perfect formula for an unfair trade law war, which now threatens to break out in the world trading system, especially between the United States and the EC. Until recently, unfair trade law had dealt primarily with a small portion of trade, mainly among intermediate industrial goods. Changes in AD and CVD statutes have increased the scope of unfair trade law coverage, and portend rocky trade relations, particularly during any future economic downturn. In the end, only an agreement among the major trading powers protecting the transparency and integrity of unfair trade law on a multilateral basis, will be able to conclusively stop the protectionist tide. A comprehensive agreement would require considerable political will on the part of the U.S. and EC governments. It is highly doubtful that an enlightened consensus can emerge before trade relations become much worse.

Appendix

Coughlin, Terza, and Khalifah (1989) criticized early studies of the determinants of the number of trade law filings by Takacs (1981) and Feigenbaum and Willett (1985) on the grounds that the OLS estimation methods of these studies biased the results. In particular, since the number of petitions filed is neither continuous nor symmetrically distributed, Coughlin, Terza, and Khalifah argue for the use of a Poisson regression, which is appropriate when the dependent variable is always a positive integer (count data) with equal mean and variance. An examination of the distribution of total AD and CVD filings (table 17) suggests the possible usefulness of a Poisson regression in the present study. The number of annual filings ranges from 10 to 167, but 55 percent of the observations are less than or equal to 36.

While the Poisson regression is designed to address this problem, the present study exhibited a chronic problem with goodness-of-fit in the estimation results, as shown in the Chi-squared statistic $\Sigma[y^i\text{-}A_i]^2/A_i$, in which A_i is the estimated Poisson parameter. Frome, Kutner, and Beauchamp (1973) suggest one possible explanation of the unacceptably high Chi-squared statistic as heterogeneity of variance. Since the Poisson model assumes that the variance of the dependent variable is equal to its mean, the fit may be improved by relaxing this assumption. The negative binomial regression modifies the Poisson model by allowing the variance to differ from the mean and calculating an additional parameter a, whereby:

$$\text{Var}\,(y_t) = E\,(y_t)\,(1 + \alpha\,E[y_t]) \tag{3}$$

and a corresponding significance level for the parameter α is calculated in the regression results (see Greene 1988). A statistically significant estimate for a

TABLE 17. Distribution of Annual Counts of Unfair Trade Petitions

Number of Petitions	Frequency	Relative Frequency	Cumulative Relative Frequency
10	1	0.036	0.036
15	2	0.071	0.107
16	1	0.036	0.143
17	1	0.036	0.179
24	2	0.071	0.25
26	1	0.036	0.286
28	1	0.036	0.321
32	2	0.071	0.393
35	1	0.036	0.429
36	4	0.143	0.571
42	1	0.036	0.607
43	3	0.107	0.714
51	1	0.036	0.75
57	1	0.036	0.786
75	1	0.036	0.821
78	1	0.036	0.857
81	1	0.036	0.893
112	1	0.036	0.929
134	1	0.036	0.964
167	1	0.036	1

Note: Total antidumping and countervailing duty petitions filed, annual data, fiscal year 1962-1989.

was found in most cases of the negative binomial regression, indicating a significant difference between the estimated mean and variance of the dependent variable.

Notes

1. See the discussion in chapter 8 of GATT safeguards reform in the Uruguay Round trade negotiations. An increase in selectivity was agreed upon, but with tight restrictions and a limit on the duration of such discriminatory protection.

2. Mueller (1992) notes the correspondence of antidumping law changes and the specific intersts of the steel industry, for example. The high political profile of the steel antidumping petitions filed since 1974, lend further circumstantial evidence to this claim

CHAPTER 6

Competition Law and Trade Policy at Loggerheads: The Case of Steel Export Restraint

One of the great tragedies of the trend toward induced export restraint is the splitting asunder of trade policy and competition policy in their joint role to protect the economy from cartels. Historically, liberal trade policy and anti-trust law both developed out of a concern to protect consumers from concentrations of economic power, and their functions were complementary and mutually reinforcing. The use of competition laws to break up cartels, trusts, and collusive arrangements acted not only to give domestic consumers the direct benefit of greater competition and lower prices, but also to dilute the political power of industries that may have a strong interest in trade restrictions. A liberal trade policy aided competition policy by extending the market past domestic frontiers, exposing domestic producers to even more competition, and thereby providing a check on any attempts to raise prices. The common principle underlying liberal competition and trade policies was the concept that competitive forces disperse economic and political power, assuring both economic efficiency and open markets, and assuring the sovereignty of consumer welfare.

To be sure, the marriage between competition and trade policies has never been a stable one. Surges of protectionist sentiment have proven to be swift and devastating home wreckers in this regard, overriding the goal of national economic welfare in favor of narrow industrial interests. The new protectionism of recent years, in particular, has split trade policy off from its competition-enhancing function, particularly through the imposition of negotiated VER export cartels, as described in chapter 2. In no industry is this phenomenon more evident than in steel. In the world's two largest steel markets, the United States and the EC, steel trade policy has been transformed into an instrument of protective industrial policy. The primary concern of established steel firms in these countries over the past two decades has been to protect the value of their capital (or for steelworkers' unions, to protect wages) from reductions in steel prices that have resulted from structural changes in steel markets. Historically, they have also attempted to achieve price and market- share stability over the business cycle, but have increasingly had to contend also with the challenge of market-share erosion due to declining long-term competitiveness.

In this context, trade restrictions in steel, usually taking the form of export restraint agreements, have been designed to guarantee market shares and profitability for domestic firms. In contrast to the earlier concept of aiding competition, such trade controls actually force foreign producers to create cartels and raise prices. Instead of dispersing political power in the marketplace and in the policy-making structure, they have created huge government bureaucracies and lobbying machines with a vested interest in restricting competition and maintaining industry rents at the expense of consumers. Even trade laws, originally conceived as a means to guarantee long-term competitive international market structures, have been manipulated and twisted to serve protectionist ends.

This chapter sets out to identify the roots of the conflict between competition policy and trade policy in the steel industry, and to identify the role of export restraint in it. We begin with an examination of the cartel tendencies of the industry and a historical review of anticompetitive trade policies and cartel activities, which together provide a long-term perspective on current steel trade problems. There follows a discussion of the development of new protectionist trade policies in the postwar period of GATT rules and constraints, including the increasing use of trade law measures (especially antidumping statutes) to achieve discriminatory, anticompetitive trade regimes. Antitrust concerns are a major problem with export restraint agreements in general, and steel provides a useful case study of the pitfalls of such measures. The chapter concludes with a set of policy recommendations and the outlook for trade and competition policy in world steel markets.

The Conflict in Historical Profile

Market Structure, Adjustment Problems, and Early
Signs of Collusion

Steel production has traditionally been highly concentrated at the national level. Although concentration levels have declined since the early years of steelmaking, the structure of national industries remains oligopolistic to this day. The share of the eight largest steel firms in production in 1990 was 56.8 percent in the EC, 56.7 percent in the United States and 71.8 percent in Japan (see table 18). The shakeout in the steel industry that occurred in the mid- and late 1980s was largely responsible for the reduction in domestic industry concentration, especially in the United States, where certain large integrated steel firms in financial trouble spun off certain steelmaking operations as a means of raising cash. As part of the structural change in the industry, mini-mills have been taking a much larger share of the market, especially in wire rod, structural shapes, and bar products, increasing their overall U.S. domestic market share from 13.5 percent in 1979 to 21.4 percent in 1988 (Adams and Mueller 1990). Mini-mills, which distinguish themselves from their integrated counterparts by their

TABLE 18. The Largest Steel Producers in the U.S., the EC, and Japan, 1984 and 1990

U.S.			EC			Japan		
Firm	Output (mNT)	World Rank	Firm	Output (mNT)	World Rank	Firm	Output (mNT)	World Rank
				1984				
U.S. Steel	15.8	2	Finsider (I)	14.9	3	Nippon Steel	32.4	1
Bethlehem	12.1	9	Brit. Steel (UK)	14.0	4	NKK	13.8	5
LTV	9.9	12	Thyssen (Ger.)	12.9	6	Sumitomo	12.5	7
Inland	6.5	17	Usinor (F)	11.2	10	Kawasaki	12.5	8
Armco	6.2	19	Sacilor (F)	7.6	13	Kobe	7.3	14
National	4.9	25	Hoogovens (NL)	6.1	20	Nisshin	3.3	36
Wheeling-Pitt	2.8	40	Cockerill (B)	5.3	21	Tokyo	3.2	38
Weirton	2.4	44	Krupp (Ger.)	4.9	24	Daido	1.9	54
Total U.S.	91.5		Total EC	132.5		Total Japan	116.4	
Share of top 4: 48.4%			Share of top 4: 40.0%			Share of top 4: 61.2%		
Share of top 8: 66.8%			Share of top 8: 58.0%			Share of top 8: 74.7%		
				1990				
USX	12.4	5	Usinor-Sac. (F)	23.3	2	Nippon Steel	28.8	1
Bethlehem	9.9	11	Brit. Steel (UK)	13.8	4	NKK	12.1	6
LTV	7.4	13	ILVA (I)	11.5	7	Sumitomo	11.1	9
National	5.2	18	Thyssen (Ger.)	11.1	8	Kawasaki	11.1	10
Inland	4.8	20	Hoogovens (NL)	5.2	19	Kobe	6.6	15
Armco	4.8	21	Cockerill (B)	4.3	22	Nisshin	3.6	30
Nucor	3.4	34	Krupp (Ger.)	4.3	23	Tokyo	3.5	32
North Star	2.5	43	Preussag (Ger.)	4.2	24	Toa	2.4	48
Total U.S.	88.9		Total EC	136.9		Total Japan	110.3	
Share of top 4: 39.3%			Share of top 4: 43.6%			Share of top 4: 57.2%		
Share of top 8: 56.7%			Share of top 8: 56.8%			Share of top 8: 71.8%		

Notes: Output measured in million net metric tons of raw steel. World rank excludes steel firms in the communist bloc countries.
Sources: Metal Bulletin (11 June 1985, p. 27); *Tekko Nenkan* (1985, pp. 610-613) (cited in Adams and Mueller, 1986); International Iron and Steel Institute (1991)

smaller scale of operations, reduced bureaucracy, aggressive cost cutting, and technological innovation, are likely to expand their scope of production to flat-rolled products in the future, previously the exclusive domain of the large, integrated mills. The upward trend in mini-mill production has also occurred in Japan and mini-mills are also beginning to appear in South Korea and Taiwan.[1] As a result of these factors, the eight-firm concentration ratio in the United States fell to 59 percent in 1990. However, in flat-rolled products and other submarkets, a few large integrated steel producers still dominate the market in most industrialized countries. Yet the degree of concentration is much lower when the world market is considered, as shown in table 18. Of the world's ten largest steel producers in 1990, four were located in Japan, four in the EC, and one in the United States (the fourth largest firm in 1990 was Pohang of the Republic of Korea). This comparison of national and world market structure suggests that a policy of open trade competition would tend to serve antitrust enforcement by diminishing national market power among steel firms.

Achieving a convergence of trade and competition policies regarding steel has been a difficult problem in practice, however, given the strong political influence of national steel industries. Since the beginnings of the modern steel-making in the latter part of the nineteenth century, the high degree of concentration in national steel industries has resulted in price-fixing schemes and other anticompetitive activities (if not outright monopolies) on domestic markets (Burn 1961). On international markets, cartel arrangements in specific steel products such as gas pipes and heavy rails can be traced back as far as the 1880s (Hexner 1943, 17–19) and private cartelization reached its peak in the International Steel Cartel of the 1920s and 1930s, to be discussed below. In most steel-producing countries, steel firms attempted to reinforce these privately managed restraints on trade with government-sponsored trade restrictions.

The tendency toward cartel arrangements and protectionist activity in the steel industry is the result of a combination of several interrelated factors, including the nature of steel production and demand, market structure, and the industry's political power. The basic structure of integrated steel production, for example, involves high fixed costs and declining unit production costs over most of the range of a producer's output. Because of the typically large efficient scale of production, the number of integrated firms in a given national market is limited, and market entry is difficult. Steel products are generally homogeneous, with some variation in quality and specifications. These factors tend to concentrate market power in a small number of firms within a country, facilitating collusion. Price discipline among the small number of firms is often considered by the industry to be particularly important in times of cyclical drops in demand, since firms with excess capacity would, under competitive conditions, have an incentive to cut prices in order to keep up capacity utilization. In a competitive market, price-cutting in a depressed market would typically continue until some firms had to shut down, at least temporarily, so that prices could finally stabilize for remaining producers. A sufficient degree of successful price discipline avoids this problem by substituting reductions in output for the drop in price. Its success depends, however, upon adherence of all major suppliers to the market to the price (or output) guidelines, explicitly set forth in a collusive agreement, or implicitly understood in price leadership arrangements or unstated pricing rules.

The incentive to collude therefore commonly occurs when demand for domestic firms' output is shrinking or has been overestimated by some firms, leaving them with excess capacity. Producers that cannot maintain production at the current market price or that have made bad investment decisions by miscalculating either the cost of capital or long-term demand trends must face the prospect of shutting down the firm or writing down the value of capital, respectively. It would of course be preferable, from the producers' point of view, to keep prices artificially high in order to validate the mistaken investment or otherwise avoid market-driven adjustment to changing market conditions. To the extent that national laws allow it, firms may thus seek to band together as a cartel and attempt to ensure for themselves a fair price above the free market level. Cartel devices include production or export quotas, market-sharing schemes, and price agreements, but in open economies, the cartel must also secure the home market from disruptive foreign competition, a requirement that inevitably entails protectionism.

Needless to say, the incursion of foreign imports not subject to the pricing discipline will disrupt the domestic industry's countercyclical strategy. The incentive to seek protection from import competition, especially during cyclical downturns, is therefore typically very strong among steel producers. Protectionist pressure intensifies when new foreign competition threatens to disrupt existing market-share patterns.

Downward pressure on prices during cyclical troughs can intensify if foreign steel producers themselves seek to maintain output by turning to export markets as an outlet for excess capacity. To the extent that domestic and foreign markets can be isolated from price arbitrage (through import barriers, for example, as well as through the natural transportation cost barrier endemic to steel trade), steel producers have an incentive to dump steel on foreign markets, that is, to sell at a high price in the protected domestic market and at a lower price on more competitive foreign markets. The demand for import protection thus feeds upon itself: if domestic producers want to dump they will need import barriers in order to succeed; at the same time, the fear of dumping by foreign rivals provides further incentives to seek protection.

Domestic steel industries have also shown a remarkable ability to achieve their protectionist goals, compared with other industries, a phenomenon that can be understood from both public choice and national-psychological perspectives. The oligopolistic structure and large scale of operations in the integrated steel industry have created large firms with considerable lobbying power and influence in government. Their dominance in the economic structure of industrial heartland regions (Pittsburgh, Ruhr Valley, Alsace-Lorraine, etc.) has enhanced their influence over national economic policy.

Yet one is struck in reviewing the history of trade policy in steel by an even more powerful, psychological factor that bolsters protectionist forces. National steel industries are closely associated with the growth of countries from preindustrial to industrial powers and with the country's military might. Steel production abounds in dramatic industrial imagery: billowing smokestacks, sinewy workers, and huge blast furnaces and mills. Steel industries are thus typically locked in the national psyche as a continuing indicator of national economic well-being, despite whatever structural changes may have intervened in the economy. From the advent of steel production to this very day, governments have often chosen to sacrifice the goal of protecting consumers from cartel activity for the narrow interests of domestic steel producers.

Thus, the distinguishing characteristics of steel production, market structure, and trade combine to provide incentives for restraining trade, both domestically and internationally. The control of such activity has depended largely on national antitrust or cartel laws, as well as a commitment to open trade policies.

In the United States, for example, antitrust laws emerged in the 1890s, concomitantly with calls for reduced tariffs. The high U.S. tariffs on steel, dating from the 1870s, fell to 15 percent or less by 1913 (Berglund and Wright 1929, 110). Trade liberalization posed little danger at the time to the then cost-efficient, internationally competitive U.S. industry, but mergers that created the dominant U.S. Steel Corporation, which in 1901 controlled nearly two-thirds of U.S. steel production, led to the close scrutiny of the U.S. Justice Department. From the time of the annual "Gary dinners" of 1907–11 (named for its president, Judge Gary, who used the occasions to encourage co-operative pricing among major steel firms) until the late 1950s, U.S. Steel and the industry in general had been the subject of antitrust investigations for their pricing practices. During this period, U.S. Steel continued to act as a price leader, and its policy of administered pricing appeared to be at least partially successful in avoiding severe price competition, especially during cyclical downturns (Adams and Mueller 1986, 91).

In Europe, commitments to antitrust regulation were less in evidence before the end of World War II, and outside of the United Kingdom, steel tariffs were a significant barrier to trade. In view of the natural tendencies for steel producers to resist price competition, the lenient attitude of most European governments before World War II toward industrial combinations, especially in Germany (the German legal system had established the validity of a private cartel arrangement in 1897), made some sort of international cartel arrangement inevitable. The perceived need in the steel industry for organizing production and trade was heightened by the expanding number of firms and countries operating on the world market, posing the threat of chaotic conditions and disruptive competition.

The International Steel Cartel of the Interwar Period

While numerous steel commodity agreements in specific products had been previously attempted, the first comprehensive market-sharing agreement came into existence on 1 October 1926 with the founding of the International Steel Cartel (ISC). Germany, France, Belgium, Luxembourg, Austria, Hungary, Czechoslovakia, and the Saar (later combined with Germany) took part in the agreement, which assigned overall steel production quotas and established a system of fines for overproduction (Hexner 1943, 70-79; Kiersch 1954, 14-15). This first cartel agreement proved to be utterly ineffective in controlling the market, however, since it did not regulate product-by-product output in sufficient detail. In addition, member national industries began bickering over their production quota allocations. Furthermore, a country's steel industry was responsible for all steel producers within its borders, whether or not they joined the national cartel, so that overproduction by any renegade firms would force that country's cartel group to pay overproduction fines. Such disputes culminated in Germany's refusal to accept its production quota in 1929, which effectively dissolved the cartel agreement.

The experience of the first international steel cartel is instructive in that it pointed out the classic problems of any such arrangement. By fixing production shares, the agreement sought to limit total production enough to sustain a stable price that would guarantee profits for all its members. Such an artificial allocation of production cutbacks creates at least two stubbornly divisive problems within the cartel. First, any success in artificially increasing price automatically tempts firms to cheat by expanding output until marginal cost equals marginal revenue, capturing profits at the expense of other members. Even if all are honest, suspicion of such behavior runs rampant among cartel members. Secondly, in the typical case where vintages of existing capital and levels of efficiency vary from firm to firm and country to country, the designation of production quotas is likely to be challenged by those firms receiving what they believe to be unfairly low shares. Market-driven production allocation would assign the greatest shares of output to the most efficient firms (thus, a multiplant monopolist would dispassionately close down an antiquated plant in favor of more efficient steelmaking capacity), but a collective market-controlling agreement of disparate firms—old, new, efficient and inefficient—inevitably resorts to political criteria in making the rules.

Yet, once tempted by the prospects of controlling the market to their own advantage, the steel producers returned to the drawing board in hopes of forging a new, improved agreement that would correct the shortcomings of the first. The persistence of the cartel mentality in attempting to overcome its natural weakness provides an eerie foreshadowing of the efforts by governments to improve their own steel cartel arrangements, after initial failures, some fifty years later (see Jones 1979). The danger of this tendency is that in order to improve a cartel's functioning, it must become even more anticompetitive and welfare damaging.

In the years immediately following the demise of the first ISC agreement, however, the incentive for steel producers to manage markets and reduce competition increased dramatically. Not only had the world steel market become increasingly competitive since 1910—with new producers entering the market and an increasing amount of steel entering export markets—but in addition the onset of the Great Depression reduced steel demand dramatically. Steel producers competitively bid down their prices, which reached a low point in 1932. Governments, even the traditionally free trade oriented United Kingdom, began to erect trade barriers in the beginning of the disastrous trade wars of the 1930s.

The introduction of protectionist measures begets yet more protectionism and the former cartel members were duly galvanized into negotiating a new, more tightly organized agreement in 1933. The new cartel concentrated exclusively on the steel export market, assigning export quotas to each member country; the members' domestic markets, in the meantime, would be protected from international competition by trade interpenetration agreements and from domestic competition by cartel agreements within individual countries. The centerpiece of the new cartel was a coordinated system of sales comptoirs, or syndicates, which controlled the marketing of individual steel products, such as merchant bars, wire rods, and heavy rails. Each comptoir was a little cartel unto itself, with a central office, a quota system, and uniform prices that applied to the comptoir's members. The reconstituted ISC thus represented an early example of an export restraint agreement, although it was motivated primarily by collusive private interests rather than national trade policy considerations. Nonetheless, later VERs in the steel industry would incorporate much of the export cartel machinery used by the ISC.

Although the ISC was organized and controlled by associations of private firms, it operated with the acquiescence—and in some cases outright approval and admiration—of national governments. Despite the anticompetitive impact of cartels, governments often looked with favor upon the effort to organize the market, replacing competition with attempts at cooperation. Perhaps one root of their attitude lay in the mounting disillusionment with the market system as violent price fluctuations, followed by the disastrous economic contraction of the 1930s, gripped world steel markets. In the absence of any comprehensive theory to explain the protracted economic crisis of the 1930s, attention was focused on the existing system of economic order and on exorcising the disruptive forces supposedly inherent in it. The ultimate purpose behind cartelization was thus to master the economic crisis by restricting the operations of markets. The cooperative marketing agreements contained in the ISC were seen as the agents of economic predictability and stability, representing a victory of mankind in gaining control over its otherwise chaotic environment. Later arguments for managing steel trade would also echo these sentiments.

The Postwar Environment

The cataclysmic events of the second world war appeared to offer an opportunity for governments in the western industrialized world to wipe the slate clean of the cartels and mercantilistic policies of the 1930s. The GATT, founded in 1947, sought to bind its members (contracting parties) to liberal trade policies. Significantly, the GATT did not contain specific antitrust or other provisions for competition policy itself (Jackson 1988). However, there was a strong feeling among the architects of the postwar economic institutions that strong national competition policies were a necessary component of a liberal economic order. This issue was particularly relevant to the discussion of economic recovery in Europe, whose governments had tolerated or even abetted national and international cartels in the interwar period.

In general, European countries strengthened national competition policies in the early postwar period, and article 65(1) of the Treaty of Paris, which founded the European Coal and Steel Community (ECSC), prohibits cartels and other anti-competitive behavior. However, the residual fear among governments of market fluctuations, especially in steel, led to the incorporation of contingency plans in the event that crisis conditions might someday overwhelm a particular industry. Under the crisis measures of articles 58 and 61, for example, the European Commission has the power to fix minimum prices and set production quotas, firm by firm, within the EC, and to impose import restrictions. These provisions for intervention in the steel market go well beyond the powers for involvement in other industries given the EC in the Treaty of Rome (Swann 1983, 168–69). The German economist Wilhelm Röpke, one of the architects of postwar German economic policy, reportedly lamented upon learning of the content of the ECSC treaty that government was creating the steel cartel all over again. The EC would in fact create a such a cartel with market-sharing import restrictions during the crisis conditions of the late 1970s. The U.S. government, as well, would play a major role in the cartelization of steel export markets, through a combination of voluntary export restraint and trade law measures.

The Anticompetitive Content of Steel Trade Policies

Voluntary Export Restraint

Export restraint arrangements are by their very nature anticompetitive in that they represent explicit collusive agreements between governments and suppliers to restrict trade. A VER typically establishes either absolute quotas or market shares assigned to specific exporting countries in the domestic market of the importing country. In steel trade, the United States and the EC have negotiated extremely detailed, product-by-product export quotas with all major suppliers. As shown in the analysis of chapter 2, the quantitative restrictions on exports prevent market responses to increased demand for foreign steel. Given the detailed product coverage of the agreements, any shortfall in the domestic supply of a specific type of steel therefore typically leads to either an increase in the offer price on available steel stocks, or severe difficulties in acquiring any supply of the good at all.

As a result, the market power of domestic steel producers increases. Mueller (1988) and others contend that the VERs have been directly responsible for price increases on steel products sold in the United States, for example. Studies of general U.S. steel price trends (see General Accounting Office 1989, 34–35) show usually modest increases in overall steel prices over the VER period, but such studies typically depend on list rather than transaction prices, aggregating data over wide ranges of steel products. Thus, spot shortages of specific types and grades of steel due to VER restrictions and associated price spikes may not always be revealed in aggregate statistics. The structure of VER agreements, in any case, makes possible the suppression of competition on individual steel transactions.

It must be noted, furthermore, that VERs virtually force foreign steel industries to form export cartels, as described in chapter 2, since effective export restraint typically requires the exporting country's government or industry association to assign quotas or market shares to each exporting firm (see OECD 1985, 53). This requirement extends the collusive nature of VERs even further into the structure of world markets. Once the cartel organization is established (or promoted) by the VER, a forum is created for yet more collusive activity.[2] The anticompetitive impact will be exacerbated by the exclusion or restriction of any new steel-producing firm from open competition in the market.

The discriminatory aspect of VERs (or any cartel agreement) thus tends to favor exporting countries and firms with established market shares, especially when they would otherwise be vulnerable to new competition in the export market. Among steel producers, the biggest losers are therefore countries or firms with increasing cost efficiency and competitive potential, which are shut out of the market by their small historical market share. In recent years, less- developed countries such as South Korea and Brazil, as well as some competitive developed country producers such as Australia, have suffered from artificially low VER market share allotments in the United States and the EC. Yet the political economy of VERs show that their discriminatory and anticompetitive aspects are closely linked with their biggest political asset: they allow the importing country to target the most efficient, disruptive export-ers in restricting trade, thereby narrowing the scope of dispute and retaliation. Unlike global tariffs, for example, which reduce trade equiproportionately among foreign suppliers without reducing their incentive to compete among each other, VERs extend the restrictiveness of the trade barrier by forcing a reduction in competition among the foreign suppliers and possibly even within foreign steel industries.

The dangers of a system of induced export restraint therefore point to the urgent need for a multilateral agreement restricting the use of such measures and promoting the adjustment in national steel industries necessary to reduce protectionist pressures in general. While the required effort to eliminate dis-criminatory trade restrictions would be great, the rewards to the world economy and the trading system would be correspondingly large. Not only would a ma-jor blockage to market-driven adjustment be removed; in addition, the environ-ment for enforcing trade laws as a set of consistent rules among trading nations would receive a new breath of life. As with any effort to liberalize trade, the difficulty lies in finding the political will among governments to make the task of trade policy (and that of achieving economic growth) easier in the future. Otherwise, they may be condemned to a future of endless petitions for new, discriminatory protectionist measures and perpetual conflict in trade relations.

Trade Law and Its Enforcement

As noted earlier, the dumping of steel in foreign markets is a common occur-rence during cyclical troughs, assuming that import barriers, transportation costs, or other trade restrictions are present, allowing the steel exporter to practice effective price discrimination between domestic and foreign markets. The con-ditions necessary for dumping suggest that lowered shipping costs (which have in fact gone down in real terms over the past two decades) and reduced trade barriers would in fact restrict the ability of firms to price discriminate, even during recessions. Yet dumping enforcement has gone well beyond the con-fines of the classical definition of price discrimination.

The dumping issue is of particular relevance to any discussion of anticompetitive practices in world steel markets since the original intent of the antidumping laws was ostensibly to protect consumers in the import market from predatory practices leading to monopoly power by foreign exporters. Simi-larly, CVD laws, which allow tariffs to be placed on imports subsidized by the foreign government, are also designed to forestall foreign government strate-gies to exploit export markets. As shown in chapter 5, however, economic analysis has always been skeptical of the ability of foreign firms or even governments to succeed in such strategies. Notwithstanding these economic objections, antidumping and countervailing duty laws would not necessarily be disruptive to trade flows or trade relations as long as the focus of enforcement was based on clear-cut and economically defensible rules on finding dumping margins and injury.

An examination of the current trade law statutes and their enforcement in the United States and the EC reveals, however, that the entire process has been transformed into a handmaiden of protectionism and cartelization, often playing the role of catalyst in causing the supplier to exercise export restraint, as shown in chapter 4. Not only does antidumping and countervailing duty doctrine refuse to consider the impact on national economic welfare of the imports in question; it has in fact evolved in recent years into a mechanism for reducing national welfare through trade intimidation.

The antidumping statutes in the United States and the EC, for example, have in many cases been formulated and applied with the specific interests of domestic steel producers in mind. The calculation of the fair value price in an AD investigation, for example, can be based on the average costs of production, rather than on the domestic price of the exporter. Thus, dumping under the alternative procedure is defined as "pricing below average cost" (see chap. 5). Since steel prices charged by both domestic and foreign producers typically fall below average cost during troughs in the business cycle, nearly all steel firms, domestic and foreign, would be found guilty of illegal pricing practices if this standard were applied domestically. The implicit cost-plus pricing rule involved in such investigations defies economic reasoning, and reflects the yearning of domestic steel firms for the oligopolistic discipline possible in bygone days through cartels or accepted rules of administered pricing. The structure of competition has changed, however, in the meantime, and all steel firms are now subjected to the discipline of an increasingly competitive world market.

Countervailing duty law is applied in such a way as to count any positive subsidies, but to ignore negative subsidies imposed by the foreign government on its steel industry, which in some cases place significant burdens on the firm. Examples of negative subsidies include domestic input purchase requirements, designation of the regional location of plants, and national laws prohibiting layoffs. While the net impact of all government policies may be neutral or negative, the CVD investigation would be structured to find positive subsidy margins.

Floating exchange rates give further opportunities to manipulate the antidumping investigation in favor of finding a violation, when in fact foreign firms are exhibiting competitive pricing behavior (see Palmeter 1988). This factor has become important in recent years, since trade flows in many standardized, commodity grades of steel are very sensitive to exchange rate fluctuations. EC rules on calculating the fair market price are also engineered to increase the probability of a positive finding of dumping (Hindley 1988), and in steel trade they have generally served the purpose of intimidating suppliers to the EC market.

The threat of administrative action under trade laws points to the most disturbing aspects of their enforcement, however. In most cases of steel antidumping charges, foreign exporters or countries have terminated the investigation after the conclusion of either a price undertaking or a quantitative trade restriction. This incentive structure tends to encourage firms to reduce imports and raise prices, and the announcement of dumping margins establishes a clear signal regarding acceptable import pricing behavior required to avoid duties. Prusa (1992) concludes that antidumping law provides strong incentives for foreign and domestic firms to come to a private settlement, in that petitions provide a means for attaining cooperative levels of profits. Withdrawn cases are thus likely to restrict trade by as much, if not more, than those resulting in actual antidumping duties.

Furthermore, Nicolaides (1991) notes that antidumping and countervailing duty laws do not take into account domestic market structure in considering the merits of the case. Thus, an unfair trade petition filed by a domestic monopoly or oligopoly, in which import competition would be of most benefit to competition in general, is treated the same as a petition by a firm or firms in a domestic industry with a low concentration ratio. Rosenthal (1982) has also identified the possibilities of domestic producers abusing antidumping laws for collusive purposes filing a complaint as a means of pressuring foreign competitors into a price-fixing or other anticompetitive arrangement, for example. Messerlin (1990b) provides evidence that EC chemical firms have used antidumping complaints to enforce cartel agreements. Such activity, if conducted domestically within the United States or the EC, would indeed be vulnerable to prosecution under antitrust laws.[3] Yet trade officials in the United States and the EC have allowed the same sort of anticompetitive outcome in the steel industry by inducing foreign governments to conclude VER agreements in exchange for a termination of the trade cases.

Given the protectionist nature of the unfair trade laws and the lack of clarity of the criteria used in the investigation, the offer of an end to trade law harassment in exchange for an agreement to increase prices or accept a designated market share becomes tempting, indeed. Government action along these lines is generally protected by special legislation, the foreign sovereign compulsion doctrine, and other legal safeguards, immunizing the resulting VERs or price undertakings from antitrust prosecution. In this manner, the unfair trade laws have promoted the cartelization of steel export markets.

Yet the prospect of increased profits through price undertakings or guaranteed quota market shares through VERs raises the question of why any foreign firm under investigation would resist the temptation to settle the case in this fashion. Political as well as dynamic factors are likely to play a role, especially in the steel industry. The foreign firm may consider the required price settlement or quota restriction to be detrimental to its long-term presence in the market, for example, especially if it is highly competitive or growing quickly. More important, it may be to the foreign firm's (or country's) advantage to resist a negotiated settlement in one case in hopes of deterring more harassment suits in the future, especially if the domestic industry uses them to gain leverage in VER or other negotiations.[4] Unfortunately, even reluctant exporters are often forced to participate in a market-sharing arrangement, and dislodging the systematically anticompetitive incentive structure of steel trade policy will require enough political will among governments to overcome the powerful and highly entrenched protectionist interests that have supported the industry in the EC and the United States for many years.

The Path to Postwar Cartelization

The generally favorable economic environment for the established national steel industries in the first two decades after the founding of the GATT were driven by postwar recovery, expanding trade, and economic growth. However, the emergence of new competition from Japan and NICs, combined with progressive industrial decline and in some cases overexpansion, caused steel market conditions for the U.S. and European industries to deteriorate and eventually reach crisis proportions. The pressures for new trade restrictions in steel increased as a result. The new protectionism in steel acquired an increasingly anticompetitive character during this time, particularly in the form of market-sharing arrangements among countries, enforced through export restraint agreements.

The drift toward discriminatory, anticompetitive trade policies in steel can be explained in part by the irony of the GATT's success in restricting the use of traditional trade barriers: import tariffs and quotas. A series of GATT-sponsored multilateral trade negotiations had reduced average steel tariffs to around 7 percent by the end of the Kennedy Round, and the use of import quotas was strictly circumscribed by the provisions of article XI. Yet the demands of steel producers for protection from increasing import competition pushed policymakers to circumvent GATT rules and develop more novel types of trade restrictions and to exploit the protectionist opportunities of existing trade measures. For example, voluntary export restraint is not specifically prohibited by the GATT (although its discriminatory and quantitative aspects certainly violate the spirit of the GATT, as shown in chap. 1), and has proven to be a politically convenient device for restricting trade from the most competitive foreign exporters.

These observations still beg the question as to what underlying economic conditions caused the steel industry crisis in the United States and Europe that led to anticompetitive trade policies. A comprehensive examination of steel market developments lies beyond the scope of this analysis (see Crandall 1981;

Barnett and Schorsch 1983; Adams and Mueller 1986; Jones 1992). In simplest terms, however, the crisis had its roots in the industry's adjustment problems, including secular changes in steel demand, uncompetitive cost structures, technological lassitude, and the emergence of new competition from both domestic mini-mills and foreign imports, whose resolution was delayed for years by the postponement of needed remedies and an interim reliance on government intervention. One further element of market structure that has played a role is the power of the steelworkers' unions, especially in the United States. The bargaining power of the United Steelworkers (USW) resulted in generous wage and benefits settlements, particularly in the early 1970s, creating cost pressures on U.S. steel firms that exacerbated the industry's crisis in the following decade (see Kreinin 1984). The political influence of the USW in Washington also played a major role in the implementation of protectionist measures, as will be seen in the following sections.

The First Negotiated Export Restraint Arrangements

The U.S. became a net importer of steel in 1959, and over the following decade experienced increasing import penetration, especially from newly competitive producers in Europe and Japan. After several decades of world dominance, the U.S. steel industry was thereby thrust rudely into a newly competitive, technologically advanced world steel market. Protectionist pressure led to legislative proposals for unilateral import quotas, and succeeded in forcing President Johnson in 1968 to seek some sort of negotiated solution in order to avoid a total breakdown in trade relations among the major economic powers. Since increased tariffs or traditional import quotas were not available as trade remedies under the GATT regime, the United States chose instead to negotiate VRAs with Japan and the EC countries.

   These first postwar export restraint agreements consisted of simple promises by exporting countries not to exceed given export levels of total steel products to the United States from 1969 to 1971. Negotiators avoided making the agreements too detailed, apparently for fear that U.S. antitrust laws would invalidate them. Yet because the controls on steel trade were so loosely defined, with no product mix specification and no comprehensive cartel arrangements within Japan or the EC, the export restraint agreements had at best a modest impact on the U.S. steel market. Steel exporters restrained by the quota limits partially compensated for the reduced tonnage by shifting to higher value-added steel products, so, for example, that while U.S. steel imports decreased in weight by 25 percent from 1968 to 1970, the value of steel imports over this period declined by just 0.5 percent (FTC, 1977, 74). In addition, not all steel-exporting firms in the EC or Japan were party to the export restraint agreements, so that overshipments of the quota levels were common. Shipments from other nonrestrained sources outside the EC and Japan also grew during the period of the first agreement, a typical result of discriminatory export restraint arrangements. Finally, the protectionist threat that originally motivated the agreements waned by 1971, so that the incentive among exporters to adhere to the agreement also declined.

U.S. steel producers appeared to be encouraged by the possibilities of export restraint to protect their domestic market, however, and pressed for a renewal, with new demands for greater detail in product coverage, as well as provisions to prevent import surges and to allow consultations during the agreement. The United States, the EC, and Japan finally adopted a renewed VRA in May 1972. The second agreement set up a much more stringent and comprehensive system of control over the steel market than did the first agreement. The attempt to create a more comprehensive and detailed system of market controls the second time around is reminiscent of the progressive cartelization of international steel markets in the 1920s and 1930s, and revealed the fascination, even obsession, that governments had acquired for attempting to manipulate and tame disruptive market forces.

The reduction in competitive forces contained in the second agreement did prompt a legal challenge, however. The Consumers' Union, a nonprofit public-interest group, filed a civil suit in 1972 against State Department officials and firms participating in the agreement, charging antitrust violations and unlawful government action under the Trade Expansion Act of 1962. Ironically, the most significant legal question regarding the VRAs—whether they represented a conspiracy in restraint of trade—was not ultimately addressed during the court proceedings, since the Consumers' Union did not have adequate funds to pursue the costly antitrust portion of its suit. On the second question, the courts exonerated government officials of any violation of the 1962 trade act, thereby affirming the right of the U.S. president to negotiate such agreements with foreign governments and firms (Lowenfeld 1979).

Despite the fact that the antitrust question was not addressed, the district court decision did specifically state that participants in the VRA would *not* in fact be immune from antitrust prosecution. The ultimate legality of the export restraint agreements was therefore still in question. For the purposes of investigating the conflict between competition law and trade policy, it is instructive to note that the U.S. government subsequently felt it was necessary to give export restraint arrangements additional legislative and legal "cover" in order to avoid future antitrust suits. The president was given more specific negotiating authority for such agreements in the Trade and Tariff Act of 1974 and the Steel Act of 1984, and subsequent export restraint arrangements negotiated by the United States in steel in 1982, 1984, and 1989 usually carried specific assurances from the Justice Department that participants in the agreements would not be liable to prosecution under U.S. antitrust law. The legal rationale developed to exempt export restraint agreements from antitrust prosecution is based on the concept of foreign sovereign compulsion, which states that if the foreign government compels its exporters to restrain deliveries (through required export licensing, for example), then the private parties so compelled will not be liable to prosecution under U.S. antitrust law. Government-to-government arrangements, furthermore, are not precluded by U.S. antitrust law (see Levine 1985, appendix I).

The Spread of Cartelization

The conclusion and renewal of the first VRAs by the United States from 1968 to 1974 encouraged further cartelization measures both abroad and at home, increasing the stranglehold of protectionist policies on world steel markets over the next ten years. Both political factors and market effects contributed to the spiral of progressively detailed market-sharing arrangements that followed. First, the U.S. policy had a significant demonstration effect, signaling the acceptability of a new trade policy instrument that could severely restrict trade in a discriminatory manner without a direct violation of the GATT. In addition, the spiraling effect of the cartelization policies followed from the perceived need to close loopholes, expand product coverage, and include more exporting countries in order to make the cartel work. Tightening the noose around steel export markets with an all-encompassing cartel became the inevitable goal of the U.S. and EC governments when it became clear that anything less than a minutely detailed, comprehensive agreement would allow shifts in product mix and transshipment schemes, offsetting the protective effect of the policy. Finally, the possibility of the diversion of exports to nonprotected markets in the wake of export restraint agreements eventually gave both U.S. and EC trade policy officials a sense of urgency in the need for protectionist measures as a defensive measure against rebounding steel exports.

The first VRAs negotiated by the United States did not in fact divert large quantities of steel from Japan to the EC countries, but European steel producers still felt that they could become vulnerable to import surges without a similar agreement. In early 1971, EC (including British) steelworkers, led by the West German firm Mannesmann, initiated talks on a cartel-like marketing arrangement with their Japanese counterparts. The negotiations, conducted by private firms without the legal umbrella of government auspices, were cut short when the West German Antitrust Office threatened prosecution (*Economist*, 6 March 1971, 91). The subsequent initiation of official negotiations by the ECSC, however, led to the first European steel export restraint agreement with Japan later that year. It is noteworthy that only the Japanese announced the agreement and that the ECSC maintained an extremely low profile during the negotiations, probably the result of efforts to show that it was truly voluntary and not collusive. After all, the official negotiations had accomplished the same result that the banned private negotiations had attempted, with the same anticompetitive implications, a source of possible anxiety among EC trade officials. Only later, in the context of formal ECSC crisis measures taken beginning in 1975, would the legal legitimacy of such arrangements be firmly established.

The steel boom years 1973 and 1974 interrupted the progression toward steel export market cartelization, as steel demand and prices soared, eliminating the industry's incentive to seek protection. The favorable market conditions of this period temporarily masked, however, the growing long-term structural crisis of the industry in the United States and the EC. The decline in steel demand in 1975 prompted the European Commission to take the first steps toward *dirigiste* control over EC steel markets by establishing reference prices, investment planning measures, and import monitoring. In November 1975, the European Commission also negotiated a VER agreement with Japanese producers. Previous threats of direct import controls by the EC, reinforced by the growing intervention of the Commission in the European steel market, provided an effective means of import intimidation and, in 1976, Japanese steel deliveries to the EC dropped by 25 percent (Walter 1979, 172).

In the United States, steel boom times were also over, and import penetration was rising. The increase in imports was due partly to secular competitive decline of the integrated segment of the industry, partly to Japanese exports diverted toward the United States by the Japan-EC export restraint agreement, and partly to the efforts of European steel producers to regain U.S. market shares lost to increasingly competitive Japanese producers. By 1977, the protectionist screw had turned again as the U.S. steel lobby demanded import quotas against Japanese steel. The U.S. government chose instead to use the antidumping laws, whose protectionist content, as described earlier, had an equally intimidating effect on imports from Japan.

The antidumping route to protectionism provided new means for reducing competition among steel exporters. In 1978, the U.S. government introduced a trigger price mechanism (TPM), which used a system of dumping reference prices to force foreign steel suppliers to the U.S. market to raise prices in order to avoid antidumping investigations. The TPM was clearly discriminatory. Under the system, the largest low-cost producers in Japan were prevented from selling at below their calculated average production cost (on which the trigger prices were based), while the generally higher-priced producers in the EC were given a free dumping margin with which to compete in the United States.

Such a minimum price scheme, severely reducing competition from the most cost-efficient producers on world markets but cloaked in legal antidumping garb, was too attractive a policy innovation to remain in the United States. The EC adopted a similar policy, the basic price system (BPS), as part of the Davignon Plan, which established an internal EC steel cartel. The continuing deterioration of steel market conditions in Europe, exacerbated by increased protectionist measures in the United States, had left the policy of stopgap measures adopted in 1975 in a shambles. The Davignon Plan established more stringent internal EC market controls, backed up by a comprehensive set of trade controls. A system of fair value import prices, inspired by the TPM, was introduced in 1978 and served as the basis for antidumping enforcement. The resulting flood of antidumping complaints provided the EC with the necessary leverage to negotiate VER agreements with most of its steel-supplying countries. The cartel noose around steel export markets was thereby further tightened.

Protectionist measures in the United States and the EC in the late 1970s failed to stem the decline in steel market conditions. Market-driven adjustment—a restructuring based on new technologies, increasing domestic competition from mini-mills, a secular decline in steel demand, and changing patterns of international competitiveness—was not promoted by the insular trade restrictions. Confronted with the failure of their previous steel policies, governments chose only to increase and refine their protectionist measures, however. In this manner, the cartelization of world steel markets proceeded as a politically logical consequence of economic policy failure.

By 1980, conditions in the EC had deteriorated to the point where a state of manifest crisis was declared, allowing even more draconian controls to be imposed on EC steel markets. Some measures actually encouraged dumping on export markets by EC firms, an incentive created by the high managed prices on insulated EC internal markets and a production quota system that raised allowable production levels if the output was exported (see Jones 1986, 134).

The EC steel strategy of export-led recovery from behind its own protectionist walls was on a direct collision course with U.S. trade policy. The TPM had eliminated Japan as a disruptive influence on the U.S. market (the United States also reportedly concluded an informal VER with Japan in 1979), but increasing market penetration by EC producers was provoking calls among U.S. steel firms for tighter trade controls. An important part of the TPM policy had been the agreement by U.S. firms not to file separate antidumping suits in exchange for automatic TPM monitoring of imports. By early 1982, U.S. steel producers had become thoroughly disillusioned with the TPM's ability to protect their market from EC imports, while EC steel exporters had begun defying the minimum TPM prices, which were subject to increasingly arcane and arbitrary manipulations by U.S. trade officials. When U.S. producers filed antidumping and countervailing duty suits against imports from the EC (Brazil and South Africa were also included in some cases) in January 1982, the TPM collapsed, setting the stage for a major trade policy confrontation between the United States and the EC (see Levine, 1985).

Once again, the trade law investigations worked their intimidating magic, due to the unpredictable nature of the methods used in determining the magnitude of dumping and subsidy margins, and the resulting uncertainty of the outcome of the investigation. At the same time, it was clear that several EC steel producers were vulnerable to antisubsidy duties as a result of heavy involvement of EC member governments in propping up their national steel industries. When it became clear that the investigations would lead to substantial countervailing duties against EC imports, the European Commission and the United States negotiated feverishly to settle the cases out of court, in an effort to avoid the trade war that might ensue if unilateral duties were imposed against the EC.

The result of these negotiations was the Washington-Brussels steel pact of 1982, a VER agreement that represented a sharp increase in international cartelization. The detailed trade law investigations of EC steel imports had created a forum for discussing product-by-product quantitative limits, which were finally set on the basis of market-share allowances. Restrictions of this sort are particularly pernicious to market forces, since they can allow domestic producers to further restrict output in an effort to raise prices, and consequently force import suppliers to cut supplies as well (see Loeb 1985); a fixed quota, in contrast, would not be subject to such fluctuations in market size. The steel pact also forced the creation of a comprehensive European steel export cartel, causing exporters to reduce collectively their deliveries to the United States in each steel category. The detailed arrangements of the pact were remarkably similar to the International Steel Cartel comptoirs of the 1930s.

In the absence of a general steel recovery, however, it became evident that a cartel would be unable to suppress competition sufficiently to avoid disruption until it encompassed not only all major products, but also all major suppliers. By reducing European steel imports to the United States, market opportunities opened up for countries not restrained by VERs, and as the steel market slump in the United States continued, imports from non-EC, non-Japanese sources rose sharply. The U.S.-EC steel pact had actually contributed to the shift in U.S. import market shares, since the EC had consequently tightened its own VER quota agreements with foreign suppliers, diverting more steel exports to the United States, in an effort to accommodate its own diverted EC steel production that would now have to seek internal market outlets. In any case, by 1984 the call was raised in the United States for formal steel VERs with Taiwan, Brazil, and South Korea as well as Japan and other countries.

The U.S. steel industry's strategy was to petition for relief from imports under section 201 of the U.S. trade laws (the U.S. version of the GATT escape clause), and thereby to receive protection in the form of a global OMA. The USITC did in fact find in favor of the domestic steel industry, but only recommended trade relief in five of nine steel subsectors, covering approximately 70 percent of all imports. Such an arrangement, of course, would leave gaping holes in steel trade barriers through which steel imports could still penetrate the U.S. market. President Reagan, for his part, was seeking a policy that would simultaneously satisfy domestic steel producers and diplomatic constraints. He was in the middle of a presidential election campaign and had already decided to provide the powerful steel lobby with trade protection in some form, but a GATT-consistent use of section 201 would have introduced complications in complying with requirements of nondiscrimination and compensation to exporting countries, as well as the possibility of having to renegotiate the EC steel pact.

The final decision, announced in September 1984, was to reject the section 201 relief plan and instead negotiate VER agreements with all other major steel suppliers to the United States, covering all major steel products, along the lines of the U.S.-EC steel pact. The policy objective was to create a cartel arrangement in which all major suppliers of various steel products would be committed to binding export restraint levels, thus eliminating the problem of import disruption from nonrestrained exporters.

Directing the formation of a comprehensive cartel arrangement is not for the faint of heart. To be sure, for those countries most vulnerable to prosecution under U.S. unfair trade laws, the incentive to join the cartel in exchange for freedom from such prosecution was clear. Yet, all major exporters not already covered by VERs would have to be brought into the plan somehow, whether or not they were guilty of unfair trade practices. There was no evidence, for example, that Japan and South Korea were violating antidumping or countervailing duty laws. For this reason, the new VER policy also announced the rigorous enforcement of section 301, an open-ended provision of U.S. trade law that allows presidential action against any foreign trade practice deemed unreasonable (see chap. 4). It is clear that the role of section 301 in the steel VER program was to provide a convenient threat to pressure recalcitrant exporters into an agreement. By late December 1984, even holdouts such as Japan and Korea came around. Of the exporting countries targeted for VER negotiations, only Argentina refused to conclude an agreement. Canadian steel producers, because of their close ties to U.S. steel user markets, and because of plans for the Canada-U.S. Free Trade Agreement, were not forced to submit to regulated VER limits, although they have apparently exercised self-restraint in supplying the U.S. market as a means of keeping U.S. protectionist sentiment against Canadian steel in check. In the end, nineteen countries and the EC concluded VER agreements with the United States under the 1984 steel program. In combination with the still strict VER limits on imports into the EC, the world steel export cartel was thus virtually complete.

Table 19 shows the sequence of protectionist policies that resulted in the cartelization of steel trade, beginning with the first postwar VER agreements negotiated by the United States in 1968. Once governments embarked upon the path of discriminatory, market-sharing trade restrictions, rebound effects and leakage problems drove trade policies toward tighter and tighter market controls.

Beginning of the End for Steel VERs?

By 1989, when the U.S. steel program was to expire, the government-enforced steel cartel arrangement had entered a new stage. Despite the promise by President Bush in his 1988 presidential campaign to continue steel trade restrictions, market forces and political factors had begun to change the environment of trade policy-making. First of all, market-driven adjustment pressures, after

Table 19. Export Restraint and Protectionist Cycles in Steel Trade

Type	Importing Area	Main Target Countries	Years of Coverage	Rebound Protectionism	Main Source of Leakage (Unrestrained exports)	Attempts to Close Leakages
VER	U.S.	EC, Japan	1968–74	Japanese export	Renegade	Tighten coverage, include U.K. in second VRA (1972–74)
VER	EC	Japan	1976	Japanese export diversion to U.S.: U.S. begins TPM	Several nonrestraining countries	VER/BPS, introduced 1978
TPM, informal	U.S.	Japan	1978–82	EC fear of trade diversion	EC	Steel pact with EC, Oct. 1982
VERs/BPS	EC	Most supplying countries	1978–92	Some exports diverted to U.S.: protectionist pressure rises	Some LDCs, other countries	Increasing VER coverage of all suppliers
Steel pact (VERs)	U.S.	EC	1982–85	EC exports diverted to home makts: EC tightens VERs	LDCs and other nonrestraining countries	Political pressure for global import quotas
Expanded VERs	U.S.	EC, Japan, NICs	1984–92	Continuation of EC VERs	Remaining nonrestraining countries	Political pressure to include Canada
Unfair trade Cases	U.S.	EC, Japan, Canada	Beginning 1992	EC cases against E. Eur.; Canada cases against U.S.	End of formal U.S. VER program	Pressure for renewed formal VER quotas

Source: Jones (1986), with updates.

years of protection-induced delay, had finally asserted themselves in the U.S. and European steel industries. The U.S. industry had by early 1989 cut capacity, reduced costs, and increased labor productivity to the point where it was competitive with most other world steel producers. The European steel industry had also shed some excess capacity and redundant labor, and European governments had reduced production subsidies and direct involvement (British Steel Corporation had even returned from nationalized to private ownership), although restructuring efforts have also involved additional aid in some cases. These developments allowed President Bush to propose negotiations on a return to more open trade policies in steel, based on an international consensus to eliminate subsidies and other unfair trade practices.

After so many years of protection-induced shortages, steel-using firms in the United States had also begun to show their open dissatisfaction with the VER program. Their intensive lobbying efforts in 1988 and 1989 against a renewal of the steel trade restrictions was the single most significant development in the political economy of U.S. trade policy in recent years. The effects of the market-sharing VER agreements on prices and availability of specific steel products in the marketplace were at last hotly debated in a public manner, with steel consumers' views finally commanding political attention.

The steel export cartel itself was also experiencing predictable tensions among its members and rumblings for liberalization of the VER quotas. Countries whose steel producers were most cost-efficient, buoyed by the developments described above, argued for larger quota allotments or exclusion from the steel program altogether. The trend toward reduced subsidization and government involvement in many steel exporting countries, as well as the newfound market viability of U.S. steel producers, had reduced the credibility of threats of unfair trade investigations, which would have to prove both a violation of the law and injury to domestic producers. The incentive structure that had brought steel exporters to the negotiating table appeared to be weakening.

In July 1989, President Bush announced a renewal of the VER program, but with a definitive termination date of 30 March 30 1992, after which U.S. trade laws would be used to regulate unfair steel imports. In the meantime, U.S. negotiators negotiated a series of bilateral consensus agreements (BCAs) with major steel-exporting countries, which included market-opening measures in the exporting members' domestic markets and a pledge to eliminate government subsidies. In order to encourage countries to conclude such agreements, President Bush offered an additional one percent of the U.S. domestic market to be distributed to countries that entered into BCAs, with additional market share increments to be added in subsequent years of the VRAs (see table 19). This gradual liberalization of the trade quotas was intended to facilitate the transition to a more open steel trading environment once the VRAs were terminated. These efforts were significant in that they represented a directed policy of eliminating VERs through a phaseout process, and differed from most other examples of terminated VER agreements, which typically lapsed only when the political crisis ended. In the case of steel, however, the high political profile of the industry and the continued potential for renewed crisis meant that considerable effort would be required to end the long-standing arrangements of export quotas.

The trend in government policy away from formal export restraint in steel continued with the termination by the EC of its VER program in December 1992. Unlike the United States, however, the EC was hardly in a position to demand an end to foreign steel subsidies as part of the deal. Instead, EC trade officials appeared to be relying on its unfair trade laws—or else informal agreements on quanitities and prices—to keep steel imports under control.

In this regard, the creation of a viable liberal trade regime in steel depended on the ability of governments to come to a comprehensive agreement on subsidies and other government involvement in domestic steel markets, since steel firms, especially in the U.S., made it clear that they would return to a strategy of filing unfair trade petitions if allegedly subsidized or dumped steel imports disrupted their markets. In addition, more open steel trade depended upon the continued market adjustment of steel firms to the changing conditions of domestic competition and the changing pattern of comparative advantage on international steel markets. This process implied the market-driven elimination of excess steel capacity, and a shifting of market shares toward more competitive imports and mini-mill producers. However, international negotiations focused only on the first of these requirements. In an effort to create a comprehensive international code of government policy rules related to steel trade, the United States sought to extend the system of BCAs by negotiating a new accord, the Multilateral Steel Agreement (MSA), within the context of the GATT Uruguay Round.

The MSA negotiations were born under an unlucky star. The recovery of the steel industry in the industrialized countries of the late 1980s, which temporarily kept protectionist forces at bay, evaporated with the slump of 1991–92. In Europe, steel prices fell 30 percent from 1989 to 1992 (*Financial Times*, 24 November 1992). Furthermore, the GATT negotiations stalled in December 1990 after the Brussels ministerial failed to resolve key agricultural issues between the United States and the EC, depriving the MSA talks of any external impetus during the final months of the VRA program. The MSA negotiations broke off in late March 1992 over the issue of which state subsidies to the steel industry would be allowed without trade law penalties ("greenlighted") on that country's exports. While all countries agreed to prohibit future operating subsidies and government bailouts, the United States insisted that state subsidies to domestic steel firms for environmental protection, research and development, worker retraining, and company closures would continue to be actionable under U.S. trade law, a position strongly opposed by the EC.

A cynical observer would claim that sectoral interests in the United States or in the EC (or both) used these remaining issues as an excuse to scuttle the MSA, whose completion would have compromised their ability to receive government protection. The subsidies in dispute account for only about 5 percent of existing state aids to the steel industry, and since their economic effect is quite distant from the point of sale, probably have little impact on current international trade flows. Ironically, the retraining and plant closure subsidies would be most likely to contribute to the long-run adjustment of the industry, whose greatest challenge continues to be the need to shut down excess capacity.

Events following the breakdown of the MSA talks lent support to the cynical view. In May and June 1992, U.S. steel producers filed dozens of antidumping and countervailing duty complaints against all major steel-supplying countries, leading in July 1993 to definitive penalty duties ranging from 1 to 154 percent against sixteen countries in thirty-two out of seventy-four cases (see *Journal of Commerce*, 28 July 1993).[5] EC steel producers, in particular, had objected bitterly to antidumping petitions being brought against imports that occurred under the VER arrangement (*American Metal Market*, 29 January 1993). The gentlemen's agreement had been that as long as foreign suppliers abided by the quotas, U.S. domestic producers would not file unfair trade petitions. The ultimate failure of the VER policy as a means of regulating unfair trade lay in the fact that it did not address the underlying problems of government subsidies and other market distortions, and therefore did not prevent a return to the use of highly disputed trade law measures, which only acted to destabilize trade relations anew.

Foreign government reaction to the final decisions in the U.S. trade law cases was mixed. More than half of the cases filed were ultimately thrown out, which represented a more favorable outcome for steel exporters than was expected. It appears that the USITC Commissioners, in voting against a final determination of injury, were finally willing to attribute the domestic industry's problems more to domestic factors—the economic downturn and mini-mill competition, in particular—than to imports. Using as a benchmark earlier cases, in which import penetration was higher, the domestic industry's case appeared to have been weaker. Nonetheless, heavy penalty duties were imposed on about $1.7 billion of steel imports, mostly plate and corrosion-resistant sheet.

The impact of the July 1993 USITC decisions on the course of steel trade relations was difficult to assess. Many observers felt that the U.S. steel industry's negotiating position was weakened, reducing the possibility of a return to VRAs (*Wall Street Journal*, 29 July 1993). However, negotiating a set of rules to reduce both subsidies and trade restrictions, including the reduction of protectionist trade law actions, as well as a framework for reducing redundant world steel capacity, remained no less difficult. It was also clear that a trade war based on escalating unfair trade law actions would be costly to all sides, as more and more countries were turning to unfair trade law enforcement as a tool of steel trade policy. Antidumping cases against U.S. exports had been filed by Mexico, for example, and Canada imposed provisional antidumping duties against imported U.S. steel sheet in retaliation for the U.S. cases against Canada (*Wall Street Journal*, 1 February and 1 April 1993). The MSA talks drifted without resolution past the end of the Uruguay Round, implying a continuation of retaliatory trade law measures as the dominant force in steel trade relations.

A manipulation of government policies thus remained a key element in the antirecession strategy of both the U.S. and the European steel industries. U.S. steelmakers, who had been trying to get price increases to stick through most of the year, were expected to have only partial success in this regard in light of the mixed rulings in the unfair trade cases. Yet the voluntary withdrawal of some steel products by European producers during the investigations, and the corresponding price increases, suggested that trade law enforcement may have created a soft cartel based on unstructured export restraint (*Financial Times*, 29 January 1993). European steel producers, for their part, pressured the EC Commission to institute a new bailout package for their national steel industries to cover redundancy and restructuring costs, including the possibility of measures for additional trade restrictions (*Financial Times*, 24 November 1992). Shortly thereafter, the EC Commission imposed antidumping duties of its own against steel imports from east European countries (ibid., 17 December 1992).

Meanwhile, a general consensus on the need for an elimination of redundant capacity in the EC had apparently been achieved, but deciding on which plants would be closed became a political nightmare, as the governments of Spain and Italy, for example, demanded that steel production in their countries be maintained for social reasons, and steelworkers rallied on the streets of Bonn to protest any cutbacks in Germany (*Financial Times*, 27 March 1993). An EC Commission plan announced in December 1993 called for overall steel capacity cuts of thirty million tons, but EC member governments were willing to cut only about five million tons from their state-subsidized plants, while federal and state authorities in Germany insisted that new subsidies be extended to plants in Brandenburg and Bremen. This state of affairs left the lion's share of capacity reduction to be absorbed by private steel producers.

Thus, while an orderly elimination of state-owned excess steel capacity was proving difficult to negotiate among EC members, an even more difficult public policy issue was emerging in how to allocate and impose collectively determined capacity cuts among unwilling private firms. In spite of offers of retraining subsidies and other government compensation in exchange for voluntary capacity cutbacks, the fact remained that the restructuring plan called for private steel capacity to be eliminated while relatively inefficient state-owned plants would continue to operate and receive subsidies. The compensation approach, it seemed, needed to be supplemented by more coercive measures. The timing of an EC Commission announcement of fines against 20 companies for price-fixing practices therefore appeared to be timed to bring additional pressure on private steel makers to accept the cutback plan (*Financial Times*, 15 February 1994). Ironically, the Commission's policy of allowing continued public subsidies had also contributed to the distortion of competition in the steel market, but the long-standing practice of EC intervention and dirigisme through Eurofer had established the predominance of central control over competition policy in its approach to the steel industry's crisis.

Whatever fears governments harbored over an escalation of retaliation and counterretaliation, the ultimate goal of liberal trade in steel remained elusive in 1994, as 50 percent of European steel capacity was still government owned, and the strategy of U.S. firms was still to pursue some sort of government protection from imports. Yet the United States and the EC had terminated their formal export restraint programs, reversing the trend of the previous twenty-five years. At the same time, the EC's willingness to continue bailing out steel indefinitely also appeared to be diminishing, as the EC Commission agreed in November 1992 to close out the remaining 750 million ECU financial reserves of the Treaty of Paris, which in the past had been used to fund steel industry crisis programs (*Financial Times*, 24 November 1992). Separate negotiations on safeguards in the Uruguay Round, in the meantime, had also resulted in an agreement to phase out all voluntary export restraints in general, as will be discussed in chapter 8.

Outlook

Prospects for a Definitive End to the Cartel

Apologists for severe trade restrictions on steel, including cartel-like market-sharing agreements, generally argue that (1) foreign steel production is hopelessly riddled with subsidies and other market distortions, and will remain so for the foreseeable future; (2) trade law cases are an inefficient and disruptive means by which to regulate unfair trade, creating so much uncertainty that they would actually reduce trade below VER levels; and (3) trade market forces are irrelevant in steel trade, and steel exporters fix prices anyway, so objections to a cartel arrangement as market distorting are superfluous. For these reasons, they argue, a managed-trade arrangement for steel is the best policy. It is instructive to view the future of steel trade policy in light of these three claims.

Regarding foreign steel subsidies, the U.S. steel lobby has gone to great lengths to document foreign government involvement in steel (see Howell et al 1988) without, however, attempting to quantify the market effects of this involvement. A 1977 report of the U.S. Federal Trade Commission (FTC 1977) suggested that 65–70 percent of U.S. steel imports at the time were free of subsidization. While the current amount of subsidized steel trade is debatable, the only way to address the problem as a trade issue will be to return to trade law as a legitimate mechanism of regulating unfair trade activity, while at the same time negotiating an end to both state subsidies and the abuse of unfair trade laws themselves. Paradoxically, the VERs, supposedly inspired by unfair trade practices, may actually have encouraged continued subsidization by guaranteeing market share access and terminating trade law investigations. Nonetheless, it has become clear to many governments that extensive subsidy programs do little to promote the health of their economies, or even their steel industries in the long run. The method of amortization of subsidies over time in countervailing duty investigations means, furthermore, that reductions or terminations of subsidy programs today would result in a steep reduction in countervailing duties over the next five years. Returning to trade law enforcement can thereby create significant incentives for reducing the problem of government involvement in steel.

Progress in this area will also reduce the disruptive aspects of trade law enforcement, which had earlier played an important role in using VERs as a negotiated solution to trade disputes. Surely, some of the uncertainty and protectionist impact of trade law enforcement derives directly from the special interest content of current trade legislation; using trade law uncertainty as an excuse to turn to VERs is therefore a disingenuous and ultimately cynical argument. Even so, it would be better to confront the issues of trade law content and enforcement directly by allowing the system to operate and reforming the unfair trade laws themselves, rather than to suppress the problem by negotiating anticompetitive, market-sharing agreements as a means of settling cases.

The final argument for the cartel solution, that prices are fixed anyway and market forces are irrelevant, is contradicted by the facts as well as by the pleas for protection themselves. Most steel markets are in fact highly competitive on a worldwide scale when they are not subject to the strictures of cartels, due to the increase in the number of steel producers, the spread of new technologies, and the secular decline in overall steel demand. To be sure, the steel market is becoming more specialized, and at any given time, particular types of steel with certain specifications or other quality attributes may be in short supply, allowing producers in an open market more price-making power. Yet it is the VER program itself that most readily promotes price-fixing by forcing the formation of export cartels and exempting them from antitrust enforcement. Indeed, an international steel cartel would have a difficult time maintaining any discipline at all if it were not for the fact that governments now enforce them. It was disturbing enough for governments to acquiesce in the formation of the privately run International Steel Cartel of the 1920s and 1930s; in the more recent VER arrangements, however, governments were actually the cartel leaders, punishing violators with the full force of law (as for example the European Court of Justice did in enforcing Eurofer pricing regulations) or threats of trade policy actions.

Conclusion and Policy Recommendations

Since the early years of steel production, large, integrated steel firms have eagerly embraced the concept of organizing markets, through pricing discipline, production quotas, and market-sharing arrangements. These efforts have often gone hand-in-hand with attempts to force the implementation of protectionist policies. Beginning in the late 1960s, the industry's political influence induced a broad and significant retreat by governments from their commitment to competition and consumer welfare. In this regard, the development of the new protectionism played directly into the hands of special industrial interests by not only restricting trade, but also by carving up export markets and insulating domestic markets from competitive market forces. Such agreements, if they had occurred under private auspices, would have directly violated antitrust laws in most industrialized countries. In 1992, both the United States and the EC terminated their formal VER programs, but the trade crisis in steel has continued.

The ultimate solution to the conflict between trade and competition policies must lie in the elevation of antitrust concepts in trade policy formulation and trade law. This consideration suggests both a legislative and an administrative agenda for change. U.S. antitrust guidelines currently exempt VER-type arrangements from antitrust enforcement as long as participating firms are subject to "foreign sovereign compulsion" (U.S. Department of Justice 1988, 33). U.S. trade legislation, in addition, gives the president specific authority to negotiate such market-sharing VER agreements in steel and other products, to the direct detriment of U.S. consumer interests. Finally, the content and enforcement procedures of antidumping and countervailing duty laws have in many cases come to serve protectionist interests, encouraging foreign exporters to negotiate market-sharing agreements as their best alternative. This combination of negotiating authority, legal guidelines, and trade law intimidation has effectively gutted trade policy of any antitrust constraints.

The lobbying efforts of those groups harmed by the trade restrictions may provide some hope of reform. In the most recent review of the VER agreements, U.S. steel-using industries appeared to play a significant role in reducing the period of renewal from the steel industry's proposal of five years to two-and-a-half years. In order to prevent the renewal or spread of legislative authority to negotiate VERs, it will be necessary at the very least to mobilize these political forces in the future. Political pressures from such groups must also be felt if there is to be any reform of trade laws. The most encouraging sign is that the stranglehold of producer interests on steel trade policy may at last be loosening; in such a political environment, antitrust law may be able to fulfill its role in protecting consumer interests in international trade as well as in domestic trade.

The functioning of trade policy in a manner consistent with antitrust law would also be enhanced by a greater role of Justice Department or competition law officials in trade policy. In the United States, from the first VER agreements in steel in 1968, Justice Department views have been subordinated to those of the larger government agencies such as the Commerce and State Departments in formulating U.S. trade policy. Overriding political interests have dictated the cartelization of steel markets and trade in the EC as well. In an interagency and legislative process of trade policy review driven by constituent interests, consumers are generally underrepresented anyway; the anticompetitive nature of proposals for VER agreements demands now more than ever a voice reminding governments of their commitment to antitrust principles, an issue to be developed further in chapter 9.

Technological developments and market forces may be able to aid the reform of trade policy and trade law. Integrated steel firms face increasing competition from small, efficient mini-mills on their own domestic markets. These firms have already made large inroads into the markets for certain nonrolled types of steel, and new technologies are likely to make them competitive in rolled products (sheets and plates) in the future. When the question of competition turns from foreign imports to the domestic market, national antitrust laws will have greater success in protecting consumers from cartelization.

Until substantial reforms in trade policy occur, however, the steel trade policy crisis will continue. Its resolution is unlikely in the absence of a strict adherence to new GATT rules forbidding VER arrangements, a workable international agreement on government involvement and unfair trade law enforcement in steel, and a commitment by government and industry to the principle of market-driven adjustment. It therefore remains for the United States and the EC in particular to resolve the conflict between trade policy and competition law, first by honoring the negotiated ban on new VER agreements in steel, textiles, automobiles and other goods, and then by subjecting trade legislation and trade law enforcement to a high antitrust standard. In the case of steel, the conclusion of a comprehensive MSA to defuse the subsidies issue is also essential, but the ultimate goal should remain one of adjustment, especially in terms of the market-driven removal of excess capacity. For as long as redundant steelmaking capacity and workers remain exposed to market pressures from either domestic or international sources, it is certain that imports will be the target of the industry's lobbying efforts.

Steel trade policy therefore plays a pivotal role in the reform of export restraint measures and the reassertion of trade policy's role as an instrument of competition policy. The challenge for governments is to link agreements on reducing subsidies and removing trade barriers to adjustment measures that will diminish the demand for protection in the future. While in the EC this goal suggests the need to turn from state subsidies to positive measures to encourage the needed plant closures, in the United States it suggests the need to reform trade policy measures that have been all too accommodating to the domestic industry over the years. The danger therefore lies in the prospect that the elimination of VERs without addressing the underlying adjustment issue will only drive trade policy toward the further creative manipulation of trade law or other administrative measures to satisfy protectionist demands. The most likely outcome would then be the replacement of hard VER cartels with informal soft cartels administered on the basis of avoiding trade law complaints. But if nations agree among themselves to enshrine such instruments of export restraint as a legitimate trade policy tool, who—or what—will be left to protect consumers from the anticompetitive impact of international collusion and price-fixing?

Notes

1. In Europe, mini-mill production is still limited primarily to the Brescia region of northern Italy. While the higher cost of electricity and scrap in Europe may be limiting mini-mill development there, it must be noted that the large role of government ownership and subsidies among the large integrated European firms may have distorted the course of the industry's development. See the *Economist*, 6 March 1993, 65–66.

2. After many years of government-enforced export cartels, it is ironic that some EC firms were accused of running a private export cartel (see *American Metal Market*, 28 July 1993). In the U.S. and EC steel industries, adherence to a private cartel agreement and violation of a government cartel agreement are both punishable, either by law or trade sanctions.

3. Prusa (1992, 6–7, notes that the Noerr-Pennington doctrine, which states that antitrust violations cannot be based on attempts by domestic firms to influence the enforcement of legislation, even if the legislation restrains trade, protects U.S. antidumping settlements from antitrust prosecution.

4. The foreign strategies involved in the 1992–93 U.S. steel antidumping cases suggest the presence of these factors, for example. See *Journal of Commerce*, 28 July 1993.

5. Definitive penalty duties were assessed against Australia, Belgium, Brazil, Canada, Finland, France, Germany, Japan, Korea, Mexico, the Netherlands, Poland, Romania, Spain, Sweden, and the United Kingdom. Provisional duties were withdrawn on steel imports from Argentina, Austria, Italy, and New Zealand.

CHAPTER 7

VERs and the Interests of Developing Countries

Curse or Blessing?

For the less-developed countries (LDCs), the export restraint issue is particularly important, not only because of the specific effects of such measures on economic efficiency, growth, and development, but also because of the broader institutional issues associated with the functioning of the world trading system. In particular, the continued use of voluntary export restraint and related instruments of trade policy threaten to institutionalize a discriminatory trade regime that may systematically harm the interests of poorer, politically weak countries. As long as political pressures in the industrialized countries result in attempts to target disruptive countries exporting politically sensitive goods for trade restrictions, it is in the interest of the targeted countries to strengthen the trade policy rules on equal market access, in other words, nondiscrimination. Otherwise, the political law of the jungle tends to assert itself, by which market access is determined in large part by political power.

The assertion of political power by large countries comes largely as a result of a failure of their adjustment processes and policies. The VER agreement has thus come to represent the inability of the major industrialized countries to adapt to structural change in the world economy—change that has often manifested itself in the shifting of comparative advantage in many politically sensitive products toward newly industrializing and less-developed countries. Constrained by the requirements of GATT rules and trade liberalization commitments in the use of protectionist measures, yet pressured by the interests of domestic producers to take some defensive action against imports, the governments of advanced industrialized countries have turned to VER agreements as a quick and politically convenient means of restricting trade. Referring back to table 1, one can identify such politically sensitive products in advanced industrialized countries in which many newly industrializing and less-developed countries have exhibited increasing comparative advantage based on lower wage rates and the spread of technology: steel, textiles, clothing, footwear, and basic electronics goods and components, among others. Such trade restrictions can be especially damaging to the process of economic devel-

TABLE 20. U.S. and EC Antidumping Case Initiations: By Target Countries

	1981	1982	1983	1984	1985	1986	1987	1988	1989	1990	1991	1992
US Filings Against:												
LDCs	2	1	0	2	3	10	3	1	0	0	6	4
NICs	1	5	26	22	27	52	12	12	8	12	17	36
NMEs	2	3	26	5	21	3	7	2	0	4	15	20
Industrial	4	40	49	35	24	20	19	27	8	11	43	51
Total	9	49	101	64	75	85	41	42	16	27	81	111
EC Filings Against:												
LDCs	0	0	1	0	0	0	0	0	0	3	2	4
NICs	4	4	4	4	2	1	6	13	13	13	5	7
NMEs	5	31	12	19	21	22	15	13	12	8	3	8
Industrial	13	9	9	21	17	12	15	23	13	6	6	4
Total	22	44	26	44	40	35	36	49	38	30	16	23

Source: USITC, OTAP (various issues)

opment in poor countries with a nondiversified manufacturing base and limited flexibility in adjusting their output to alternative products.

In addition to structured VER agreements, unfair trade law measures or unreported threats and clandestine agreements also restrict the exports of developing countries. Finger and Murray (1990) report that 34 percent of all antidumping and 40 percent of all countervailing duty cases initiated from 1980 to 1988 in the United States were filed against LDCs. A 1988 World Bank study indicates that 39 percent of antidumping cases initiated from 1980 to 1987 in the EC were targeted at imports from NICs and LDCs (Messerlin, 1988, 28). The trend in antidumping case filings against this group of exporting countries has increased since 1980 (see table 20). In addition, since the share of NIC and LDC imports in the EC, for example, was about 18 percent during the period, unfair trade law has been targeted disproportionately at these countries.[1] These numbers probably understate the negative impact of antidumping and countervailing duty investigations for LDCs in particular, which often have a lower degree of flexibility and diversification in shifting production and exports to other goods once trade law petitions close the door on major sources of export earnings. In addition, the unpredictable, arguably arbitrary character of trade law investigations and decisions may intimidate a much larger portion of trade than is actually subjected to formal petitions by causing exporters to exercise unstructured restraint, as described in chapter 4, in order to avoid investigations.

In distorting the market-driven pattern of trade, export restraint has forced the targeted exporting countries to adjust their production, investment, and trade strategies. Particularly in the developing countries, these distortions have major consequences for the economy's resource allocation, income distribution, and growth, and for the government's policy approach to these economic goals. In this regard, the major questions that arise out of the proliferation of such agreements are these: What is the economic impact of VERs on developing countries? What do they imply about the future role of poorer but aspiring exporting countries in the world economy? Does orderly trade management through discriminatory VERs offer these countries any better chance of advancing economically than does a liberal trading order and its reliance upon open markets?

These questions deserve careful consideration in light of the apparent economic successes of export restraining countries. Japan, for instance, provided an example of apparently successful modern trade diplomacy by a low-cost, efficient producer rapidly increasing exports to large, politically powerful countries. Whenever surges in its exports threatened to trigger protectionist responses abroad, the established Japanese producers appeared willing to restrain their deliveries to such politically sensitive markets in order to keep trade peace. On a broader scale, individual VER agreements appeared to pave the way for the integration of Japan into the GATT trading system by providing the quid pro quo for a disinvocation of GATT article XXXV, which had allowed several countries to refuse to apply GATT rules and extend general nondiscriminatory market access to Japan. These restrictions on Japan's access to certain markets appear not to have hindered its phenomenal economic growth in the postwar period. Furthermore, in addition to the strategic success of VER agreements in securing general access to major world markets, the control of the restrictions by exporters has also allowed them to capture quota rents, as described in chapter 2.

More recently, several NICs have faced similar problems of market access leading to VER agreements. These countries exhibit high rates of economic growth and a rapid expansion of manufacturing exports, sometimes contributing to market disturbances for established industries in the advanced industrialized countries. The most successful countries in this group, the "four dragons," South Korea, Taiwan, Honk Kong, and Singapore, as well as other countries in Asia and Latin America, have concluded numerous VER agreements. Are export restraint agreements a detriment to development in the exporting country, as suggested by a traditional view of protectionism, or have they provided a means by which "these less powerful exporting countries have found a way to turn an adverse situation into advantage"? (Yoffie 1983, 9)

For the LDCs, the policy issue of whether to control or ban VERs from the trade policy arsenal is therefore not as straightforward as it may first appear. Since the GATT rules cannot eliminate developed country protectionism itself, as implemented currently through VERs and other export restraint devices, the policy debate has focused on how existing developed country protectionism can best be contained and channeled. The evolution of commercial policy suggests, in fact, that a ban on VERs would drive countries toward other, even less transparent policy measures, such as a greater reliance on antidumping and countervailing duty law enforcement, a trend that is already apparent in recent trade policy developments. Alternatively, Uruguay Round negotiations have confirmed that an agreement to eliminate VERs within the GATT is acceptable to importing countries only if there are some changes in GATT rules to allow more freedom in the use of safeguard measures, particularly in terms of targeting the most disruptive exporters. It is not clear that LDC interests would be well served by such trade-offs.

Trade, Export Restraint, and the Development Process

Trade Theory Perspectives on Development

Whether individual developing countries, or the LDCs as a whole, are better off as a result of the proliferation of export restraint agreements in recent years, is a complex question. Even in the presence of net static welfare gains from VER quota rent transfers, it is possible that other effects may detract from these gains. For example, the rent seeking that grows out of the export cartel organization accompanying VERs may promote a system of corruption that retards efficiency and market-driven economic growth. Furthermore, the establishment of VERs tends to lock into place rigid market shares, not only for individual exporting firms, but also for exporting countries. Some countries may gain from the market sharing while others, usually the latecomers to the market, may lose. Finally, the initiation of LDCs into a world trading system marked by a network of negotiated trade restrictions may, through its example, also taint the trade policies of the exporting countries, inhibiting long-term growth.

Harry Johnson described the general concept of development in terms of a continuous process requiring fundamental transformations of political and social structures:

> The development problem of the less developed countries is one of converting a "traditional" society predominantly based on subsistence or near-subsistence agriculture and/or the bulk export of a few primary commodities, in which per capita income grows slowly or may even be declining as a result of population pressure, into a "modern" society in which growth of per capita income is internalized in the social and economic system through automatic mechanisms promoting accumulation of capital, improvement of technology, and growth of skill of the labor force. (Johnson 1967, 44)

Over the years, economists have attempted to identify the links between international trade and development. The classical economists, including Smith, Ricardo, and Mill, emphasized the role of trade in creating a vent-for-surplus to bring unused resources into production, offering opportunities for specialization and improved resource allocation, increasing savings and capital accumulation, transferring technology, skills, and entrepreneurship, and instilling new wants and tastes. More recent contributions to the development literature have focused on export-led growth and the role of trade in boosting factor supplies and productivity (Meier 1984, 489–92), and in providing the proper price signals and incentive structures (see Riedel 1991). Beyond the contributions of trade itself to development, trade policy has also been recognized as an important input in the development process, especially in its significance in directing the country's resources toward their most efficient and productive use, as determined by the existing pattern of comparative advantage (see Krueger 1980, 288–92 and Balassa 1981).

The general link between trade and development suggests that the greater the availability of export markets and trade opportunities and the greater the exposure to international competition, the better will be the environment for development. The direct policy implication is that any trade restrictions imposed by either the importing or exporting country, and in the form of either tariffs, import quotas, or VER agreements, will tend to misallocate resources and reduce the gains from trade.[2]

The role of trade in development also commonly appears in the pattern of debt and the balance of payments. As a growing economy attempts to build its infrastructure, increase its stock of physical capital, and acquire technology, it will often borrow funds from abroad. At certain stages of development, the poorer country will thus typically run a deficit on current account, offset by capital inflows in the form of loans. As the development process continues, however, the loans are normally financed through the economic growth they presumably made possible, in the form of exports of manufactured and other goods. Trade restrictions of any sort by the industrialized countries—currently most often in the form of induced export restraint—thus short-circuit the market-driven resolution of the debt crisis in many developing countries.

VERs, Trade Strategies, and Development

Notwithstanding the economic objections to VERs in general, it is remarkable that the roster of exporters most often targeted under VER arrangements includes the most economically successful developing countries, such as the Republic of Korea, Taiwan, and Hong Kong. It seems that entering into a VER agreement is virtually tantamount to a badge of economic success in entering world export markets, and the participation in such trade restrictions does not appear to have diminished these countries' economic performance. It is also undeniable that VERs often create new profit opportunities for exporters because they generate scarcity and higher export prices, as shown by the economic analysis of chapter 2. By restricting export deliveries in a limited range of products against a limited number of exporters, opportunities for product upgrading, transshipment, and investment in unrestrained countries arise, all of which could contribute to industrial development and trade among countries clever and quick enough to take advantage of the situation. In addition, VERs often give existing exporting firms guaranteed shares of the protected market, reducing the risk to market incumbents of new entry.

Yoffie (1983) takes this idea further by presenting VERs as part of a comprehensive strategy that can serve as a model for LDCs in their trade relations with industrialized countries. In particular, he identifies five strategic elements in maximizing the exporting country's benefits from a VER negotiation and its implementation: (1) focusing on long-term economic opportunities and the accompanying need for production flexibility, so that economic resources can shift toward unrestrained, high-growth product categories or industries after the VER is in place; (2) bargaining to maximize ambiguity and flexibility in the terms of the VER agreement, so that the exporting country has the greatest leeway in complying with the VER; (3) using cross-issue linkages or bargaining chips to improve the terms of the agreement for the exporting country; (4) discreet, but calculated, cheating on shipment volumes and shipment origins as a means of circumventing the quota restrictions; and (5) exploiting splits within the importing country's government, placing competing bureaucratic and policy interests at loggerheads to enhance the exporting country's bargaining position.

Yoffie goes on to cite several examples of how exporting countries have successfully managed trade relations and economic growth policies under VERs. Japan's management of textile trade relations with the United States in the 1950s (ibid, 44–64), Hong Kong's adeptness in cheating on quota limits under the Long-Term Arrangement, and Taiwan's and Korea's decision to shift textile production toward synthetics (ibid, 110–16) all proved to be successful strategies in terms of the countries' economic development. Similarly, Korea and Taiwan skillfully negotiated favorable terms under the OMA in footwear with the United States in 1977 (ibid, chap. 5). Mexico, Taiwan, and Korea exploited the market vacuum created by the color television OMA negotiated by the United States with Japan in 1977 to increase their shipments to the protected market (ibid, 217–20). Similar stories of successful exporter trade performance and benefits are likely to be found in other VER arrangements, although Yoffie notes that miscalculations by exporting countries facing VER negotiations can be equally disastrous, especially Hong Kong's mishandling of textile trade negotiations with the United States from 1959 to 1962 (ibid, 64–80, 85–88).

Yet, despite the skill shown by certain industrializing countries in successfully adapting to VER constraints, there are serious problems with setting up

VER-type arrangements as a model for trade strategies among developing countries in general. The drawbacks stem in part from the fact that VER-induced profit opportunities are not uniformly distributed, and their benefits may be denied to many LDCs. More serious is the danger to the trading system from establishing a coalition of protection among exporting and importing countries, especially when such a discriminatory regime is likely to evolve and mutate according to the dictates of national political power, whereby smaller countries, including NICs and LDCs in general, will be the losers.

Economic theory, supported by Yoffie's observations, suggests that the magnitude of economic benefits of VERs to exporters are closely tied to the market position and production flexibility of the targeted and nontargeted exporters, as well as the nature and scope of the VER arrangement itself. If the VER exporting country coverage is limited, for example, then nonrestrained exporters are in a position to exploit the VER-induced increase in price and increase shipments to the protected market. To the extent that this shift in trade patterns occurs, however, the loose VER policy will be ineffectual politically because of its porosity. A similar problem arises when the VER product coverage is loose, allowing product shifting or upgrading. If the product in question is sufficiently sensitive, the policy response is likely to be a tightening of the quotas and of country coverage, but in this case the largest benefits will accrue to the market incumbents, whose market performance typically results in the largest quota shares.

Balassa (1981) has extended the traditional analysis of comparative advantage to explain the apparent shifts in comparative advantage that occur from country to country over time. Particularly in developing countries, the large relative endowment of labor suggests that exports of manufactures in the early stages of development will be labor-intensive. As the development process continues along the lines of Johnson's description, not only will capital accumulation occur, but the fledgling economy will be able to establish the economic and social infrastructure necessary to sustain growth. Typically, more capital will be added to the production process, educational and skill levels will increase, wages will rise, and the increasing complexity of the economy will make possible (or make necessary) a shift in comparative advantage toward more human and physical capital-intensive production. Thus in order to understand the pattern of trade in the developing world, one must differentiate between developing countries according to their current stage of comparative advantage. Countries that entered world trade in manufactures as exporters of low-wage products, such as textiles, may then graduate to comparative advantage in higher-skill, more capital- intensive products, such as steel and electronics goods. This is the pattern followed by Japan, and it is also visible in the rapid development of the Republic of Korea, Hong Kong, and Taiwan, all of which began as exporters of textiles and light manufactured goods and have since diversified their exports into increasingly sophisticated products.

In this regard, the discriminatory nature of export restraint agreements may seriously distort the pattern of trade and harm the development process. Export restraint gives the early entrants in manufactures trade among developing countries an advantage not enjoyed by the latecomers in that the former can negotiate market shares based on historical performance while the latter are typically locked out of the growing share of exports they would otherwise enjoy.

The dynamics of export restraint agreements such as the MFA illustrate this point. Trade in textiles and clothing did not become a political problem for the industrialized countries until first Japan, and then Hong Kong, the Republic of Korea, and Taiwan emerged as major exporters of these goods. As the MFA took shape, these early entrants in the market for a politically sensitive traded product were able to establish large enough market shares to consolidate their position in the major importing countries. At the same time, these are the very countries whose success in textiles trade had already made possible the further development of their economies, providing the flexibility to switch production and exports toward other sectors still open (for the time being) to trade.

William Cline's study of the world textile industry supports this point by concluding that a return to free trade would probably cause the major east Asian textile exporters to lose market shares to other LDCs (Cline 1990, 58, 143). In this case, the evolution of a highly restrictive trade regime in textiles has succeeded in locking in market shares based on historical trade performance, an allocation system that is inherently biased against latecomers in the market. Jones, Nguyen, and Whalley (1990) lend further support by calculating the global welfare effects of removing textile quota restrictions, concluding that the biggest losers would be established exporters with large quota shares: Hong Kong, Macao, Thailand, Peru, and Taiwan. Exporting countries that would gain include those underrepresented in the MFA quota system: China, Mexico, India, Bangladesh, and Indonesia. Whereas the evolving pattern of comparative advantage would call for apparel exports, for example, to shift significantly from the more advanced industrializing countries to those with a greater relative endowment of labor, the rigid quota system of the MFA tends to block such a natural change in trade patterns. This negative effect for the LDCs is caused in part by the elements of time and progressive cartelization in the evolution of export restraint policy: as the trade restrictions become more and more institutionalized and controlled by zealous leagues of government bureaucrats, the bargaining power of newcomers to the game tends to diminish. Although there may still be opportunities for the latecomers to exploit remaining loopholes and imprecision in the bilateral agreements, the scope for taking advantage of the trade regime will be limited when the largest market shares have already been assigned. In addition, the lost opportunity that may result from the premature stifling of an expanding textile-apparel sector at an early stage of economic development, which may otherwise serve as a springboard for further development (by using increasing export earnings and sales as a basis for capital accumulation, education, and skill development of the workforce, etc.), may cripple such countries' development prospects for years to come. The LDCs do not typically enter into trade talks on such sensitive goods with the same degree of production flexibility or bargaining acumen as did Japan, Taiwan, or Korea, and are therefore not in as auspicious a position to benefit from the trade restrictions through strategic long-run production shifts or product upgrading.

In this environment of managed trade, many of the least-developed countries face the formidable task of entering markets that have already been carved up in favor of established producers. Spinanger (1987) has examined the case of Bangladesh as a case in point. Among the poorest countries in the world, Bangladesh nonetheless had a fledgling textile and clothing industry, largely the result of Korean investment, and had begun to export to the United States. By 1985, clothing represented 12.5 percent of exports from that country, and more production facilities were being planned. Yet under the MFA market disruption provisions, the United States, France, the United Kingdom, and Canada all severely restricted imports from Bangladesh, despite the fact that its share in these markets was miniscule compared with the established exporters. The result of these restrictions in a country in the early stages of development, with limited opportunity for a redeployment of resources to other sectors, was wide-scale shutdown and the idling of workers and machinery.

The situation of new entrants to markets protected by export restraint arrangements also explains why developing countries with established positions in the market often favor such trade restrictions. Since they already have locked in market shares in an industry where natural comparative advantage is shifting toward the least-developed countries, their interests clearly lie in keeping the competitive newcomers out. Thus export restraint creates conflict not only between exporting and importing countries, exacerbating north-south tensions, but also pits established exporters against aspiring exporters.

Economic Effects of VER Protection

An analysis of the welfare effects of VERs and other instruments of export restraint on exporting countries, particularly developing countries, must consider both the benefits, such as the associated rent transfers, as described in chapter 2, and the costs of allocative inefficiency associated with the market distortion. While empirical evidence of the net welfare effects of export restraint on developing countries is scant, an overview of the direct and indirect economic effects, especially as they relate to the development process, suggests ambiguous results at best.

VERs and Resource Misallocation

Insofar as protectionism of any sort distorts market-driven patterns of production and consumption, VERs can be expected to inflict allocative efficiency costs upon the exporting country. To the extent that an export restraint measure or agreement reduces output and makes investment in a particular export industry in which the country has comparative advantage less attractive, resources will be idled or redeployed toward other, presumably less productive, activities. The discriminatory nature of export restraint arrangements may also shift production of protected goods toward a higher-cost developing country not covered by existing restraints (the quota-hopping effect), causing the latter country to overproduce the protected good (see Cable 1986, 312). In countries where exports are restrained, economies of scale may be lost as output in the restrained industry drops, thus increasing production costs for remaining output.

In addition, the rents created by VER and similar agreements may generate rent seeking (see Krueger 1974), which refers to activities among the exporting firms geared toward the acquisition of the valuable rights (usually in the form of export licenses administered by the government) to ship the restricted good and thereby capture the scarcity premium. In the process, firms may use up real resources, whose diversion from their market-driven destination represents an economic efficiency cost. The inefficient allocation of export quota shares based on political influence or other noneconomic criteria also damages the welfare of the exporting country. Even more economic waste would result if the exporting firm (or firms) managed to acquire a monopoly or near-monopoly on exporting rights of the restricted good and "short-ship" the good, thus lowering production (as described in chap. 2). The efficiency cost here comes from the restricted production of the monopolized good and may be offset by the increase in rents extracted from the foreign importer by the increase in price. This possibility is brought on because export restraint agreements normally require the establishment of an export cartel apparatus that would otherwise not exist. However, further damage to the exporting country's economy could occur if the export cartelization also facilitated a domestic cartel (see Keesing and Wolf 1980, 128). Other unproductive behavior that accompanies the establishment of monopoly or cartel practices includes X-inefficiency, a situation in which the firm fails to obtain maximum output from its inputs due to the weakened incentives and less efficient management that accompany reduced competition (see Leibenstein 1966). The sum of effects described above represents the static welfare losses to the economy due to export restraint arrangements, lowering the developing country's GNP in the current period.

De Melo and Winters (1990) present a model that suggests that resource misallocation, combined with losses by labor, may actually offset the rents earned by exporters in a VER agreement. If the labor market is perfectly competitive, the VER quota tends to reduce the value of marginal product of labor, which then typically causes the affected industry in that country to contract. Labor in the exporting country loses absolutely in this case. The net welfare effect on the industry in the exporting country depends on the ease with which sales can be diverted from restricted to unrestricted markets, and the share of the relevant labor market that participates in the affected industry. If price elasticities of demand for the restricted export goods are high and labor supply elasticities are low, the losses suffered by labor may in fact outweigh the gains from the VER-induced scarcity rents. Their study goes on to show that such contraction appeared to occur in the Korean footwear industry as a result of the U.S. VER agreement from 1977 to 1981, and that reasonable assumptions about parameter values suggest that the VER may have caused the industry to suffer a net loss. In any case, the income distribution implications of the VER for the exporting country are clear in the context of a perfectly competitive labor market: the gains in economic rents to owners or stockholders of the exporting firms are at least partially offset by the losses of labor.

Gains from Export Restraint

There are at least two factors that may mitigate or even reverse the negative static welfare effects listed above. First, the opportunity cost of foregone production due to the trade restriction will be reduced by the degree and ease of substitutability of resources into alternative uses of comparable economic value. Thus, if South Korea can adjust to the forced reduction in textile production due to the MFA by redeploying capital, labor, and other factors of production toward the electronics and automobile sectors, for example, then the efficiency cost of the restrictive trade policy will be lessened. This will depend on the net change in the social value of the country's output due to export restraint. Certainly, those developing countries with an established economic infrastructure and educational system will have a greater ability to adjust more smoothly to such production shifts than the least-developed countries, whose economies remain at an early stage of development, limiting opportunities for alternative production. In many of the NICs, for example, economic development and industrial diversification have kept step with the exigencies of the protection-induced reallocation of resources.

Some have argued, furthermore, that export restraint has actually brought net benefits to those countries forced to switch to higher value-added products (see Cable 1986, 312 and Keesing and Wolf 1980, 123–24). The reasoning here is that trade restrictions force entrepreneurs in the exporting country to consider greater profit-making opportunities (in higher value-added items, for example) that they would not have recognized under free trade. This proposition would indeed be dubious in an environment of perfect information and fully functioning, well-developed capital and product markets. In the context

of rapidly growing economies with a fledgling and perhaps inexperienced entrepreneurial class, however, it suggests a plausible process of learning and
adaptation that is likely to be part of a successful strategy of sustained growth.
It should also be noted that an environment conducive to foreign investment in
the developing country will tend to enhance this adjustment process, since international capital generally flows quickly toward new profit opportunities.

The second element that may offset welfare losses is the rent transfer that
typically accompanies an export restraint agreement. A partial measurement of
the rent transfer will show up in the terms-of-trade effect of the trade restriction, as illustrated in chapter 2. If sufficiently large, such transfers may overwhelm the static welfare losses described at the beginning of this section and
leave the exporting country better off (in terms of static welfare) as a result of
export restraint. One might extend this argument to say that, in certain industries, the rent transfers may help to fund research and development, or otherwise promote technological progress.

Table 21 tabulates some estimates of rent income to Hong Kong, Taiwan,
and the Republic of Korea due to export restraint in textiles, footwear, and
steel. Tarr's estimate (Tarr 1987) of the net annual gain to Korea of $32.4
million reflects the most detailed evaluation of welfare effects in that it takes
into account inefficiency costs of deadweight loss, suppressed prices, and lost
rental income in unprotected markets, and changes in domestic consumer surplus. According to these estimates, it appears that the deadweight and other
losses incurred by VER agreements do not outweigh the substantial rent incomes generated by the quota premiums. This is not a surprising result in view
of the political economy of VERs, in which the rent transfer is a quid pro quo
for the export restraint.[3] In this regard, one can state in any case that a negotiated VER arrangement will leave the exporting country better off than a tariff
or unilateral quota without rent transfer that restricts exports to the same level.
If protectionism is inevitable, then export restraint will be favored by the exporting country, no matter what its level of economic development.

The Systemic Cost of VERs to Developing Countries

Undermining the Multilateral Distribution of the Gains from Trade

Notwithstanding any gains that VERs offer over alternative trade restrictions,
the systemic damage done by the export restraint regime may be of even greater
concern to the interests of developing countries than the economic considerations discussed so far. There are two aspects to this problem: the conflict that
VERs create between the winners and the losers among exporting countries in
the VER regime and the defeatism that such devices have engendered in terms
of trade policy reform. The additional conflict comes from the interests of VER

beneficiaries among exporting countries, which may form an unlikely coalition for protection with the importing countries, as opposed to the interests of the latecomers and other countries that benefit much less—or even lose—from the VER regime. Since the importing countries, such as the United States and the EC member states, that induce the export restraint are usually large, politically powerful players in world trade, and since some of the major exporters may not be inclined to push for reform, the smaller, politically weak LDCs, which are least likely to gain from VERs, have a correspondingly small voice in opposing the VER regime.[4]

An additional impediment to progress in eliminating VERs as a trade policy instrument is the apparent defeatism that has grown, especially among cynical observers of trade relations, since such discriminatory measures have become popular. In part, the trade policy pessimism is linked with the perceived benefits of minimizing risk through a guaranteed VER quota or market share in an otherwise closed market. Thus small, politically weak countries may favor VERs as the best way to gain any benefits from export trade when protection of some sort is inevitable and the alternative is a unilateral restriction without the transfer of scarcity rents. Hindley (1987) has put the VER issue into the perspective of trade policy reform by noting that LDCs should not be forced to give up anything for the elimination of VERs, since they are less damaged by them than they would be by suggested alternative measures, such as allowing GATT-legal discrimination in the unilateral imposition of article XIX measures.

The False Hopes of Trade Policy-Driven Transfers

Insofar as export restraint tends to improve the exporter's terms of trade, the gains from VER protection to the exporting country are of the same type as optimum tariff gains for an importing country. The difference between the two types of gains from protection lies in the fact that the importing country internalizes the optimum tariff gains into its policy decision; it independently asserts its market power by imposing the tariff unilaterally.[5] The rent transfer to the exporting country through a VER, on the other hand, results essentially from a policy decision by the importing country. The exporting country cannot, therefore, internalize the gains as the result of its own policy decision, since it does not independently capture the gains from restricted trade (if it could, a VER agreement would not be necessary).

This distinction is instructive in that it underscores the link between the choice of the protectionist policy instrument in the importing country and economic welfare in the exporting country. In this regard, the gains to less developed (and other) countries from export restraint may be tenuous indeed. Already, some GATT countries have argued for a revision of GATT article XIX (the escape clause) that would allow discriminatory application of safeguard measures. This would in principle allow importing countries to target disrup-

TABLE 21. Estimates of Rent Income to Export Restraining Countries

Product	Country	Year	Annual Rent Income	Source
Textiles	Hong Kong	1982	$217.8m	Hamilton (1986)
		1983	$506.8m	
Textiles	Hong Kong	1983	$263.9m[a]	Morkre/Tarr (1984)
Footwear	Taiwan & Rep. Korea	1977–79	$176m to 248m[a]	Hufbauer, Berliner, and Elliot (1986)
Footwear	Taiwan	1977–79	$43.6m[a]	Pearson (1983)
Steel	Rep. Korea	1984	$32.4m[b]	Tarr (1987)

[a]Rents from U.S. sales only during the period.

[b]Net gain (rent minus efficiency loss).

tive exporters with unilateral trade restrictions and still remain within GATT rules, weakening the desirability of negotiated agreements on export restraint, which provide a framework for the rent transfer (Hindley 1987). Many economists have recommended other policy reforms, including the retariffication of existing trade restrictions (Hufbauer 1982; Branson and Richardson 1982) and the auctioning of global import quotas as an alternative to export restraint (Bergsten et al. 1987). Both of these proposals would remove quota rent transfers to exporters.

It thus appears that the main advantage of export restraint to LDCs depends upon the current welfare-reducing trade policies of major industrial countries. The major policy question that arises from this situation is whether developing countries should continue to base their economic decision making on the assumption of the persistence of negotiated export restraint. Clearly, many of the NICs (or at least their export industries) are currently benefiting from substantial quota profits and have a vested interest in protecting those gains, as shown by the distribution of MFA quota rents, for example, but the record of developed country measures to manipulate trade policy or trade policy rules to help poorer countries in a systematic way is not encouraging. The only major effort along these lines has been the GSP, which officially allows discriminatory trade policies (in the form of lower tariffs) favoring developing countries. Despite the avowed goal and open commitment of the developed countries in the GSP to give developing countries preferential access to their markets, the practical benefits of this measure have been small. Aside from the theoretical problems the GSP itself poses for economic welfare and efficiency (see Johnson 1966), developed countries have gutted much of its substance by excluding sensitive items (textiles, steel, footwear, etc.) and inserting safeguard measures in case of import surges.

Compared to the GSP, export restraint agreements have been superior in their welfare effects on certain developing countries by transferring concentrated quota profits to exporters. However, this result has come as a side effect, rather than as a policy goal of VER agreements. The problem with induced export restraint as a tool of trade policy is that there are no rules to govern it: there are no gains to exporters from VERs that could not generally be removed unilaterally by the importing countries either by renunciation of the agreements, by retariffication, or by the auctioning of quotas.

Article XVIIIB and Balance-of-Payments Measures

Another systemic problem with VER arrangements is their linkage to the special and differential treatment contained in article XVIIIB of the GATT, which allows developing countries to impose trade restrictions as a means of correcting balance-of-payments problems. As discussed in chapter 1, such provisions have always been problematical within the larger framework of GATT principles. Article XVIIIB specifically allows a developing country with external financing difficulties the right to impose and maintain discriminatory, quantitative trade restrictions. Developed countries have complained that abuse of this provision allows developing countries to impose sectoral protectionist measures without the accompanying disciplines of article XIX (safeguards) or XVIIIC (infant industry protection), although the 1979 Declaration on Trade Measures Taken for Balance-of-Payments Purposes, negotiated in the Tokyo Round, provides for consultations, monitoring, and guidelines to prevent abuse. However, GATT rules still do not allow exporting countries adversely affected by article XVIIIB actions to seek compensation or to retaliate. Furthermore, there is no mechanism within the GATT to force countries using such measures to address the underlying macroeconomic problems that typically cause sustained external imbalances. Thus, article XVIIIB provides the formula, in theory at least, for countries to impose long-standing protectionist measures with no incentive to end them (see Whalley 1989, appendix D). At the same time, developing countries have pointed to protectionist policies in the developed countries as a major cause of their balance-of-payments difficulties, especially as a result of export restraint agreements targeted specifically against them. As far as GATT disciplines are concerned, article XVIIIB at least contains provisions for monitoring and consultations, which is more than can be said for gray area VERs taken outside the GATT. The link between article XVIIIB-based trade restrictions and VER agreements was not lost on the negotiators at the Uruguay Round, during which the possibility of trading off GATT rights under this article by developing countries for a ban on VERs by developed countries was discussed (see chap. 8).[6]

The Trade Policy Demonstration Effect

Finally, and perhaps most detrimental for long-term resource allocation and growth, the use of discriminatory trade restrictions by the developed countries appears to create a strong and negative demonstration effect for trade policy in developing countries. As described above and in chapter 1, the GATT itself has exacerbated this problem by exempting developing countries from certain GATT disciplines and, in general, perpetuating the attitude that opening one's markets is a concession lost in trade negotiations. The unfortunate result is that many LDCs continue to be highly protectionist in their own import policies (International Labour Office 1987, 31–35). These countries typically apply the protectionist approach as a part of a broad import substitution strategy, which protects not only those sectors in which a natural comparative advantage exists, but also extends to other sectors of comparative disadvantage. Yet the insistence by industrial countries on managed trade in sensitive sectors thus provides the developing world with neither the example nor the incentive to conduct trade policy on a market-driven, nondiscriminatory basis. In this manner, the actions of the industrialized countries directly contradict their stated objectives of integrating the developing countries into the world economy and stimulating growth through trade.

Outlook

In summary, we return to the conundrum that dominates the policy discussion of trade reform implications for developing countries. If protectionism is inevitable, why not allow the VERs to exist peacefully in the GATT system as a means of transferring at least some benefits to the exporting countries in an imperfect protectionist world? Indeed, if one defines the issue simply as a matter of choosing between unilateral tariffs or quotas on the one hand, and a negotiated VER on the other, the choice for many exporting countries is usually clear: the transferred rents typically make VERs more attractive. Yet the purpose of the GATT is not merely to eliminate certain types of objectionable trade policies, but ultimately to reduce trade barriers and promote adjustment to trade in general. In this regard there would be no meaningful benefit to LDCs of eliminating VERs unless there was a guarantee that they would not be replaced with GATT-legal unilateral measures with no compensation.

The role of the GATT in providing a framework for trade relations is relevant to this situation of vulnerability for developing countries. The GATT was originally established with the goal of creating a system of trade policy rules governed by consistency, transparency, and predictability. Only then could a world trading order succeed in protecting all member countries from abuses of political power that typically culminate in discriminatory trade policies. The derogation from GATT rules through VERs should remind the developing countries that any gains from such agreements are subject to the policy choices of more powerful trading partners. Induced export restraint is an attempt to manage markets through ad hoc trade restrictions governed by power politics, and thereby carries the dangers of any breakdown of order to the less powerful countries: it provides no protection from abuses of power.

Economic considerations cast further doubt on the desirability of VERs for developing countries, especially those that are latecomers in protected trade markets. Economic costs of the misallocation of resources and possible anticompetitive practices may in some cases even outweigh the benefits of the quota rents. In short, theoretical, empirical, and political observations suggest that developing countries would benefit from a negotiating strategy based on a package of policy reforms that relinquishes their GSP status and severely circumscribes their ability to apply article XVIIIB measures and, at the same time, eliminates VERs, removes the intimidating aspects of unfair trade law enforcement, and introduces market liberalization in textiles and agriculture. A 1985 report to the GATT underscores the shortcomings of the GATT preferences system:

> Developing countries receive special treatment in the GATT rules. But such special treatment of limited value. Far greater emphasis should be placed on permitting and encouraging developing countries to take advantage of their competitive strengths and on integrating them more fully into the trading system, with all the appropriate rights and responsibilities that this entails. (GATT 1985, 44)

As will be discussed in the next chapter, the Uruguay Round of trade negotiations has shown that many market-oriented trade policy reforms favoring developing country interests are within reach, specifically in the areas of eliminating VERs and liberalizing agricultural and textile trade (unfair trade law reform is the exception to this trend and will probably have to wait). Open and equal access to markets abroad, combined with liberal trade policies at home, are more likely to promote economic development than a preferences regime based on false hopes, unfulfilled promises, and contingency protection through export restraint.

Notes

1. Messerlin (1988) calculates an exposure ratio to antidumping investigations in the EC by dividing the share of an exporting country in EC antidumping cases by its share in extra-EC trade. The exposure ratio for industrialized countries from 1977–87 is 0.46, while for LDCs the ratio is 3.24 and for NICs is 1.97.

2. Optimal trade policies for developing countries may need to take account of market failures and policy constraints, suggesting the utility of government intervention in some cases. An overview of the issues is provided in Krueger (1984).

3. One must consider, however, the possibility that the government of the exporting country may not aim to maximize national welfare, but rather to satisfy political interests represented by the domestic beneficiaries of quota rents. The possible losses of labor (see De Melo and Winters (1990) and discussion in this chapter) may actually outweigh the gains without altering the exporting country's acceptance of a VER arrangement.

4. This array of exporter interests does not preclude the possibility that potential VER beneficiaries such as the NICs will push for more liberal trade, including the elimination of VERs altogether, as Korea, for example, has done in the Uruguay Round. However, in sectoral trade negotiations, where the focus is on maximizing the gains from existing trade restrictions for narrowly defined exporter interests, the conflict between exporters with stronger and weaker bargaining positions becomes much clearer. On the other hand, the general support by many NICs as well as LDCs for a GATT ban on VERs may cast doubt on the proposition that they are net beneficiaries from export restraint policies, an inference that would call into question Yoffie's (1983) general trade strategy recommendations.

5. The gains from the optimum tariff are subject to erosion from retaliatory tariffs and other costs of protection, and to the underlying assumptions of the model. See Corden (1984b, 82–95).

6. Article XVIIIB, paragraph 10, in conjunction with article XIV-sanctioned deviations from MFN requirements for quantitative restrictions, gives qualified GATT approval to the use of product-by-product, discriminatory import quotas by developing countries. Their resemblance to gray area VER agreements is unmistakable.

CHAPTER 8

Export Restraint, Public Policy, and GATT Reform

Policies that induce export restraint to curb disruptive imports have evolved over the years from stopgap measures designed to settle temporary trade disputes into extensive and detailed networks of discriminatory export quotas that have in some cases effectively cartelized world trade in the protected good. The increasingly sophisticated use of export restraint as a trade policy instrument, incorporating protectionist manipulations of trade law and other intimidating measures, has made such devices a subject of high priority in trade negotiations and a matter of increasing concern in public policy. This study has linked export restraint with disruption and conflict in trade policy, losses in economic welfare in the importing country, and damaging effects to the economies of many exporting countries, particularly among the least-developed countries. Export restraint tends to have a regressive impact on income distribution, even more so than traditional types of trade policies, and conflicts with the goals of competition policy in protecting consumers from monopolies and cartels. In view of the deleterious effects of export restraint agreements, there is a pressing need for trade policy reform, as well as measures to encourage and promote adjustment in the industries subject to increased import competition. This chapter sets out to place export restraint in perspective as a second-best (or worse) policy tool in an imperfect world subject to strong protectionist pressures. In addition to an evaluation of the role of VERs in the multilateral trading system, the chapter also offers a review of Uruguay Round reforms that pertain to export restraint issues, and concludes with a proposal for progressive, GATT-based economic integration.

Export Restraint and Its Alternatives

Policy Choice in an Imperfect World

Governments introduced VERs under the implicit assumption that, in order to maintain the rules of liberal trade, one must sometimes break them. Despite the damage that VERs have inflicted, it is necessary to consider the argument that export restraint represents a minimum sacrifice of liberal trade principles required to maintain the political viability of an otherwise liberal trading system. One could argue, for example, that VERs in manufactured products have represented the least of the protectionist evils that have threatened world trade in politically sensitive products. Without co-operative export restraint arrangements in textiles, it is argued, protectionist pressures could have kept Japan (and perhaps other countries) out of the GATT system through the use of article XXXV, which allows an individual Contracting Party to declare that the GATT does not apply to its trade relations with a particular country. Such negotiated trade restrictions in textiles, apparel, and steel may also have saved various rounds of trade negotiations from collapse. Japanese export restraint in automobiles may have prevented the passage of domestic content legislation in the United States and the EC, which would have undermined the entire basis of multilateral trade. This view is common among pragmatically minded trade officials, who must inevitably balance the interests of strong protectionist lobbies with the national interest in the implementation of trade policy.

To these arguments it is tempting to add that the market adjustment following VERs often vitiates their protective effect. Chapters 2 and 3 showed, for example, that the structure of export restraint agreements often allows product upgrading, trade diversion, and quota hopping as means of at least partially circumventing the trade restriction. To the extent that exporters can adjust to the VER in this manner, the trade restriction does in fact lose some of its bite. Evidence of this result appears in the refocusing of protectionist sentiment against imports of higher value-added products, nonrestrained exporters, and even against the incursion in the importing country of foreign investment in the wake of VER agreements. Baldwin (1982) has argued that, for these reasons, VERs have often been inefficacious as protectionist policies, Bhagwati (1987) has described their effect as "porous protection" and Yoffie (1988) has maintained that VERs are viewed as the ideal trade policy for situations where "mixed motives" cause government officials in the importing country to balance national economic welfare against protectionist interests. The political utility of VERs, according to this reasoning, is that they allow governments to impose what appears to be protection, satisfying domestic demands for trade restrictions, while in fact allowing trade to continue largely undisturbed, although there are inevitably some market distortions associated with the shifting of product mixes and sources of production.

While these two sets of views—the "minimum sacrifice" and the "porous protection" arguments—do not embrace VERs as an ideal policy, they do suggest that their damage is usually minimal, or at least lower than one would expect from more drastic protectionist alternatives, which are presumed to be inevitable. One can in this regard point to export restraint agreements negotiated by the United States under article XIX in footwear and televisions as cases of onetime trade restrictions that defused protectionist sentiment while allowing circumvention through product upgrading and investment shifting and, ultimately, a termination of the trade restrictions after a few years.

However, the key to this acceptance of VERs as a politically efficient trade policy tool is the temporary and isolated nature of the trade restriction. If in fact the negotiated export restraint agreement puts the question of trade restrictions to rest, ensuring the overall integrity of an otherwise nondiscriminatory, open, multilateral trading system, while allowing nearly open trade in the disputed good, then such an approach can be accepted as a legitimate stopgap device. In those cases where the domestic import-competing industry adjusts to the underlying shift in comparative advantage, or where for other reasons the political profile of the industry diminishes, VERs have proven to be a politically effective trade policy. The main caveat to this positive view is that their effectiveness as an instrument of liberal trade would greatly diminish with overuse.

It is quite a different story in cases where the initial VER does not quell protectionist sentiment, and the severity of the export restraint increases. It is instructive to note that initial economic assessments of many early export restraint agreements were positive, with no hint of their later transformation into quasi-permanent, monstrous export cartel arrangements. The glow surrounding negotiated settlements of international trade disputes in the 1968 steel VERs and in the 1971 textile MFA appeared, for example, to have brought trade relations to a new level of cooperation. Yet, as this study has shown, the market effects of VERs used to protect declining industries stubbornly resistant to adjustment tend to cause export restraint to spread in both product and country coverage. One cannot, therefore, accept the general proposition that VERs facilitate liberal trade, unless their use can be restricted to cases where adjustment or a diminishing political profile ensures a timely termination of the trade restriction. Who among policymakers has such a crystal ball?

This criticism of long-term VERs expanding into export cartels still begs the question, however, of how to maintain the multilateral trading system in the face of seemingly overwhelming protectionist sentiment in high-profile industries such as steel, automobiles, textiles, and apparel. Clearly, the role of a system of trading rules under the GATT in this regard is to provide governments with both a framework for channeling protectionist sentiment toward safety valves such as antidumping, countervailing duty, and safeguard measures, and a set of constraints that will allow governments to argue effectively that more draconian measures prohibited under the GATT would threaten the integrity of the trading system and national economic welfare. Insofar as the GATT has not been able to prevent the safety valve devices, particularly unfair trade law measures, from being manipulated toward protectionist ends, and has allowed governments to stray from at least the spirit of GATT rules in concluding export restraint agreements, it has not fulfilled its purpose. It has therefore become evident that governments will be unable to deal with the problem of export restraint and its erosion of the GATT system without reform of the governing trade rules themselves.

The Larger Systemic Issue

The GATT itself has increasingly come under attack in recent years as disillusionment with the ideals of a multilateral trading system has spread. Rapidly advancing structural change in the industrialized countries, particularly in the United States, has put severe pressure on many established manufacturing industries to adjust, and the associated encroachment of imports has come to be viewed in many quarters as a threat to national economic security. The large U.S. trade deficits of the 1980s and early 1990s have been widely viewed as a sign of economic weakness. The unquestioned supremacy of the United States in the world economy of the early postwar period has diminished, albeit largely as a result of postwar recovery and economic growth in other industrialized countries rather than from an absolute decline in U.S. economic growth. Ironically, the very benefits of an open, multilateral trading system have achieved the major U.S. foreign policy goal of establishing economic prosperity in Europe, Japan, and elsewhere, only to lead to a widespread internal perception of the United States as a "diminished giant" (see Bhagwati and Irwin 1987). This perception is important, for the early success of the GATT depended in large part on the leadership of an economically self-confident United States. The decline of U.S. confidence in the world economy has inevitably led to a decline in its support of GATT principles, as expressed, for example, in the spread of VER agreements and other methods of induced export restraint.

In contrast to the liberal-neoclassical view of trade as an engine for growth and a means of transforming a country's resources more efficiently into goods and services, the loss of confidence has led to a defensive view of international commerce. The emergence of economic nationalism in this context has led to the attitude that access to domestic markets must be jealously guarded against foreign incursion, and that trade policy is essentially a political weapon that can leverage concessions on market access from other countries. Bilateralism thus becomes the key to trade policy. "The GATT is dead," according to Lester Thurow (1990); sectoral and balance-of-payments trade pacts are the wave of the future. The proliferation of VERs and free trade pacts are offered as evidence. For the bilateralists, VERs are just the beginning. The United States in this new age of trade politics should develop and use new trade policy devices, of which "super-301" provisions of the 1988 trade act provide the prototype, to force other countries to open their markets. Other countries would be forced to practice voluntary import expansion as a counterpart to VERs. Such provisions are already part of the semiconductor price-floor agreement between the United States and Japan. Bilateral trade balance agreements along the lines of the

Gephardt amendment, which proposed to use import restrictions to reduce trade deficits with particular countries, would presumably allow the United States to regain control over its own economic destiny. World economic interdependence is, for economic nationalists, a frightening development, and managed trade is in their view the only way to secure economic prosperity in the future.

Such ideas are not really new. They typically emerge among those who wish to use a country's political power as a means of capturing or recapturing economic power, without necessarily assuring increased economic welfare. Managed trade was practiced in the form of several commodity cartels in the 1920s and 1930s. The International Steel Cartel, described in chapter 6, was hailed as the dawn of a new age of cooperation in the world economy, replacing the evil uncertainties of the marketplace. Bilateralism in trade relations dominated the same period. Far from forging any lasting cooperation, however, this trade regime fostered suspicion, resentment, cheating on the quotas, and retaliation. Managed trade has proven itself to be a destabilizing force in the world economy.

The GATT, on the other hand, is not dead, notwithstanding the animadversions of its detractors. Despite the presence of VERs, bilateralism has not yet dismantled the multilateral structure of the trading system. Progress has even occurred in the phasing out of VERs in steel, described in chapter 6, and textiles and apparel (see discussion in the following section). Free trade agreements between the United States, Mexico, and Canada, for example, and further economic integration in 1992 as set forth in the Single European Act are not, in themselves, inimical to the GATT system, despite the dangerous link between GATT-sanctioned customs unions and discriminatory trade restraints established in chapter 1. GATT has always viewed customs unions as a two-steps-forward, one-step-backward approach to trade liberalization. An economic assessment of economic integration sets out to measure its net effect on the member countries' economic welfare from trade creation, trade diversion, and economies of scale, as well as dynamic economic effects. While article XXIV of the GATT cannot guarantee that customs unions and free trade areas will indeed improve welfare according to this economic standard, it does require that essentially all trade be covered, so that such agreements do not become mere vessels for sectoral, discriminatory trade pacts between countries. With this proviso, the GATT assumes—perhaps idealistically, but with some justification—that countries freely engaging in economic integration will do so according to their own economic self-interest, which will also serve the interest of the world economy as a whole.

While there are concerns in some cases about the trade-diverting aspects of economic integration (particularly the U.S.-Mexico component of the North American Free Trade Agreement) and the possible creation of new protectionist barriers based on fears of a "fortress Europe" in the wake of the 1992 reforms, the trend in economic integration appears, on balance, to be a positive development for the world economy, and even for the GATT. The trade pacts embodied in such integrative measures differ significantly from the sectoral and accounts-clearing schemes typical of managed trade in that markets, not governments, dictate the final flow of goods and resources. In this regard bilateral trade liberalization has the opposite effect from bilateral trade restrictions such as VERs. As long as economic integration is established on the basis of expanding, rather than blocking, trade opportunities, they will move the trading system in the right direction, with the ultimate goal of integrating all markets. One can even argue that free trade areas spur on multilateral trade liberalization, in that they encourage countries outside a particular zone of integration to negotiate their way into it. In addition, regional trade integration negotiations must broach many of the most difficult and new issues involved in multilateral trade relations, including unfair trade law enforcement, dispute settlement, standards, services, and investment. To the extent that these negotiations can tear down political barriers to regional trade, the battle for more general multilateral trade can be made easier. A daisy chain of such agreements could form the basis for a GATT-Plus trade area, as described below.

The Uruguay Round

Overview of the Issues

The issues of discrimination, gray area measures, and process protection that are linked with induced export restraint played a central role in the Uruguay Round. The major driving force behind the start-up of the Uruguay Round was in fact the dangerous drift away from GATT rules that put existing world trade in manufactures at risk, and at the same time threatened to poison the trading environment for new areas not previously covered by the GATT, such as services, intellectual property, and investment-related trade. In order to maximize the benefits of trade in the future, and in particular those associated with these new areas, it was necessary to establish an agenda to shore up the GATT system and to renew the contracting parties' commitment to GATT principles of non-discrimination, the transparency and progressive reduction of existing trade barriers, multilateral and balanced reciprocity in trade negotiations, and the peaceful and GATT-consistent resolution of trade disputes. In addition, the developed countries realized that progress in the new issues mentioned above, especially with regard to market access in the LDCs, required that they bring a broad range of issues to the negotiating table, including many GATT articles and politically sensitive sectors untouched in previous GATT talks.

In this regard, the conclusion of the Uruguay Round in general, and the disposition of the issue of gray area and process protectionism in particular, must be considered in terms of the packages of agreements that were negotiated. For example, the negotiating issues linked with export restraint included the new antidumping, subsidies, and safeguard agreements;[1] balance-of-payments provisions in the GATT; liberalization of textiles and agricultural trade; and rules and procedures regarding dispute settlement. The problem of the observed crossover of protectionist actions from one policy instrument to the other, discussed in chapter 4, is particularly applicable to the evaluation of the Uruguay Round negotiations. Meaningful progress in reducing the backdoor protectionist actions of recent years will be impossible unless the GATT system provides an effective means of closing loopholes in the rules and channeling protectionist sentiment toward measures that are consistent with GATT principles. It would be futile, for instance, to implement a tighter safeguards agreement if governments were free to stretch the use of antidumping or other unilateral measures as a means of satisfying protectionist demands.

The following discussion will focus on the impact of the Uruguay Round on induced export restraint arrangements, particularly in terms of the incentive structure provided by GATT reforms for policymakers to choose among various policy instruments to deal with import disruptions and other trade disputes. The difficulty of negotiating away the use of export restraint devices resides in the fact that they are so appealing politically. Whether in the form of officially negotiated restrictions on exports or withdrawals of exports from the market due to threats of trade law or unilateral measures, such arrangements have shown that they can get protectionist lobbies off the backs of policymakers (at least for awhile) while keeping foreign governments from triggering widespread retaliation. In previous negotiations, the key to a successful GATT round was to harness the interests of exporters in market access and liberalization as an effective offset to protectionist interests. To the extent that export restraint devices have become institutionally entrenched in trade law and commercial relations, however, domestic and foreign export interests alone are not sufficient to dislodge them. In addition, the introduction of unilateral measures by governments to pursue market opening (under section 301 in the United States for example) has compromised exporters' vested interest in multilateral tariff reductions (see Finger 1991). It has proven much more difficult for the GATT negotiations to combat protectionist processes and institutions than to tear down tariff walls.

Yet the usefulness of the GATT from a policymaker's point of view remains in the fact that it is helpful to have international obligations as a means of deflecting protectionist demands at home, with the assurance that similar strictures on other governments will act to maintain open markets worldwide. This is indeed the core principle of the GATT, providing the politically pragmatic modus operandi that has the power to keep participants returning to the negotiating table. The decade following the Uruguay Round will therefore be crucial in the struggle for the soul of the GATT, that is, for the fight to maintain the integrity of the multilateral system of rules governing world trade policy. The most likely alternative to the multilateral obligations of the GATT system is a free-for-all patchwork of discriminatory trade relations and restrictions and a return to the law of the jungle and the beggar-my-neighbor policies of eternal commercial conflict witnessed in the 1930s.

References to the text of the Uruguay Round agreement in the following sections are drawn from the *Final Act Embodying the Results of the Uruguay Round of Multilateral Trade Negotiations* (GATT 1993), concluded on 15 December 1993. The *Final Act* established a new GATT agreement (referred to as GATT 1994) and created the World Trade Organization (WTO), which was designed to oversee GATT activities, as well as new trade policy agreements in services and intellectual property.[2] Given the many complexities in agriculture, services, and other new areas of trade policy coverage in the *Final Act*, the discussion will concentrate on reforms of existing GATT articles, and measures that pertain to trade in manufactures. These elements provide the core of a framework for trade relations in the future, and will play a large part in determining the role of export restraint in commercial policy into the twenty-first century.

The Safeguards Complex

The *Final Act* (GATT 1993) reflects the many compromises that one would expect in an undertaking of this magnitude. With regard to gray area and process protection measures, it offers a mixed bag of reforms, some reaffirming GATT principles, others legitimizing protectionist manipulations of GATT principles, especially in the area of unfair trade law.

The centerpiece of efforts to restrict the use of voluntary export restraint and other gray area trade restrictions was the agreement on the use of so-called safeguard measures, as contained in article XIX. In these negotiations, the major disputes were over allowing selectivity (discrimination) in safeguard actions, compensation to exporters, degressivity and adjustment requirements, compensation to exporting countries, and the treatment of existing VER agreements. On the export restraint issue, the article XIX reforms come down squarely in favor of GATT principles. Notable in this regard is the prohibition of voluntary export restraints and related measures in section XIX:

> a contracting party shall not seek, take or maintain any voluntary export restraints, orderly marketing arrangements or any other similar measures on the export or the import side ...Any such measure in effect at the time of entry into force of the Agreement Establishing the WTO shall be brought into conformity with this Agreement or phased out . . . (paragraph 22b)

Existing VER arrangements are to be eliminated or brought into conformity with the revised article XIX rules within four years of the entry into force of the new safeguards agreement. A maximum of one exception per importing contracting party is allowed, subject to GATT approval, and must not extend beyond 31 December 31 1999 (paragraph 23). This provision allowed a longer phaseout period for the EC-Japan automobile export restraint agreement that was part of the consolidation of automobile import policies among EC member states under the Single European Act. No other exceptions are mentioned in the draft agreement, although other contracting parties are still entitled to maintain one VER measure in the interim.

In order to increase the attractiveness of the new safeguards regime, however, the agreement also removes the right of compensation to the exporting country in most cases for the first three years of a legitimate safeguard measure (paragraph 18). VERs, with their built-in selective compensation in the form of transferred rents to the targeted exporting country, had been an attractive alternative to legitimate MFN safeguard measures, since the latter required compensation across the board to all affected exporters. However, other provisions in the draft agreement on article XIX impose additional discipline on the importing country by limiting the duration of safeguard actions to four years (paragraph 10), requiring evidence of adjustment to applications for extensions (paragraph 11) and progressive liberalization of the trade restriction if it lasts more than one year (paragraph 13), placing restrictions on repeating safeguard actions (paragraph 14), and restricting their use against developing countries (paragraph 19). Somewhat weaker rules on the duration and renewability apply to safeguard measures imposed by developing countries (paragraph 20).

The most significant part of the agreement, however, is the explicit requirement subjecting all safeguard measures to MFN treatment (paragraph 5). The question of whether the original provisions of article XIX allowed discrimination had been vigorously debated over the years, especially since requests for emergency action sanctioned by this article most often arose as a result of import surges from one or from a small number of foreign sources. While the lack of specific requirement of MFN treatment had left the issue open to debate, the actual application of article XIX actions by the contracting parties had generally reflected an implicit assumption of nondiscrimination, perhaps out of fear that setting a precedent of discriminatory use would backfire as other trading partners would reciprocate with GATT-legal discriminatory safeguards of their own. In any case, the GATT strictures on targeted safeguards established the incentive structure that gave rise to negotiated bilateral export restraint agreements and to the manipulation of unfair trade laws as new protectionist devices. The reaffirmation of MFN treatment and the official ban on VER agreements in the new safeguards agreement appear to have shut down the first of these protectionist policy instruments, suggesting an even greater shift toward the use of unfair trade laws.

Antidumping

Indeed, the negotiations on a new antidumping agreement took place in a political environment much less conducive to liberal trade principles. Notwithstanding the ban on VERs contained in the safeguards agreement (which may reflect changing government strategies in commercial policy, to be discussed later in this chapter), the article XIX reforms were negotiated at little political cost to those importing countries most likely to be affected by them, the United States and the EC members. First of all, the reforms required little in the way of new conforming trade legislation in these countries, and secondly, escape clause actions had become much less numerous compared with other actions in recent years. The practical impact of safeguard reforms may therefore be quite limited in practice. In the case of unfair trade laws, by contrast, the political stakes were much higher. In the period 1981–92, there were 624 antidumping cases alone in the United States, compared with 28 safeguard cases. A similar preponderance of antidumping cases is evident elsewhere: from 1981 to 1992 there were 422 antidumping cases in the EC, 577 in Australia, and 651 in Canada (see table 10). In these countries, trade legislation had already pushed the administration of unfair trade laws toward protectionist misuse, and negotiators were put in the position of defending their decidedly illiberal status quo, and in many instances seeking GATT legitimacy for the more flexible use of unfair trade laws.

The problems of dumping as traditionally defined (i.e., based on price discrimination), for example, are much easier to deal with in multilateral trade negotiations because firms have increasing difficulty isolating markets and setting differential prices as world markets become more integrated and other national trade barriers fall. The progressive liberalization of world trade is therefore consistent with—and indeed, instrumental in—the resolution of classically defined dumping as an issue in international commercial relations. In contrast, the introduction of technical criteria into the determination of dumping makes progress in negotiating a liberal trade regime much more difficult because they often tend to punish rational economic behavior even by competitive firms in world industries where monopoly pricing is unlikely. Once such criteria become established in unfair trade law and accepted as consistent with the GATT, the devil's work is accomplished through the minutiae of administrative practices.

Within this enforcement framework, the issue of de jure unfairness wreaks havoc in the world trading system. The single most pernicious protectionist aspect of antidumping law is that it began with a narrowly defined agenda of preventing predatory behavior and leveraged the accepted legitimacy of this purpose as a means of expanding the definition of what is unfair. The actual incidence since the GATT was established of predatory activity from dumping, in the form of a realistic attempt to eliminate competition in a target foreign market, is regarded by most knowledgeable trade officials as practically nil. Nonetheless, as soon as import competition is subjected to allegations of dumping, the mystique of legally defined unfairness tends to intimidate antiprotection activity.

As was shown in chapter 4, antidumping laws are exceedingly difficult to defend from the point of view of national economic welfare, and any political benefits they may previously have provided as a safety valve for residual protectionist sentiment have been largely washed away by the inherently anti-import bias of many provisions of the laws. It is important to remember that the GATT brought upon itself a large part of the blame for this state of affairs by opening this Pandora's box in article VI, particularly in its inclusion of cost-of-production criteria (paragraph 1.b.ii). As Destler (1991) notes, it was only a matter of time before U.S. legislators, especially those most exposed to lobbying on trade issues, would realize the political advantages of using unfair trade laws to redirect protectionist demands away from their branch of government. These same legislators were adamant in their opposition to any liberalization of GATT antidumping provisions in the Uruguay Round, and were in a position to hold ratification hostage to an agreement that would afford the flexibility of trade law enforcement and administration that had evolved in recent years. In addition, the EC, which has made increasing use of unfair trade laws in recent years, took a strong position against liberalization.

Given the prevailing strength of political forces opposed to liberalization, the scope for antidumping reform favoring exporting country interests in the Uruguay Round was small. Among those participants arguing for greater disciplines on the use of antidumping laws were countries that have recently been the targets for expanded antidumping measures: Hong Kong, Japan, Korea, the Nordic countries, and Singapore. In addition, Canada and Australia, which have active antidumping enforcement regimes, as well as some developing countries that are in the process of setting up antidumping enforcement, also favored liberalization measures (see Messerlin 1990a, 112). It is notable that the countries just now introducing unfair trade law enforcement are probably doing so in part as a means of gaining bargaining power against the United States and the EC on this issue, a trend that is likely to continue.

In spite of the heavy political artillery put in place to protect antidumping laws, the smaller countries did in fact succeed in introducing some changes to protect their interests. The most significant of these progressive reforms in the *Final Act* include:

- a tightening of requirements that must be met before a case can be initiated (Agreement on Implementation of Article VI, art. 5);

- the explicit inclusion of industrial users and/or consumers of the product under investigation in the submission of evidence (art. 6.12);

- a "sunset" provision requiring the phase-out of antidumping duties in five years, unless a prior review shows that removal of the duties would result in a continuation of dumping and injury (art. 11.3);

- guidelines governing the use of "best information available" (article 6.8 and annex II) and the use of averages in calculating dumping margins (art. 2.4.2).

- establishing the *de minimus* dumping margin level at 2 percent and the negligible level of dumped imports at 3 percent of the market in the importing country, or 7 percent for a group of countries (art. 5.8).

These provisions will tend to prevent the further proliferation of induced export restraint to the extent that they diminish the intimidating effects of antidumping law that operated through harassment and uncertainty, and also provide for a more open, transparent process of reviewing evidence. Rules regarding the method of comparing export prices with an average of domestic fair value prices, for example, made it possible to find dumping when no price discrimination had actually been practiced, thereby increasing the pressure on the exporter to reduce shipments or submit to a price undertaking. The failure of foreign firms to meet extensive and complicated information requirements imposed by the domestic investigative authority often led to its resort to the "best information available," as provided by the domestic applicant in the case and possibly biased against the foreign exporter. Establishing a *de minimus* dumping margin of 2 percent will eliminate many positive dumping determinations based on margins as low as 0.5 percent, which, despite the small implied initial duties, nonetheless would subsequently allow much larger duties to be imposed (Palmeter 1989, 190).

Yet the basic machinery of intimidation in antidumping law remains unaltered by the Uruguay Round, including cost-of-production criteria, provisions for price undertakings to terminate a case, a wide scope of flexibility in administrative guidelines, and perhaps most important, the stigmatizing impact of the unfairness label. Other proposed reforms were weakened or removed. For example, an effort to provide a check on antidumping abuse by making decisions reviewable under a GATT dispute settlement procedure was watered down by restricting GATT panels to an examination of the procedures used in the disputed case, thus precluding a GATT review of the facts of the case (art. 17.6).

In addition, the new antidumping agreement allows the continued use of anticircumvention provisions aimed at "screwdriver plants" in the importing country that are used to assemble products where antidumping duties have been levied.[3] If an imported item is subject to antidumping duties, for example, the foreign exporter may try to avoid the duty by delivering the components of the item into the importing country for assembly, typically involving little value added to the component parts, a case first litigated in the EC in 1987 (McDermott

1988). Such market-driven efforts to get around existing antidumping laws are reminiscent of the trade diversion strategies used to avoid formal export restraints. The broadening of country coverage in VER arrangements or tightening of customs inspections used to plug up the leakage thus has its counterpart in the tightening of antidumping law, the "protecting of protection," as Messerlin (1990a) puts it. In both cases the constant tightening of restrictive measures raises the fundamental question of whether the underlying trade policies are in the national economic interest, given the persistent efforts undertaken by exporters and importers to get around the rules. As long as antidumping law suppresses international exchange that would otherwise be considered normal domestic commercial activity, trade policy officials can expect exporters to seek out new avenues of circumvention activity and to raise international diplomatic disputes over the enforcement of unfair trade law.

The pure economic view of reform, in terms of maximizing national welfare based on market principles, remains one of eventually replacing antidumping statutes with traditional antitrust law enforcement, in which no distinction would be made between threats to competition from imports or from domestic sources.[4] For example, to the extent that international dumping constitutes a monopoly threat, the matter could ultimately be handled as a competition issue under national antitrust or competition laws, since there is no clear economic rationale for discriminating between international and domestic commercial practices (see Barcelo 1991). The next-best economic solution would be to allow antidumping statutes to remain on the books, but to require them to give national treatment to foreign firms, that is, to treat any instance of price discrimination or pricing below the cost of production, for example, in the same manner regardless of whether it occurred domestically or internationally. Many international disputes over dumping would be alleviated by applying the principle of national treatment to the cost-of-production criteria, which are widely regarded as the most unfair aspect of the unfair trade laws. Further down the economic hierarchy of GATT policy reforms would be a further tightening of the guidelines used in determining injury and dumping margins, to avoid spurious dumping determinations based on the manipulation of such factors as exchange rate data, averaging techniques, and bureaucratic requirements on information submissions.

As noted earlier, the Uruguay Round agreement did in fact achieve some tightening of antidumping guidelines. However, these reforms can only be expected to deal with the problem of antidumping law enforcement in trade relations at the margins. The sweeping changes suggested on economic grounds are perhaps important to hold up as ideals for rational trade policy, but they will remain for the foreseeable future nothing more than a hopeful, if credulous, vision of reform. In light of the political constraints on a head-on dismantling of antidumping and other trade laws at the international or domestic level, a possible alternative strategy is to incorporate consumer interests more systematically into the decision-making process of the law. This approach will be discussed in chapter 9.

Subsidies and Countervailing Duties

Trade restrictions sanctioned by the GATT to countervail trade-distorting subsidies have also led to induced export restraint arrangements, especially in steel. Yet the problem antisubsidy laws pose to the trading system differs from the antidumping dispute to the extent that government subsidies (as opposed to the private subsidies implied in antidumping cases) distort trade, and that the reductions in or elimination of subsidies would improve world welfare, and almost always national welfare in the subsidizing country. The economic case against countervailing duties lies in the fact that subsidized trade benefits consumers in the importing country and, on balance, usually benefits that country's economic welfare as a whole (see Corden 1974, 244–46). In addition, domestic subsidies in foreign countries may be justified on economic grounds if they are used to correct a market failure (ibid, chap. 2).[5] Yet there is a compelling political argument against forcing one's domestic producers to compete with the treasuries of foreign countries, which is now well established by several decades of countervailing duty law enforcement. The prohibition of direct export subsidies, in particular, is enshrined in the GATT as a basic ground rule of commercial policy. Still, the enforcement (or threat of enforcement) of such laws to countervail against domestic subsidies has the potential for restricting trade as a protectionist device, either by finding subsidy-induced trade distortions when none exist,[6] or by inducing foreign governments to agree to export restraint agreements, or both. In other words, the world may indeed be a better place in terms of economic welfare if U.S., EC, or other CVD laws motivate foreign exporters to dismantle subsidies (an argument also made on behalf of section 301 measures), but if in the meantime their intimidating effects distort trade through negotiated export restrictions—often including much broader product categories than were originally targeted by the CVD investigation— then reforms of the law are in order.

The main goal in any international regulation of antisubsidy measures should be that they are clear in defining which state interventions are actionable, what minimum subsidy margin will result in a punitive duty, and what criteria and thresholds will be used in determining injury and subsidy margins. The system of remedies should not allow incentives for concluding export restraint agreements as a means of terminating the investigation, since these measures are likely not only to distort trade further, but also would allow the subsidy—and the potential for trade disputes—to continue. In terms of the Uruguay Round negotiations, the main issue for opposing parties was one of discipline on subsidy activities by governments versus discipline on antisubsidy measures taken by governments (Hufbauer 1990).

The Agreement on Subsidies and Countervailing Measures deals mainly with disciplines on subsidy activities. In addition to the continued prohibition of export subsidies, the new agreement defines as actionable those foreign domestic subsidies that cause injury to import-competing producers, nullification or impairment of GATT benefits, or serious prejudice to the interests of other signatories (article 5). Serious prejudice is presumed to occur whenever ad valorem subsidization exceeds 5 percent, or whenever subsidies are used to cover continuing operating losses or debt repayments (art. 6). Nonactionable subsidies include those that are nonspecific, those that support research (up to 75 percent of basic industrial research or 50 percent of pre-competitive development activity), and those that represent assistance to disadvantaged regions (art. 8). Prototype or product development subsidies, however, are deemed actionable, but subsidies provided by the EC for Airbus Industrie are excluded from the new disciplines (USITC 1992, 11). LDCs are to receive "special and differential treatment" (art. 27) in that they may under certain circumstances use export subsidies and are subject to more lenient standards in determining which subsidies are actionable. The *de minimus* subsidy level, below which the subsidy effect is presumed to be negligible, is set at 1 percent (art. 11.9).[7] The new agreement also includes guidelines regarding information gathering and calculation methods (appendixes II–VI).

The subsidies agreement does impose some additional discipline upon governments in their use of countervailing duty law, in that actionable subsidies and administrative guidelines are more clearly defined. Yet it is not surprising that political pressures, especially in the United States, caused the agreement to maintain the ability of governments to use CVD law as a tool of intimidation, notwithstanding the prohibition of formal export restraint agreements in the safeguards agreement. Provisions for price undertakings (art. 18) will still allow soft cartels to develop, and the scope of administrative discretion in CVD calculations and enforcement is still wide enough to exaggerate the actual trade effects of subsidies and to impose high levels of risk on importers. In particular, offsetting negative subsidies are not allowed to enter the calculations, and uncertainties regarding the imposition of bond requirements on importers, even if preliminary estimated duties are small, may be enough to choke off trade in the product. It is safe to say that as long as political pressure in developed countries to maintain strong unfair trade laws continues, the scope for international liberalization of these measures will be small.

Textiles

The *Final Act* provides a sort of ten-year "methadone" program for liberalizing textile protection, beginning in 1995. Given the long history of textile protection in the developed countries, it is not surprising that they have insisted on such a slow and deliberate phaseout of the MFA. The basic liberalizing element of the agreement is a plan to increase progressively the growth rate of bilateral textile quotas[8] during the three stages of the ten-year period. In stage 1, covering the first three years after entry into force of the Uruguay Round agreement, the textile quota growth rates prevailing in bilateral agreements in the immediately preceding year will be increased by 16 percent; during stage 2, covering the subsequent four-year period, the stage 1 growth rates will be increased by 25 percent; and during stage 3, during the final three years of the ten-year program, the stage 2 rates will increase by 27 percent (art. 2, paragraphs 13 and 14). Thus, if the 1994 quota growth rate is 6 percent (typical for most textile and clothing products), then in stage 1 the annual quota growth rate would be 6.96 percent each year; in stage 2, 8.7 percent; and in stage 3, 11.049 percent. Simultaneously, importing countries are required to integrate an increasing number of product categories into full GATT disciplines during the agreement: 16 percent of 1990 textile and clothing imports (by volume) at the beginning of stage 1, an additional 17 percent at the beginning of stage 2, and another 18 percent at the beginning of stage 3. The complete sectoral liberalization of textile and clothing will therefore require as much as 49 percent of product categories to enter the GATT system fully at the end of the transition period, although it should be noted that the expanding quota allotments, in themselves, are intended to achieve de facto liberalization in the meantime. The text of the agreement ends with a hopeful provision for final termination of the long-standing regime of textile protection:

> This Agreement and all restrictions thereunder shall stand terminated on the first day of the 121st month that the Agreement is in effect, on which date the textiles and clothing sector shall be fully integrated into the GATT 1994. There shall be no extension of this Agreement (art. 9).

The ability of the developed countries, especially the United States and the EC, to comply with this final provision will depend largely on an effective process of adjustment in their respective domestic textile industries and a corresponding diminution of protectionist pressure. In an effort to minimize such pressures during the course of the transition period, the agreement also includes safeguard provisions that allow importing countries to impose selective quantitative restrictions upon disruptive suppliers (art. 6). Safeguards are limited to three years without renewal (art. 6.12) and require progressive liberalization if they last longer than one year (art. 6.13). The provision for discriminatory safeguards was championed by the EC, indicating the particularly high degree of political sensitivity associated with textiles there. The existence of the textile safeguards system also foreshadows a difficult, protracted adjustment process for domestic producers in the United States as well as the EC, where the many years of protection had allowed firms to avoid market-driven adaptation to international competitive conditions.

The growth rate in the quotas themselves, combined with the stepwise integration of subsectors into the GATT, is consistent with progressive liberalization in textiles trade.[9] Actual liberalization will depend on the management of the safeguards system, adherence to the timetables, and the continuing commitment to the goals of the agreement. To the skeptic, the plan opens up the possibility for importing countries to file multiple safeguard petitions that would effectively delay liberalization for years. Furthermore, if governments use numerous safeguard measures and delay GATT integration in politically sensitive sectors, an importing country may find itself required to go "cold turkey" on the full GATT integration of these difficult sectors at the end of the ten-year period, raising possibly irresistible political opposition to the consummation of the liberalization process. Ten years is in fact such an eternity in political terms that the endurance of the required political will to carry through on the agreement may come into question. In this regard, another issue that casts a long shadow over any eventual agreement is the prospect of China joining the GATT. In view of China's major role in the textile and clothing export market, it is likely that a special protocol of accession will be necessary to avoid serious conflicts with the trade liberalization process encompassed in the textile agreement. In summary, the agreement marks a significant milestone in trade liberalization in that it creates a framework for terminating a highly distorting, long-standing, and seemingly self-perpetuating arrangement of co-operative protection. Yet its final success will surely depend in part on the ability of the GATT to inspire confidence in its ability to achieve real trade liberalization in general and to regulate trade disputes and international adjustment problems effectively.

Article XVIIIB and Balance of Payments Measures

As noted in chapter 7, Uruguay Round negotiations over balance-of-payments measures became linked with the VER issue, suggesting a package combining a prohibition on VERs with a tightening of article XVIIIB disciplines. New measures in the Understanding on Balance-of-Payments Provisions in the *Final Act* build on the 1979 declaration by committing those countries using balance-of-payments provisions to announce publicly timetables for their removal (art. 1), and to give preference to price-based, transparent measures rather than quantitative or other nontariff restrictions (art. 2-4). Use of GATT article XVIIIB is subject to GATT review and countries must enter into consultations with the GATT Committee on Balance-of-Payments restrictions if they impose new or more restrictive balance-of-payments trade barriers (art. 5-7). While the reforms do not eliminate the use of GATT balance-of-payments provisions, they do establish tighter guidelines, opening a channel for dispute settlement in cases of alleged abuse. As a negotiated package, the ban on VERs is thus counterbalanced with commitments to refrain from protectionist use of balance-of-payments measures, subject to GATT review. This outcome may not completely balance concessions by developed and developing countries, but it is a step in the right direction. A logical next step would be to introduce official IMF approval and review into the use of article XVIIIB. Such a requirement would have the advantage of linking developing country trade policies to their monetary, fiscal, and exchange rate policies, an element absent in current GATT rules. The connection between trade and macroeconomic policies suggests furthermore the benefits of a more formal link between GATT rules and IMF conditionality in cases where IMF loans are involved.

In a broader perspective, the issue of special and differential treatment of developing countries with regard to GATT obligations is likely to remain burdensome for peaceful trade relations for the foreseeable future. The conflict is the result not only of discrimination in the GATT rules but also of the implicit denial that internal trade liberalization and its associated incentive structures benefit all countries, not just the developed ones. In future trade rounds, it would be most beneficial to all GATT contracting parties to circumscribe even further the scope for exceptions to GATT principles and the liberalization process, so that trading rules can achieve more consistency and integrity as an economic institution. To the extent that the GATT continues to exempt certain countries from obligations that apply to its other members, the basis for general compliance with the GATT will be in danger of eroding.

Dispute Settlement

The importance of dispute settlement procedures cuts across all other areas of the Uruguay Round agreement, since the effectiveness of any negotiated reforms will depend upon a credible framework for resolving trade conflicts. For example, the new safeguards agreement presumably makes the introduction of any new VER arrangement actionable under GATT article XXIII (nullification or impairment) and the new dispute settlement guidelines. The phaseout of textiles protection is bound to raise conflicts over the proper application of discriminatory safeguard measures and guidelines for product integration into the GATT. New guidelines for antidumping and countervailing duty investigations may bring disputed trade law practices and administrative procedures before the GATT. In addition, the future integrity of the GATT system itself will depend upon its ability to channel trade dispute resolution into a multilateral, rules-oriented forum, and away from unilateral punitive and trade-intimidating measures or negotiated bilateral trade restrictions that gave rise to many VER arrangements in the past.

In particular, it is crucial that the GATT dispute settlement process provide an effective modus vivendi with national retaliation legislation such as the U.S. section 301 and similar measures in the EC. The main problem with such unilateral measures, as noted by Robert Hudec (1990), is not that they violate GATT rules in a technical sense, but that they are one-sided: they impose a purely national view of what is unreasonable, which in U.S. legislation refers to practices that are not illegal under the GATT, but nonetheless allegedly harm U.S. interests. U.S. congressional impatience with the weak enforcement mechanism and often dilatory proceedings under the GATT dispute settlement process has played a large role in the formulation of new section 301 measures, which include tight timetables for review and mandatory retaliation if the offending foreign practice is not corrected. It is in fact true that GATT panels have often been ineffective in resolving trade disputes, especially when the subject of the investigation is a politically powerful contracting party, such as the EC. Yet the United States itself has also blocked adverse panel reports and requests for retaliation, has imposed conditions on other countries before agreeing to panels, and has temporized over measures to bring its own legislation or policies into compliance with panel rulings (see Hudec 1990, 204).

The key to a successful dispute settlement reform is therefore the eventual channeling of all trade complaints toward a systematic and effective multilateral review process. As far as the danger of induced export restraint is concerned, the submission of all disputes to effective GATT disciplines would remove the element of intimidation based on threatened unilateral measures that has forced the acceptance by foreign governments of VERs, soft cartels, and other trade restraining devices in the past. As a means of promoting a multilateral dispute settlement mechanism, the Understanding on Rules and Procedures Governing the Settlement of Disputes contained in the *Final Act* introduces reforms that favor the completion of definitive panel decisions in dispute settlement cases. Specifically, the consensus rule, which allowed any single party in the GATT Council (usually the alleged violator) to block the course of a dispute settlement case, has been turned around to require agreement by consensus of all parties to block the proceedings. For example, review panels must now be established upon request by a complaining party (following a consultation period) unless a full consensus disagrees (art. 6.1). Panel reports may now be appealed to a newly formed appellate body (art. 17.1) but the appellate report must be adopted by the GATT Council unless all Council members reject it (art. 17.14). If the ruling is not implemented within a "reasonable period of time" (art. 22.1), the GATT Council will grant the complaining party the right to appropriate retaliation within thirty days of its request, again subject to a veto that would require a consensus of all GATT Council members. Timetables are also established, generally not to exceed nine months from the formation of a panel to the panel's report, or twelve months if appealed (art. 20). In order to prevent unilateral retaliation outside the GATT, contracting parties are required to submit all cases of alleged GATT violations to the GATT panel decisions (art. 23). There is also a new provision for a less formal GATT review of cases where no GATT violation exists, but in which there is an alleged nullification and impairment of GATT benefits (art. 26). This provision is clearly designed to cast the GATT net as widely as possible in bringing renegade unilateral measures (such as U.S. section 301 cases based on allegedly unreasonable foreign practices) into GATT disciplines.

The changes in the dispute settlement process impose increased formal discipline upon retaliatory measures taken by governments within the GATT system and have the power to increase the credibility of the GATT as a forum for negotiating trade disputes. To the extent that the GATT's credibility improves, the politics of intimidation will become less effective in forcing countries to restrain exports (or increase imports) as a means of ending trade disputes. However, the bottom line of GATT's enforcement capability, as starkly stated by Hudec (1990, 180), is that GATT rules impose no direct legal restraint on government officials. This formal weakness does not, to be sure, indicate that the GATT system is powerless in getting governments to change their ways, since the political force of international legal obligations under the GATT, reinforced by the threat of retaliation, give the GATT powers beyond its own ability to enforce the rules. Nevertheless, countries that in the past have blocked the dispute settlement process must now be prepared to "bite the bullet" and accept and implement panel reports if the GATT process is to fulfill its role in regulating trade relations.

Taking Stock of the Uruguay Round Reforms

On balance, the Uruguay Round results suggest a future movement away from formal, bilaterally negotiated export restraint agreements between governments and toward informal export restraint measures by firms (perhaps with some persuasion from their governments), such as soft cartel price undertakings or quantitative restrictions, as a means of avoiding trade law prosecution or other unilateral import restrictions. In this regard, the revealed preference of governments seems to indicate that informal induced export restraint will remain an attractive way of dealing with trade disputes, while official VER agreements have largely been policy failures. The economic consequences of VERs, as documented in this volume, are crystallized in Bhagwati's statement (1987) that such measures provide at best "porous protection." The political point lies in the observation that, as a regime for regulating unwelcome import competition, VERs promised more than they could deliver. To the extent that they caused markets to adjust through import surges from unrestrained suppliers, encouraged transshipment schemes, and fostered product upgrading strategies, for example, VERs led to at least a partial circumvention of the intended protective effect. To the extent that such problems led to the progressive cartelization and tightening of the restrictions in industries with high political profiles and chronic adjustment problems, they only introduced new policy headaches and recurrent trade disputes. Based on these observations, a cynical view of the GATT safeguard reforms would be that governments had little to lose by bargaining away the practice of negotiating VERs and have already tilted trade policy practice toward other measures. At this juncture in the course of trade policy practice, it seems that redefining the import issue as a problem of technical trade law administration is a trend that is gaining momentum. For legislators and trade policy officials, such an approach has exhibited the political benefit of getting protectionist lobbies off their backs, while allowing them to claim a pure heart according to the GATT rules.

Notwithstanding the negotiated ban on VERs, the danger of export restraint for the world trading system thus continues. As noted in chapter 4, trade law enforcement and other threatened unilateral measures restrict trade largely through intimidation. The process of market adjustment to this trade regime, followed by further policy adaptation, is therefore also likely to continue. For example, firms have already tried to avoid antidumping enforcement by establishing assembly operations either in the final import market or in offshore facilities, only to be met with new anticircumvention countermeasures. Renewed efforts by foreign exporting firms to avoid trade restrictions may include the transplantation of more value-added production in the final import market, as well as increased cross-investment linking foreign firms with domestic firms.[10] Such efforts, which are already extensive in the automobile and steel industries, are intended to build up political capital in the importing country as a means of offsetting protectionist sentiment from import-competing firms. Domestic competitors may then demand higher and higher domestic content rules, increased restrictions on foreign investment, or further restrictions on output or components imports based on the location of corporate headquarters.[11] New crises in commercial diplomacy loom on the horizon as this cycle of trade restrictions and circumvention continues.

Yet there is another, even more dangerous turn that trade policy could take in the direction of export restraint: forced bilateral trade account balancing. Many politicians in the United States, for example, are convinced that the real problem in trade relations lies in the unfair trade surpluses of certain trading partners, particularly Japan, but also possibly including newly industrializing countries such as the Republic of Korea, Taiwan, and Singapore. Legislation that would force specific countries to reduce bilateral trade surpluses—either "voluntarily" or through unilateral general import restrictions—has already been introduced in the U.S. Congress and could reappear if the U.S. trade deficit continues and protectionist pressures are sufficiently strong. Such policy measures, which harken back to the account-clearing schemes of nonmarket economies, are a sign of frustration turned into contempt for the GATT system among policy makers, particularly legislators.[12] They are, however, a logical extension of the political concept behind export restraint in general, which is that national economic power has the legitimate goal of bending trade flows to its will. The gains from trade are thereby subordinated to—if not quashed by—the assertion of national power by the strong over the weak as the goal of trade policy.

If forced trade balancing schemes ever were implemented, the GATT would indeed cease to exist and trade relations would revert to the discriminatory, adversarial relationships of the 1930s. But such a gloomy prognosis is probably premature. Whatever their dissatisfaction with the GATT, governments still appear unwilling to scuttle the trading system that brought them unprecedented levels of prosperity in the postwar period. At the same time, the GATT reforms in the Uruguay Round present a clear challenge to its contracting parties: either adhere collectively to the principles of nondiscrimination, transparency, progressive liberalization of trade barriers and dispute settlement, or else risk unraveling the system that harnesses trade as an engine of growth.

The Way Forward: Re-Inventing the GATT

The founders of the GATT clearly did not foresee the dangers of VERs to the world trading system. Until their recent proliferation, VERs were for the most part regarded as temporary, isolated trade restrictions of limited scope that could be used from time to time to avoid larger trade disputes. In the meantime, however, their increasing popularity with governments has in fact created trade disputes and seriously eroded the GATT's ability to regulate trade policy. The increasing use of unfair trade law to induce export restraint has further undermined the GATT principles of nondiscrimination and transparency and its credibility as an instrument of trade liberalization. The control or elimination of induced export restraint in all its forms, combined with domestic policies to promote adjustment and diminish protectionist sentiment at home, will be necessary if the GATT is to establish and maintain an orderly trading system.

Yet the reform measures negotiated in the Uruguay Round provide no guarantee that governments will abstain from using discriminatory devices of induced export restraint when GATT principles become politically inconvenient. The intractability of the problem of selective discrimination under existing GATT measures, furthermore, indicates that general GATT reform—such as a formal ban on VER agreements—will diminish the use of export restraint only insofar as the political will to enforce it exists. The evolution of export restraint devices themselves, for example, illustrates the vulnerability of GATT principles to domestic political pressures. In addition, the discussion of the safeguards complex earlier in this chapter revealed the tendency of governments to channel protectionist pressures toward available measures of least political resistance, such as unfair trade law measures. The history of deviation from GATT principles through the clever use of alternative means of trade restriction, in any case, casts doubt on the utility of formal GATT reform alone.

A more fruitful approach would lie in the progressive economic integration of the major economic powers—including but not limited to the United States, the EC, and Japan—based on the elimination of discriminatory trade restrictions against each other (see Banks and Tumlir 1986; Wolf 1986a). This and other proposals for forming a "GATT Plus" (see Atlantic Council 1976) would go beyond the existing GATT by first of all requiring MFN treatment in all trade policy measures (including, ultimately, the dismantling of antidumping and countervailing duty laws in trade among the members), and by preventing the substitution of other barriers to trade to circumvent the MFN requirement. Ideally, the agreement would be structured to allow any other country to join. Once the large countries join, furthermore, the smaller countries would have a strong incentive to join also, insofar as they are most often the targets of discriminatory trade restrictions. Politically, it appears that the provisions of a GATT-Plus agreement would have to be applied on a conditional MFN basis in order to avoid the problem of free riding (see Wolf 1986, 13–14). A precedent for a conditional MFN approach has already been established in the GATT codes negotiated in the Tokyo Round (Hufbauer, Erb, and Starr 1980, 59). A GATT-Plus agreement would also have the character of a broad-based customs union, for which there is ample precedent under GATT rules and growing interest as a means of economic integration.

Such an agreement would also require that any existing sectoral trade restrictions be renegotiated (if not eliminated) in order to conform to the MFN rule, if trade liberalization in these areas does not occur in the meantime. Efforts at regional trade integration, such as the NAFTA and the EC, including EC-1992 trade reforms, have shown that progress on such difficult questions is possible among members of the trade agreement. Furthermore, once the door to regional reform has been opened, broader multilateral reforms may be possible. Intermediate steps could include the conversion of existing trade restrictions to a single, global tariff, or to the less attractive alternative of competitively auctioned import quotas. Yet a general agreement on universal application on MFN would be the sine qua non of any meaningful progress in eliminating protection in these sectors anyway, and is therefore a logical first step toward the resolution of sectoral trade disputes.

The inclusion of further measures would strengthen the attractiveness and acceptability of the GATT-Plus agreement. Wolf (1986a) has noted that a comprehensive agreement guaranteeing liberal and nondiscriminatory trade would require a broad range of specific agreements on all nontariff barriers, dispute settlement, and antidumping and countervailing duty measures. Agreement on unfair trade law provisions is particularly important because of the close link between their enforcement and discriminatory export restraint and because of the tendency to manipulate such laws for protectionist purposes. Barcelo (1991) notes that progressive economic integration, culminating in the treatment of intraregional trade as internal trade, provides a framework for eliminating unfair trade laws and replacing them with general antitrust measures. In this manner, member states of the EC eliminated antidumping law enforcement on intra-EC trade, for example. The binational review panel for antidumping and countervailing duty disputes under chapter 19 of the U.S.-Canada FTA represents an intermediate step in this direction by introducing a supranational body into trade law enforcement. A package of such rules and dispute resolution arrangements would, in fact, be necessary to assure adherents to the agreement that substitution of other, less transparent, bureaucratically mandated protectionist measures for existing policies would not occur.

In the absence of an immediate free trade arrangement, an agreement requiring retariffication of all existing trade restrictions would introduce additional incentives for concluding a GATT-Plus trade area. Aside from promoting transparency, it would make the price effects of protection more visible, increasing public pressure for tariff cuts. In addition, retariffication would permit countries to negotiate tariff rebates (Tower 1987). For example, countries adhering to the agreement might agree to rebate tariff revenues openly to each other. This would tend to foster further political incentives for trade liberalization, and at the same time would increase dramatically the benefits of joining the agreement. Tariff revenues could alternatively provide a source of funds to finance adjustment assistance, subject to specific sunset provisions.

Outlook

The preceding discussion suggests that the prospects for international trade policy reform are real, but limited. After several years of experience with VER agreements, governments can now see more clearly the pitfalls they create, not only with the GATT system, but also with the conduct of a country's trade relations. These concerns became serious enough to create a general consensus on eliminating VER agreements, as negotiated in the new safeguards agreement. The dispute settlement process has also been given a more credible system of identifying GATT violations and expediting their resolution in the agreement. Specific international trade disputes that have become institutionalized in the form of multifiber and multisteel export cartel arrangements have finally become burdensome enough to governments to motivate serious efforts to terminate them. The MFA, subject of the specific Uruguay Round negotiations, appears to be subject to a lengthy but—one hopes—definitive phaseout process. The multilateral steel talks, discussed in chapter 6, have been more contentious and have not created a formula for ending trade disputes in that sector, mainly because of the transfer of trade restrictions from VERs to unfair trade law enforcement.

It is in the area of unfair trade laws, the emerging "chemical weapons" of trade policy,[13] that the most work in international trade policy and GATT reform has yet to be done. Trade law statutes have over the many years since their inception generated a sense among the governments using them that the basic content of such measures is sacrosanct, exempt from the trade negotiations agenda. Yet their progressive manipulation for protectionist purposes, and their ability to accomplish protectionist ends, makes them particularly dangerous as trade policy instruments, and therefore a vital issue in future trade negotiations.

One possible route for further reform is to continue to try to negotiate the details of trade-distorting laws and policy measures, which was the approach taken in the Uruguay Round. Governments are most comfortable in dealing with trade issues and disputes in this manner (this is a major reason why lawyers have come to play such a large role in trade policy), since it slows down the reform process, affords interest groups a continuing voice in the negotiations, and creates possibilities of numerous negotiating trade-offs in the details of both the narrower and broader issues being discussed. At the same time, these very elements diminish the prospects for major reforms. More far-reaching measures, such as the proposed GATT-Plus trade area, or other fundamental institutional changes, are much more difficult to achieve without a large reservoir of political will, vision, and leadership in the major trading countries: the United States, Japan, and the EC member states. Beneficial as such a sweeping measures would be to the world trading system, they will probably have to wait for internal political conditions in those countries that are more resistant to protectionism.

In this regard, any progress toward the elimination of discrimination in trade policy will require domestic policies that diminish the motives for such discrimination and for protectionism in general. While this study has generally focused on how export restraint creates *international* conflict and instability in trade relations, the real political battle in this case, as in nearly all cases of trade policy in democratic societies, will occur on the home front. It is to this crucial issue that the final chapter turns.

Notes

1. Unlike earlier codes on dumping, subsidies, etc., the new agreements in the Uruguay Round are integrated into the final agreement, thus preventing selective adherence.

2. See GATT (1993) for a full description of the WTO (originally named the Multilateral Trade Organization). A preliminary report, the so-called Dunkel Draft (GATT 1992), contains most of the agreements contained in the *Final Act*, but shows how particularly controversial proposals for reform were either dropped or watered down in the final days of the negotiations, particularly in the antidumping agreement.

3. A draft proposal to regulate anticircumvention measures, contained in article 12 of the Antidumping Agreement in the the Dunkel Draft (GATT 1992), was eliminated from the Final Act, thus allowing current practice in the United States and the EC to continue. Such practices could be challenged in subsequent GATT antidumping discussions, however.

4. This seemingly radical judgement does not deny the possible benefits of trade law measures that would act as a safety valve for protectionist pressure, as envisioned by the founders of the GATT. However, such measures need not be unfair trade laws, especially if the real problem lies with adjustment, not with a manifestly unfair business practice. See the recommendations for adjustment assistance and compensation in chapter 9.

5. There is legitimate economic skepticism that governments are able to identify market failures, and if they do, to calibrate the subsidy in a sufficiently accurate manner as to make the country better off. However, countervailing duty laws themselves do not recognize the possibility that subsidies, including those that affect trade (if only indirectly) may improve net world welfare.

6. Domestic subsidies will produce a trade effect to the extent that they alter the output or price of the product under investigation. Francois, Palmeter, and Anspacher (1991) discuss ways in which the CVD investigation under U.S. law is biased in favor of finding trade effects when none may exist.

7. Current U.S. practice uses a *de minimus* standard of 0.5 percent. See Francois, Palmeter, and Anspacher (1991, 131).

8. Any quotas outside the existing MFA would be reported to the GATT and incorporated into the phaseout agreement. See GATT (1992, "Agreement on Textiles and Clothing," art. 2).

9. See Cline (1990), who estimates that rates of global quota growth of less than 7 percent would increase the level of apparel protection.

10. Messerlin (1990a) suggests the possibility that domestic firms may use antidumping complaints as part of an anticompetitive investment strategy. If the antidumping complaint artificially lowers the foreign plant's market value, the complainant may have the opportunity to acquire it cheaply and then reap windfall gains by withdrawing the antidumping petition.

11. The EC has negotiated automobile quotas with Japan, for example, that do not differentiate between imported units and units produced locally by transplants in the EC. See Schott (1990, 21 and n. 23).

12. For a critical view of the GATT and proposals for managed trade regimes, see Jerome (1992) and Dornbusch (1990). A prominent supporter of bilateral trade balancing measures in the U.S. Congress is Richard Gephardt (1988).

13. The *Economist*, 16 September 1988, quoted in Bovard (1991, 107).

CHAPTER 9

Export Restraint under Public Scrutiny: Can the "Dracula Effect" Save Liberal Trade?

Despite the encouragement provided by Uruguay Round negotiations on eliminating VER agreements from the arsenal of trade policy measures, the use by governments of discriminatory, trade-intimidating measures continues. Renewed rancor over steel and automobile imports, in particular, has cast doubt upon the ability of policymakers to relinquish their use of managed trade policies when protectionist pressures increase, notwithstanding their international commitment to the contrary. In the end, GATT reform can go only part of the way in generating a lasting solution to the problem of discriminatory protectionism, as embodied in policies of induced export restraint. Yet such policies are ultimately the product of a political process of concealing the economic effects of protection from consumers (as suggested in the political economy analysis of chapter 2) through the cloaking of collusive market-sharing agreements and price increases in the garb of a mutually agreeable, negotiated settlement or by a legal manipulation of the adjustment problem into an unfair trade issue. It is therefore both logical and necessary to return to the economics of domestic trade policy formulation itself in seeking a more comprehensive plan to control the new protectionism.

The conduct of trade policy in recent years has shown that protectionism grows fastest and most dangerously in the dark, in the interstices of administrative processes and in the smoke-filled rooms of clandestine agreements. It feeds upon obfuscatory regulations and the politics of backroom deals, which serve to satisfy the special interests of a favored domestic industry while shrouding the economic costs and transfers in a cloud of legal impenetrability or diplomatic argot. Under cover of darkness, trade policy-making of this sort abandons accountability and allows trade officials and legislators to grant favors, to intimidate foreign exporters, and to distribute the economic costs discriminatively; government becomes at once bully and patron, enhancing the power of trade policy arbiters in the absence of public scrutiny and open debate. Such is the policy environment that has brought forth voluntary export restraint agreements and the detailed regulations of unfair trade laws as the major instruments of trade restriction. This new protectionism has rotted much of the foundation of the liberal trade order established by the GATT and several rounds of multilateral trade negotiations, while weakening the link enshrined in democratic societies between public policy and the public interest.

What can be done against these insidious forces that have come to dominate trade policy? Bhagwati (1988, 85) suggests that the "Dracula effect" is the best antidote to such gray area and process protectionism: exposing such policies to the daylight of public scrutiny will tend to bring about their downfall. This strategy requires, however, that the economic effects of trade restrictions be made more transparent, and that the interests of groups negatively affected by them gain a more prominent voice in trade policy. The political process of trade policy formulation, in other words, must do a better job of exposing the protectionist content of the policies, mobilizing antiprotection forces and restoring accountability to trade policy.

This final chapter sets out to examine the possible role of a mandated trade impact statement on policy debates over trade restrictions, particularly induced export restraint devices. It begins by identifying the conflicting forces involved in the policy debate, and then traces the recent changes in the trade policy environment that have weakened the liberal trading order. This discussion leads to a proposal containing the essential elements of trade policy review that can represent consumer and national economic interests. Among other reforms, it argues for requiring a statutory economic impact statement for all trade restrictive measures (including those taken under unfair trade law regulations), whose purpose would be not only to expose the costs and dangers of the protectionist policy, but also to identify the amount and destination of compensatory trade adjustment assistance that could be used to buy off opposition to open markets. The antiprotection strategy rests on the basic political requirement of creating an effective protrade coalition to counteract the focused support of protectionist lobbying.

The Tenuous Liberal Trade Coalition

Trade Policy and Interest Groups

Trade policy formulation may be described as a process involving competing groups within the economy that seek to assert influence with policymakers. The traditional approach has been to concentrate on the strength of protectionist forces as the primary determinant of protectionist policy (see Baldwin 1985), but it is clear that antiprotection forces may also be prominent in the policy debate (Destler and Odell 1987). Within this political framework, a policy of governmental nonintervention is regarded as the status quo, which sectoral protectionist interests attempt to change. Protectionist forces must therefore achieve a requisite threshold of influence in order to cause policymakers to implement trade restrictions, while antiprotection interests seek to counteract these forces by raising the threshold level. The critical stage in the trade policy process is the determination of whether protectionist pressures are sufficient to pass the threshold of influence necessary to implement the trade restriction. In the course of the debate, institutional factors, the ideological disposition of trade officials, and general economic conditions also influence the threshold level. The overall goal of each interest group is to create resonance with the appropriate policy makers so that they will represent that group's interest in the policy debate (see Walter and Jones 1981).

The foregoing description of the policy process suggests that a policy of liberal trade depends upon a sufficient mustering of antiprotection interests, reinforced variously by institutional forces (such as trade laws and regulations conducive to liberal trade), the supporting liberal trade ideology of policymakers, and general economic conditions that will favor widespread support of liberal trade. To the extent that the antiprotection forces are sufficiently strong, the threshold of influence will be high enough to prevent policymakers from succumbing to protectionist demands. While a protrade government ideology and institutions, and continually robust economic conditions may in some instances be enough to secure an open trade policy, it is more typical that antiprotection political influence must be mobilized in order to keep protectionist forces in check.

Destler and Odell (1987, 30–59) have identified two broad types of antiprotection constituencies:

> *general* free trade interests, including household consumers, multinational corporations and international banks, and business coalition organizations; and

> *special* antiprotection interests, including exporters currently producing for foreign markets, import-consuming industries, retailers and other trade-related services, and governments and producers in the exporting countries.

The incentive structure of trade policy discussed above suggests that general free trade interests will rarely take collective political action in resisting protectionism. The costs of individual consumers, multinational corporations, or banks to lobby or otherwise take steps to influence policy decisions in favor of free trade are unlikely to outweigh the benefits. Similarly, the benefits to a multinational corporation or a bank from lobbying for free trade are usually small relative to the costs, unless it has a strong free trade interest in a particular import-export issue (ibid, 33). Business coalitions and consumer organizations may speak or testify on behalf of liberal trade in general terms, but do not offer the sort of focused opposition to trade restrictions that can counterbalance, for example, a concerted protectionist campaign organized by industries and labor unions directly affected by import competition.

Special antiprotection interests, in contrast, have a direct and identifiable stake in liberal trade. Some groups would suffer direct harm from specific protectionist actions themselves, such as steel fabricating firms that have opposed steel export restraint programs and clothing retailers that have opposed the textile and apparel quotas. Others see their trade interests jeopardized by possible retaliation against protectionist measures, such as major exporting industries, especially those in politically sensitive sectors. Foreign antiprotection interests—governments as well as industries and corporations—also have a clear stake in specific trade policies, and even though they have no direct political representation in the government, they can assert considerable influence through lobbying activities, especially through the State Department or Foreign Ministry. The irony of this configuration of antiprotection activities is that domestic consumer interests are often best represented in their own countries by foreign exporters arguing on the basis of corporate interests.

It is useful in this regard to consider the governmental bodies involved in policy formulation, where pro- and antiprotection interests clash directly. Lobbying groups seek constituency status among legislative representatives and within executive branch departments or ministries in order to achieve resonance with their representatives and thereby maximize their impact on the policy-making process. The outcome of the process is typically determined in large part by the balance of pro- and antiprotection influences. One must add that ideological and historical factors may play a significant role in the outcome, especially if trade policy is controlled principally by the executive branch or by a unified party platform. Thus a U.S. president committed in principle to open trade policies will often be in a position to tip the balance in favor of antiprotection interests in interagency policy deliberations. In contrast, an entrenched policy of protection (or protectionist procedure, such as trade law enforcement) is likely to have established a strong foothold within the government agencies that administer it and strong supporting constituencies within the legislative branch, making it difficult to remove the protection, regardless of the president's trade ideology.

In this regard, trade laws and regulations that are tilted toward protectionist interests, for example, automatically lower the threshold level of influence needed in order to force the implementation of trade restrictions. In fact, when protectionist sentiment is channeled through such technical-track measures, in which decisions by governmental bodies on dumping, subsidization, and injury are based on legislatively mandated technical criteria, the requirement of achieving political influence in individual cases is greatly diminished. The successful efforts by protectionist forces to change the details of the trade laws in their favor and move their case to the technical track may therefore provide a politically expedient substitute for the separate protectionist campaigns that would otherwise be required in order to achieve the threshold of political influence taken on high-profile, political-track measures in each case. Such institutional reform facilitates protectionism by removing the process from public scrutiny, diminishing or eliminating the role of open policy debate, which acts as a useful check on government market intervention in general.

The Era of Trade Liberalization

The political process of trade policy formulations suggests that the period of generally open trade policies among the major trading countries from the inception of the GATT in 1947 until the 1970s was the result of a confluence of political, economic, and institutional factors conducive to liberal trade, especially in the United States. The disastrous trade policies of the depression years of the 1930s, culminating in world war, had cleared the way for more liberal policies at the end of the war. The United States itself had prepared the way for a viable process of trade opening through the major institutional reforms of the Reciprocal Trade Agreements Act of 1934, which transferred trade policy-making power from the legislative to the executive branch of government and freed trade relations from the logrolling quagmire of particularist protectionist interests (see Schattschneider 1935). Yet the viability of the GATT system itself depended on a coalition of protrade interests, especially among exporters and import-consuming industries, a commitment by governments to the concept of open trade, and the ability of the political process to neutralize protectionist forces. In this regard, the rapid economic growth of the postwar period was probably the greatest ally of trade liberalization, simplifying the adjustment problem of increased imports by providing growing domestic and international markets to absorb displaced workers.

At the same time, trade liberalization did not occur across the board. Agriculture, and later textiles, were excluded from many of the GATT rules. As was discussed in chapter 1, the GATT itself had built in a number of safety valves to prevent protectionist pressure from building up as a result of increased imports, including the escape clause (art. XIX), antidumping and countervailing duty provisions (art. VI), and balance-of-payments protection for less developed countries (art. XVIII.B). From an economic point of view, such measures can be regarded as a means of buying off the opposition to trade liberalization by providing a set of rules to protect them from increased import competition. Their economic usefulness as part of the framework of trade policy therefore lies not in eliminating market distortions arising from trade but rather from securing the requisite level of political support needed for trade to expand. To the extent that the safeguard measures and GATT exceptions reduced opposition to trade liberalization without severely restricting trade in most manufactures—agricultural trade being the major cost of the political balancing act— one could argue that they were economically justified. During the first few decades of the GATT, government officials indeed felt that such measures were absolutely necessary in order to secure a viable agreement and make possible broad trade expansion. They apparently did not foresee the monsters that would grow out of these measures, such as the ever-renewable multifiber agreement in textiles, antidumping law abuse, and voluntary export restraint arrangements as substitutes for GATT-sanctioned safeguards.

Erosion of Liberal Trade

After two decades of postwar expansion and six rounds of successful multilateral trade negotiations, trade tensions increased dramatically in the international trade environment in the 1970s. Ironically, the very economic growth in Europe and Japan linked to expanding trade contributed to the tension by closing the income gap with the United States, diminishing its relative position in the world economy. The "diminished giant" syndrome (see Bhagwati 1988), coupled with the challenges of structural economic change, inflation, unemployment, and the increasing economic interdependence of the United States with other national economies, moved the United States into an increasingly defensive posture in matters of trade policy. Europe also was suffering from the ravages of an ossified industrial structure buffeted by structural change and chronic unemployment.

In the face of these adjustment challenges, policymakers became more open to arguments that imports represented a threat to national welfare. The political fallout from these adjustment problems became increasingly difficult to control because existing GATT-sanctioned safeguard measures were proving incapable of fulfilling their political role to channel domestic protectionist sentiment effectively. In the absence of such safety valves, the perceived threats of unemployment, trade deficits, and allegations of foreign machinations against U.S. trade generated new calls for protectionism.

The deterioration of the trade policy environment had three major effects on the trade policy process in the United States. First and most important was the shift in trade legislation toward the use of technical criteria as the basis for trade restrictions beginning in the U.S. with the 1974 trade act. In view of the inadequate protection afforded by existing trade laws, a key strategy of those groups seeking protection, especially in the automobile and steel industries, was to make the trade laws more responsive to petitions for relief from import competition. Thus, the definition of dumping has been progressively broadened in trade legislation, injury criteria in escape clause cases has been relaxed, and stricter timetables for executive action have been imposed. When trade statutes themselves are tilted toward the interests of domestic import-competing petitioners, then the political debate and its requirement of achieving a threshold of influence the direct trade measures, in which protectionist and antiprotection forces are on a more equal footing, can be avoided.[1]

A second factor, also involving new trade legislation, is that exporting industries, normally linked perforce with antiprotection interests, now have in many cases an incentive to seek foreign market opening through section 301 or super-301 measures. The expanded provisions of section 301, designed to protect U.S. export interests from foreign trade restrictions or practices, have the ability to siphon off a major source of antiprotection influence from the debate over import restrictions. Finger (1991) identified this factor in the stalled progress of the Uruguay Round, but its impact is likely to extend to individual trade policy cases as well.

Finally, the deteriorating trade policy environment, as well as gray area measures themselves, have eroded the liberal trade ideology that had under pinned trade policy in the postwar period. To be sure, protectionist sentiment had never ceased to play a prominent role in trade policy deliberations, but its reach had generally been confined to special interest politics, leading to the perceived need to carve out textiles and agriculture, for example, from the GATT system. The advent of the widespread structural change, increased economic interdependence, and large trade deficits fostered, however, a more general disillusionment with the liberal, multilateral trading system as represented by the GATT. Mercantilistic arguments began to reappear, this time clothed in the rhetoric of strategic trade restrictions, industrial policy, and forced reciprocity. The supposed benefits of focused government intervention—including trade restrictions—to support specific industries in Europe and (especially) Japan won committed adherents in the United States. According to this view, foreign market intervention required managed trade solutions. New developments in trade theory suggesting the possibility of welfare-increasing trade intervention, while widely abused in policy debates, nonetheless fueled protectionist fires. The rallying cry was Lester Thurow's pronouncement that "the GATT is dead." The impact of neo-mercantilist trade ideology was to increase the resonance of protectionist arguments among policymakers, especially if the debate could be turned toward allegedly unfair Japanese trade surpluses, "predatory" foreign efforts to undermine national high-technology industries, and the need for a level playing field.[2]

An important early indication of the decline of liberal trade policy could be seen in the proliferation of trade restrictions outside of GATT disciplines beginning in the late 1960s, as noted in earlier chapters. The United States concluded the first VER agreement in steel with Japan and the EC in 1968. Protectionism in textile trade, which had festered throughout the 1960s, led to the MFA, establishing an elaborate network of export quotas to cover most textile and apparel trade, in 1973. Throughout the next two decades, VER and other cartel-like agreements would spread to footwear, consumer electronics, machine tools, and automobiles, among other industries. What had been justified earlier in the textile quotas as a necessary departure from the GATT rules had become a virtually uncontrolled tool of protectionism. These deviations from GATT disciplines have further eroded the liberal trade ideology by setting precedents for discriminatory, managed trade solutions to trade disputes.

Toward a New Balance: The Role of an Economic Impact Statement

The challenge of protecting a liberal trade order today is to shore up the existing institutional structure of trading rules in such a way as to provide the means for governments to resist protectionist pressures more effectively. The analysis of the preceding sections suggests that shedding needed light upon obscure neo-protectionist measures will require governments to introduce new means of achieving openness in trade policy. The key is to bring the policy debate back to one of opposing interests competing in the light of public debate, for then the political calculus can more accurately weigh the impact of trade restrictions on the entire economy. To this end, a comprehensive economic impact statement would represent a valuable tool in restoring a liberal trade coalition. Ideally, trade policy reform would require that an impact statement be completed before *any* new trade restrictive measure—including those emanating from unfair trade law investigations and changes in trade statutes—came into effect.[3] An independent fact-finding agency such as the U.S. International Trade Commission or the Congressional Budget Office would be responsible for issuing the report.

Table 22 presents a checklist set of items that a comprehensive economic impact statement should include, as well as the linkages of each item with the trade policy-making process.[4] The usefulness of an economic impact statement of trade measures therefore goes beyond the traditional role of merely identifying the costs and benefits of protection. As part of a political process, it should (1) increase the public profile of the issue and educate the public on its impact; (2) improve the transparency of the policy instruments being proposed, in terms of both the positive economic effects of the trade intervention and the distribution of the gains and losses to specific groups; (3) suggest alternative policy measures that would allow adjustment to proceed at lower economic cost; and finally, (4) act as a blueprint for assembling an effective coalition of anti-protection interest groups to counterbalance the protectionist lobby.

Basic Welfare Analysis

The economic impact statement begins with the traditional static welfare analysis: estimating the effects of the proposed trade restriction on the prices of imports and the protected domestically produced goods, as well as domestic output of the protected good. From these figures estimates of changes in consumer and producer surplus, as well as deadweight economic loss, can be made. These are the typical measures of the market effects of trade protection that are estimated only after they have been in place. A key to the success of an economic impact statement as an antiprotection device is to identify and estimate welfare effects in advance, in order to provide a requisite amount of informa-

TABLE 22. Economic Impact Statement: Essential Elements

Category	Items	Antiprotection Links
1) Primary market impact	Domestic and import price effects Import quantity Domestic output	Cost of protection Effect on price level
2) Transfers	Change in consumer and producer surplus Rents transferred to foreigners	Identify consumer cost Identify rent-seeking Cost of bribe
3) Income distribution	Product upgrading effect Income effect by income group Distribution of producer surplus	Product availability Burden on income groups Gains to workers and owners of capital
4) Production cost	Effective protection: import consumers Allocative impact: input markets	Export competitiveness Shift to indirect imports? Negative impact on other sectors Investment distortion
5) Systemic	Prospects for retaliation Discrimination Precedent effect Conformity with GATT obligations	Export interests Spread of protection Disruption of trade system Disruption of trade system Erosion of trade rules
6) Adjustment	Record of industry's market performance Secular market trends in industry	Endless protection Identify mismanagement Identify nontrade factors Identify long-term viability
7) Market structure	Impact on domestic competition Impact on foreign competition	More monopoly power? Negative employment impact Cartel formation Collusion with domestic producers
8) Nontrade impact	Environmental impact of domestic output Contribution of trade to reforms and democracy in foreign country	Domestic environmental gains from trade Foreign policy benefits Resonance among domestic interest groups
9) Alternatives	Relative economic cost of alternative policies to protection	Identify policy hierarchy Identify groups for least-cost payoffs

tion to draw the beneficiaries of liberal trade into the policy debate over protection. In this regard, new protectionist devices such as VERs and trade law enforcement have introduced new and often unexpected elements into the policy calculus, such as impacts on market structure and the system of trade relations, which may have perverse market effects, particularly in terms of income distribution and the adjustment process. This consideration makes an economic impact statement all the more important as a means of exposing the political economy of protectionism to public scrutiny.

Transfers

The magnitude of the transfer to domestic producers of the protected good effected by protection is not typically a matter of public debate during the phase of policy formulation, since most estimates of the transfers occur ex post facto, in order to assure more statistically defensible results based on observed data. Yet in order for economic analysis to maximize its role in the policy debate, the transfers and their probable magnitudes must enter the debate in high public profile before the protectionist horse is out of the barn. As a practical matter, various market scenarios would have to be presented and the full range of possibilities discussed, but any reasonable economic forecast of the transfers will typically provide a measure of political embarrassment to the seekers of protection. The perverse effect of gray area and trade law-induced restrictions on the trading system has in fact been caused in large part by their ability to camouflage the damage done to consumer and national economic welfare. The sunlight of the impact statement and the associated "Dracula effect" would achieve political potency in this regard not merely by showing what consumers lose, but also by exposing the rent-seeking activities of protectionist lobbies and the clandestine industrial policy of the government in providing massive subsidies to selected industries, financed by higher prices.[5]

Part of the cooperative nature of the new protectionism that has contributed to its erosion of the GATT system includes the transfers made to the foreign country or its exporters. VERs, in contrast to traditional tariffs and quotas controlled by domestic trade authorities, are set up in such a way as to shift control over the trade restriction to the exporters, and thereby allow them to raise the export price of the product. This arrangement can be described in blunt language as a bribe to foreigners for their cooperation in restricting trade.[6] Quantitative agreements and price undertakings to terminate unfair trade cases tend to have the same effect. Thus, the trade restriction's premium value is collected by the foreign exporter and represents a transfer from consumers in the importing country to producers in the exporting country. Again, such transfers have usually been estimated only *after* the actual protective effects can be measured. Identifying and estimating them for the public record in advance of the trade restriction would allow the policy debate to consider consumer interests, which are typically deprived of direct representation in cases of negotiated trade restrictions.

Income Distribution

The assessment of consumer welfare effects should also include the policy's impact on the availability, quality and choice of the protected product, not only to determine the trade restriction's impact on consumer welfare in general, but also to identify possible differential impacts on income groups. Quantitative restrictions, in particular, tend to cause exporters to shift their product mix toward higher value-added products within the quota category, with a corresponding increase in the relative price of the low value-added item, a phenomenon that has been documented in automobile, steel, textile, and footwear VERs.[1] As a result of the value escalation effect, certain items exported by the foreign country under free trade may be withheld or disproportionately limited under an export restraint agreement. The differential impact of trade restrictions on product groups within quota categories therefore points to a potentially powerful income distribution argument against new protectionist trade policies. To be sure, protectionism in general has usually targeted cheap imports, implying a greater relative loss to lower-income groups in the importing country. However, the targeting of the lowest-cost producers in VER arrangements, combined with the value escalation effects discussed above, tends to shift the burden of consumer cost more heavily onto poorer consumers. Furthermore, the absolute cost to poorer consumers, when concentrated in this manner, may indeed be substantial in some items. The U.S. automobile VER arrangement with Japan, for example, was estimated to increase the cost of Japanese imports by about $1,000 and American models by about $600 per unit, a substantial sum in terms of the budgets of lower-income consumers (USITC 1985). As was shown in chapter 3, textile quotas are estimated to cost families in the lowest quintile of income groups about 4 percent of their income each year. The income distribution effects are of course largest, and the associated antiprotection argument most compelling, when the protected item is a necessity good (Cline 1990).

In addition, the beneficiaries of protection in the economy are not always the workers, on balance. In the case of textiles, the largest beneficiaries have been the owners and stockholders of domestic textile firms, so that textile trade protection has led to welfare transfers away from the poorest quintile and toward the highest quintile of the population (ibid.). In addition, depending on the domestic product and labor market structure in the protected industry, the protection-induced gains from higher prices may not be passed on to workers. In short, a thorough examination of income distribution effects for the purposes of discussion and public debate is a largely unused weapon in the antiprotection arsenal.

Effective Protection and the Costs of Production

For those domestic producers that use the protected good as an input, the special interest motivation to oppose the trade restriction is clear, and such interests can play a crucial role in the antiprotection coalition. The estimated price effects of the trade restriction determine the possible negative effective protection on industrial users of the protected good when it is an input into a final product. To the extent that there is a deleterious impact on U.S. export competitiveness, the political weight of the antiprotection argument is likely to be even stronger. For example, domestic steel fabricating firms face higher input prices from steel quotas and must simultaneously compete on highly competitive world markets for the final product. Trade restrictions on semiconductors and other inputs into computers and high-technology products have also raised production costs and decreased the international competitiveness of many U.S. manufacturers.

Less conspicuous but nonetheless important are the domestic resource allocation effects of protection that raise input costs. If protection diverts input factors toward the protected industry, and if these resources are not supplied elastically to other firms competing for their use, the costs of nonprotected industries using the inputs will rise. Furthermore, protection tends to distort the incentive structure for investment among firms in related industries, so that potential candidates for capital investment in nonprotected firms would suffer. This element of the cost of protection may be particularly important in high-technology industries, where selective protection tends to shift scarce high-skill, technical, and scientific labor toward the protected sector, and may also divert capital away from otherwise promising new ventures. Any nonprotected firm or potential entrant potentially has a strong interest in opposing such a diversion of resources.

Retaliation and Erosion of the GATT System

Foreign trade policy effects of the trade restriction represent another well-known consideration among policymakers, but take on added significance in the context of new protectionist measures. For example, the negative impact of foreign retaliation has traditionally assumed reciprocal tit-for-tat tariff escalation. When a government imposes new and discriminatory types of trade restrictions, however, retaliation in kind may threaten the entire trading system. The protectionist manipulation of unfair trade law measures has been matched by similar trade reforms in the EC and is now spreading to other countries as well. In addition, the EC has threatened the use of its own unilateral trade restrictions to punish unfair trade practices as a response to the U.S. use of section 301 measures.[8] In the case of VERs, the discriminatory targeting of low-cost producers for export restrictions may cause that country's exports to be diverted to unprotected markets. The fear alone of such trade diversion may be enough to cause third countries to set up their own protectionist barriers, a phenomenon that encouraged the spread of VER-type trade restrictions in steel and automobiles, for example. The escalation of new, anti-GATT protectionism through retaliation may culminate in international cartel agreements (textiles, steel) and in any case contributes to the erosion of the trading system. A timely examination of such scenarios before new trade restrictions are introduced is now possible, based on past experience, and as part of an economic impact statement may prevent the first protectionist steps from being taken down the path of deteriorating commercial relations and managed trade.

Adjustment and the Industry's Track Record under Protection

The traditional approach to evaluating the costs of protection already incorporates so-called dynamic efficiency effects, based typically on the perverse adjustment incentive structure provided by protection. Usually, this argument is limited to calling attention to the potential for the induced entrepreneurial lassitude that may result from reduced competition. Such effects are difficult to predict, especially since they will depend upon the trade restriction's impact on market structure and the nature of competition in the industry, as well as firms' management of the resulting changes in the market. Since many firms and industries petitioning for protection base their argument at least in part upon the need for breathing space to become more competitive, their case would be considerably weakened if doubt could be cast upon their intentions or abilities to adjust. An economic impact statement should therefore consider the available evidence that the firm will adjust, or be able to adjust, in light of the firm's or industry's history of adjustment under protection, or the adjustment record of comparable domestic or foreign industries. Golding (1982), for example, examined the adjustment path of five U.S. industries that received escape clause protection and concluded that the typical pattern was for protection to slow the inexorable decline of the protected industry, rather than to lead to modernization and increased competitiveness. In the context of predicting the industry's adjustment prospects in an economic impact statement, an economic evaluation of the industry's long-term competitive position on world and domestic markets should indicate its potential for revitalization.

The adjustment question is even more crucial in cases of industries that have received protection in the past. In some instances, such as in steel and textiles, protection has become virtually institutionalized, and the renewal of trade restrictions has proceeded with little regard for the industry's adjustment measures (or lack of them). A comprehensive review of the protected industry's performance record may reveal not only the industry's failure to adjust, but also many nontrade elements of the underlying adjustment problem. An economic analysis showing that either (1) domestic or international market forces point to the inexorable decline of the industry anyway, (2) poor market performance has been the result of mismanagement, or (3) adjustment could proceed in the absence of protection will weaken the argument for the trade restriction based on claims of the benefits of protection.

Market Structure

One of the great ironies of the trend toward gray area and process protectionism is that such policies are typically in direct conflict with the intent of antitrust provisions of domestic law. It is instructive to note, for example, that many voluntary restraint agreements can be concluded only after the importing country's government agrees to waive antitrust enforcement. Similarly, many trade statutes often allow quantitative import limits or price undertakings as a means of terminating an unfair trade petition, when such an arrangement among domestic producers would result in a violation of antitrust law. As a matter of public policy, it is important that an economic impact statement make clear the effects of reduced competition that are likely to result from the particular type of trade restrictions being considered. In particular, it is important to identify those markets being considered for protection that are most vulnerable to reduced competition when imports are restricted. In this regard, there is also clearly room for an expanded role of the Justice Department and other agencies dealing with competition policy in trade policy review.

There is a growing literature tracing the effects of new protectionist measures on market structure. VER arrangements, for example, often force foreign firms to form a cartel, and because of their quantitative limits on trade may increase the price-making power of the domestic protected industry as well.[9] A thorough review of the trade restriction's impact on both foreign and domestic competition and output is therefore in order. Empirical evidence suggests that the anticompetitive effects of VER agreements on automobile exports to the United States, for example, may actually have either reduced U.S. domestic automobile production and employment or left them unchanged (Collyns and Dunaway 1987; McKinney and Rowley 1986). The possibility that a proposed trade restriction may actually reduce domestic employment in the protected industry provides a particularly compelling political argument against its implementation.

Cultivating Nontraditional Alliances

In order to serve its antiprotection goals most effectively, it is important that the economic impact statement be as comprehensive as possible in identifying potential liberal trade allies. It may be possible, for example, to mobilize nontraditional support for liberal trade through the environmental, cultural, social, or political effects of trade. Groups advocating the protection of Florida wetlands, for example, have a common interest with the reduction of sugar protection that encourages cultivation of such areas. The negative economic impact of trade restrictions on the new democracies of eastern Europe provides a motive for related ethnic groups in the United States to oppose such measures.

To be sure, such interests could in some cases also take the protectionist side of the issue, as demonstrated, for example, in the antitrade platform of some environmental groups and the outcry against the alleged prison labor content of Chinese exports. However, it is ultimately in the best strategic interest of antiprotection forces to have a full public accounting of the welfare and market effects of proposed trade restrictions, based on the idea that maximizing the amount of information generally contributes positively to the economic content of public policy. Another political consideration is that the entire concept of an economic impact statement is likely to have a greater chance of being implemented if it incorporates information that could support protectionist, as well as antiprotectionist, arguments. It is in any case important that antiprotection forces be able to cast their net as widely as possible in forming a coalition to oppose specific proposed trade restrictions.

Contribution to the Policy Debate

One may argue that much of the information contained in the proposed legislatively mandated economic impact statement already enters the policy debate through the deliberations of the interagency review process that typically accompanies major trade policy decisions. Various departments and agencies representing liberal trade interests do in fact provide economic analyses to buttress their arguments, which then often play an important role in solidifying an antiprotection stance among senior government officials. Yet this observation misses an essential point regarding the policy-making process. The liberal trade policies of the postwar period have, in retrospect, depended on a tenuous coalition of special antiprotection lobbies and government officials committed at least to the concept that open trade is good public policy. When trade legislation such as the super-301 statute begins to peel away antiprotection support, and a new status quo of gray area and process protectionist measures create government bureaucracies to defend them, it is no longer clear that antiprotection forces will be well represented. Political winds within the administration may change, and consumer and other antiprotection interests may find themselves with a diminishing voice in the debate. In view of the erosion of liberal trade institutions, a statutory requirement for a comprehensive analysis of trade measures would provide a framework for giving the antiprotection arguments a public hearing in each case. Such a rule would serve the same beneficial purpose that many existing GATT articles do, that is, to provide governments with a rule requiring openness as a means of resisting protectionism.

In the area of unfair trade law enforcement, the need for an antiprotection counterbalance is particularly acute, since allegations of unfair trade often stigmatize antiprotection forces. It is therefore important to extend the requirement of economic impact statement to unfair trade investigations, not just to the high-profile discretionary trade measures that are subject to policy review. Once the trade issue falls into the black hole of trade law regulations and procedures, antiprotection interests are at a severe disadvantage, since the law focuses on injury to domestic import-competing producers, without systematic regard given to consumer or other economic interests. The Canadian proposal, included in the Draft Final Act of the Uruguay Round, to incorporate the interests of *all* interested parties in antidumping investigations would, for example, be well served by an economic impact statement.[10]

Finally, the impact statement provides information that could act as the basis for proposing alternative policies designed, for example, to compensate displaced workers while still promoting a market-driven adjustment process. By pinpointing the welfare losses and transfers, an impact statement reveals the underlying political economy of the proposed trade restriction, and thereby allows policymakers to identify specific groups they may be able to buy off without undue transfers to other groups and further damage to the economy. To the extent that the end result is a trade policy of lower cost to the economy and the trading system, the added economic information of an impact statement will improve the political process.

Summary and Outlook

In the unforgiving realm of politics, there is nothing quite so contemptible as a policy position without an effective constituency to represent it. The recent erosion of liberal trade principles and institutions within the policy-making process now threaten the ability of antiprotection forces to muster an effective coalition to oppose trade restrictions, especially in areas where trade legislation and negotiated trade restrictions have tilted the trade regime toward intervention. It is therefore important to give maximum exposure to the broad spectrum of welfare and efficiency implications of proposed trade restrictions or trade law reforms, especially those that have received little attention in the debate, such as regressive income distribution and anticompetitive effects. The proposed requirement of an economic impact statement is designed to provide information that will facilitate the coalition building that is often crucial in maintaining open trade.

It must be emphasized that making the economic information available through a statutory requirement is only part of the battle against protectionism. The task of creating a viable framework for promoting liberal trade will be a complex and arduous political process, requiring, for example, the establishment of more effective means for promoting adjustment among declining industries, the elimination of existing quantitative restrictions or their conversion to negotiable tariffs, and the reform of trade laws to remove their more egregious protectionist elements. Yet the introduction of a required economic impact statement has the singular systemic benefit of bringing the entire process of trade policy formulation into the light of public review, and it is doubtful, in view of the current institutional environment, that much meaningful progress in securing a liberal trade order can be made without it. To the extent that a comprehensive economic impact statement can reveal the obscure and unfamiliar aspects of trade policy, it can keep our protectionist Dracula in the sunlight, and he may be forced, if not to shrivel away, then at least to confine his movements to the dusky shadows of his coffin.

Notes

1. See chapter 4. In U.S. trade law, final decisions in unfair trade cases are based on technical criteria regarding fair value and injury. In escape clause cases, the U.S. president can accept or reject the recommendations of the International Trade Commission to implement trade restrictions (which are also based on technical criteria), but a presidential rejection of the USITC's recommendation can be overridden by congressional resolution.

2. Among the major arguments put forward by skeptics of an open trading system are (1) gains from multilateral trade liberalization are vastly overestimated, and (2) a national-economic-power approach to trade relations is superior to a liberal trade regime, because it presumably gives the domestic government power over its own economic destiny. See Jerome (1992) for a collection of anti-GATT essays in this vein.

3. Given the potentially volatile nature of trade policy issues, the proposed economic impact statement will, in itself, provoke much political opposition. One need only consider the outcry against outgoing USTR Carla Hills's request for a review of the economic effects of U.S. unfair trade law, (*Financial Times*, 12 March 1993) to reach this conclusion. This chapter does not delve into the political strategies that may be necessary to pass such reforms, but the identification of antiprotection interests may provide the framework for organizing a coalition of interests in its favor. The support of the U.S. president is also likely to be crucial.

4. See *International Trade and the Consumer* (OECD 1986), in which a task force compiled a similar checklist of items for the assessment of trade policy measures.

5. Consider, for example, the political reaction to the 1981 U.S.-Japan automobile VER negotiation if the possibility of massive increases in U.S. automobile profits that occurred when demand rebounded could have entered the public debate beforehand.

6. As such, the foreign country or foreign producers may oppose removing the trade restriction, especially if it also reduces market risk or market competition, a topic to be discussed in this chapter under "Market Structure." This information may also lend support to antiprotection arguments based on domestic economic interests.

7. See the discussion of value escalation in chapter 2 and of associated income distribution effects in chapter 3. Empirical studies include Aw and Roberts (1986) for footwear, Feenstra (1985) for automobiles, and Boorstein and Feenstra (1987, 1991) for steel.

8. See Council Regulation EEC 2641/84, *Official Journal of the European Community*, no. L252 (1984, 1) and *Bulletin of the European Communities* (1984, point 2.2.5, p. 51).

9. See the discussion in chapters 5 and 6. OECD (1984) provides a collection of articles on the link between competition policy and trade policy. For a theoretical discussion, see Krishna (1985), who examines the market effects of VERs in a duopoly. Messerlin (1989) and Prusa (1992) examine the anticompetitive effect of antidumping law enforcement.

10. See Hufbauer (1990, 106) and GATT (1993), Antidumping agreement, article 6 (Evidence), F.10–F.14.

Bibliography

Adams, Walter, and Hans Mueller. 1986. "The Steel Industry." In Walter Adams, ed., *The Structure of American Industry*, 7th ed. New York: Macmillan.

————. 1990. "The Steel Industry." in Walter Adams, ed., *The Structure of American Industry*, 8th ed. New York: Macmillan.

Aggarwal, Vinod K. 1985. *Liberal Protectionism: The International Politics of Organized Textile Trade*. Berkeley: University of California Press.

American Iron and Steel Institute (annual). 1962–81. *Annual Statistical Report*. Washington, D.C.: AISI.

Anderson, James E. 1985. "The Relative Inefficiency of Quotas." *American Economic Review* 75:178–90.

Applebaum, Harvey N. 1988. "The Coexistence of Antitrust Law with Antitrust Policy." *Cardozo Law Review* 9(4):1169–73.

Atlantic Council 1976. *GATT Plus: A Proposal for Trade Reform*. Washington, D.C.: Atlantic Council.

Aw, Bee Yan, and Mark J. Roberts. 1986. "Measuring Quality Changes in Quota-Constrained Import Markets: The Case of U.S. Footwear." *Journal of International Economics* 21:45.

Balassa, Bela. 1981. *The Newly Industrializing Countries in the World Economy*. New York: Pergamon Press.

Baldwin, Robert E. 1982. "The Inefficacy of Trade Policy." Princeton University Essays in International Finance, no. 150. Princeton: Princeton University.

————. 1985. *The Political Economy of U.S. Import Policy*. Cambridge: MIT Press.

Banks, Gary, and Jan Tumlir. 1986. "The Political Problem of Adjustment." *The World Economy* 9(2):141–52.

Barcelo, John J. 1991. "A History of GATT Unfair Trade Remedy Law—Confusion of Purposes." *The World Economy* 14(4):311–34.

Barnett, Donald F., and Louis Schorsch. 1983. *Steel: Upheaval in a Basic Industry*. Cambridge, Mass.: Ballinger.

Barshefsky, C., and R. O. Cunningham. 1981. "The Prosecution of Antidumping Actions under the Trade Agreements Act of 1979." *North Carolina Journal of International Law and Commercial Regulation* 6:307–62.

Berglund, Abraham, and Philip G. Wright. 1929. *The Tariff on Iron and Steel*. Washington, D.C.: Brookings Institution.

Bergsten, C. Fred. 1975. "On the Non-Equivalence of Import Quotas and 'Voluntary' Export Restraints." In C.F. Bergsten, ed., *Toward a New World Trade Policy: The Maidenhead Papers*. Lexington, Mass.: D. C. Heath.

Bergsten, C. Fred, K. A. Elliott, J. Schott, and W. Takacs. 1987. *Auction Quotas and United States Trade Policy*. Washington, D.C.: Institute for International Economics.

Bhagwati, J. N. 1965. "On the Equivalence of Tariffs and Quotas." In R. E. Caves, H. G. Johnson, and P. B. Kenen, eds., *Trade, Growth and the Balance of Payments: Essays in Honor of Gottfried Haberler*. Chicago: Rand McNally.

————. 1982. "Directly Unproductive, Profit-Seeking Activities." *Journal of Political Economy* 90:988.

————. 1986. "The Political-Economic-Theoretic Analyses of International Trade: VERs, Quid Pro Quo DFI and VIEs." *International Economic Journal* 1(1):1–15.

————. 1988. *Protectionism*. Cambridge and London: MIT Press.

————. 1990. "Aggressive Unilateralism: An Overview." In J. N. Bhagwati and Hugh T. Patrick, eds., *Aggressive Unilateralism: America's 301 Trade Policy and the World Trading System*. Ann Arbor: University of Michigan Press.

Bhagwati, J. N., and Douglas Irwin. 1987. "The Return of the Reciprocitarians: U.S. Trade Policy Today." *The World Economy* 10(2):109–30.

Bhagwati, J. N., and T. N. Srinivasan. 1976. "Optimal Trade Policy and Compensation under Endogenous Uncertainty: The Phenomenon of Market Disruption." *Journal of International Economics* 6:317–36.

Boltuck, Richard, and Robert E. Litan, eds. 1991. *Down in the Dumps: Administration of the Unfair Trade Laws*. Washington, D.C.: The Brookings Institution.

Boorstein, Randi, and Robert C. Feenstra. 1987. "Quality Upgrading and Its Welfare Cost in U.S. Steel Imports, 1969–1974." National Bureau of Economic Research Working Paper Series, no. 2452. Cambridge, Mass.: NBER.

————. 1991. "Quality Upgrading and Its Welfare Cost in U.S. Steel Imports, 1969–1974." In Elhanan Helpman and Assaf Razin, eds., *International Trade and Trade Policy*. Cambridge: MIT Press.

Borcherding, Thomas E., and Eugene Silberberg. 1978. "Shipping the Good Apples Out: The Alchian and Allen Theorem Reconsidered." *Journal of Political Economy* 86:131–38.

Bovard, James. 1991. *The Fair Trade Fraud*. New York: St. Martin's.

Brandis, R. B. 1982. *The Making of Textile Trade Policy*. Washington, D.C.: American Textile Manufacturers Institute.

Branson, William H., and J. David Richardson. 1982. "Capacity, Competitiveness and Capital Mobility in the World Economy: Challenges to U.S. Policy." Report of a National Science Foundation project. Washington, D.C.: U.S. Government Printing Office.

Brenton, Paul A., and L. Alan Winters. 1993. "Voluntary Export Restraint and Rationing: U.K. Leather Footwear Imports from Eastern Europe." *Journal of International Economics* 34:289–308.

Bronckers, M. C. E. J. 1985. *Selective Safeguard Measures in Multilateral Trade Relations: Issues of Protectionism in GATT, European Community and United States Law*. Deventer, Netherlands: Kluwer Law and Taxation Publishers.

Burn, Duncan Lyall. 1961. *The Economic History of Steelmaking, 1867–1939*. Cambridge: Cambridge University Press.

Cable, Vincent. 1986. "The Impact of EEC Trade Policies on Developing Countires." In H. Giersch, ed., *Free Trade in the World Economy: Towards an Opening of Markets*. Tubingen: J. C. B. Mohr.

Caine, W. K. 1981. "A Case for Repealing the Antidumping Provisions of the Tariff Act of 1930." Law *and Policy in International Business* 13:681–726.

Cline, William R. 1987. *The Future of World Trade in Textiles and Apparel*. Washington, D.C.: Institute for International Economics.

———. 1990. *The Future of World Trade in Textiles and Apparel*, rev. ed. Washington, D.C.: Institute for International Economics.

Collyns, C., and S. Dunaway. 1987. "The Cost of Trade Restraints: The Case of Japanese Automobile Exports to the United States." *IMF Staff Papers* 34(1):150–75.

Corden, W. Max. 1974. *Trade Policy and Economic Welfare*. Oxford: Clarendon Press.

———. 1984a. "Market Disturbances and Protection: Efficiency Versus the Conservative Social Welfare Function." Discussion Paper No. 92. Canberra: Australian Centre for Economic Policy Research.

———. 1984b. "The Normative Theory of International Trade." In R. W. Jones and P. B. Kenen, eds., *Handbook of International Economics*, vol. 1. Amsterdam and New York: North-Holland.

Coughlin, C. C., J. V. Terza, and N. A. Khalifah. 1989. "The Determinants of Escape Clause Petitions." *Review of Economics and Statistics* 71(2):341–47.

Crandall, Robert W. 1981. *The U.S. Steel Industry in Recurrent Crisis*. Washington, D.C.: The Brookings Institution, 1981.

———. 1984. "Import Quotas and the Automobile Industry: The Costs of Protectionism." *The Brookings Review* 2(4):8–16.

Curzon, Gerard. 1965. *Multilateral Commercial Diplomacy*. London: Michael Joseph.

Dale, R. 1980. *Antidumping Law in a Liberal Trade Order*. New York: St. Martin's.

Dam, K. 1970. The GATT: *Law and International Economic Organization*. Chicago: University of Chicago Press.

Deardorff, Alan V. 1987. *Why Do Governments Prefer Nontariff Barriers?* Carnegie-Rochester Conference Series on Public Policy, vol. 26. Rochester, N.Y.: University of Rochester.

————.1989. "Safeguards Policy and the Conservative Welfare Function." In *Protection and Competition in International Trade: Essays in Honor of W.M. Corden*, H. Kierzkowski, ed. London: Blackwell.

De Melo, Jaime, and L. Alan Winters. 1990. "Voluntary Export Restraints and Resource Allocation in Exporting Countries." *The World Bank Economic Review* 4(2):209–33.

Destler, I. M. 1991. "Comment." In Richard Boltuck and Robert E. Litan, eds., *Down in the Dumps: Administration of the Unfair Trade Laws*. Washington, D.C.: Brookings Institution.

Destler, I. M., and John S. Odell. 1987. *Anti-Protection: Changing Forces in United States Trade Politics*. Washington, D.C.: Institute for International Economics.

Diewert, W. E. 1976. "Exact and Superlative Index Numbers." *Journal of Econometrics* 4:115–45.

Dietrich, Ethel B. 1940. *Far Eastern Trade of the United States*. New York: Institute of Pacific Relations.

Dinopoulos, Elias, and Mordechai E. Kreinin. 1989. "Import Quotas and VERs: A Comparative Analysis in a Three-Country Framework." *Journal of International Economics* 26:169–78.

Dornbusch, Rudiger. 1990. "Policy Options for Freer Trade: The Case for Bilateralism." In Robert Z. Lawrence and Charles L. Schultze, eds., *An American Trade Strategy: Options for the 1990s*. Washington, D.C.: Brookings Institution.

Economic Report of the President. 1982. Washington, D.C.: U.S. Government Printing Office.

Erzan, Refik, and Paul A. Holmes. 1990. "Phasing Out the Multifibre Arrangement." *The World Economy* 13(2):191–211.

Esthus, Raymond A. 1966. *Theodore Roosevelt and Japan*. Seattle: University of Washington Press.

Evans, John W. 1956. Lecture before the Bologna Centre of the School of Advanced International Studies of Johns Hopkins University, 20 February.

Falvey, Rodney E. 1979. "The Composition of Trade Within Import-Restricted Product Categories." *Journal of Political Economy* 87:1105–14.

Farley, Miriam. 1940. *The Problem of Japanese Trade Expansion in the Post-War Situation*. New York: Institute of Pacific Relations.

Federal Trade Commission. 1977. *Staff Report on the United States Steel Industry and Its Rivals: Trends and Factors Determining International Competitiveness*. Staff report of the Bureau of Economics. Washington, D.C.: U.S. Government Printing Office.

Feenstra, Robert C. 1985. "Voluntary Export Restraints in U.S. Autos, 1980-81: Quality, Employment and Welfare Effects." In R. E. Baldwin and A. Krueger, eds., *The Structure and Evolution of Recent U.S. Trade Policy*. Chicago: University of Chicago Press.

————. 1987. "Automobile Prices and Protection: The U.S.-Japan Trade Restraint." *Journal of Policy Modeling* 7:47–68.

Feigenbaum, Susan, and Thomas D. Willett. 1985. "Domestic versus International Influences on Protectionist Pressures in the United States." In Sven W. Arndt, Richard J. Sweeney, and Thomas D. Willett, eds., *Exchange Rates, Trade and the U.S.Economy*. Cambridge, Mass.: American Enterprise Institute and Ballinger.

Feinberg, Robert M. 1989. "Exchange Rates and Unfair Trade." *Review of Economics and Statistics* 71(4):704–7.

Feinberg, Robert M., and Barry T. Hirsch. 1989. "Industry Rent Seeking and the Filing of 'Unfair Trade' Complaints." *International Journal of Industrial Organization* 7:325–40.

Finger, J.M. 1981. "The Industry-Country Incidence of 'Less than Fair Value' Cases in U.S. Import Trade." *Quarterly Review of Economics and Business* 21(2):260–79.

————. 1991. "That Old GATT Magic No More Casts Its Spell: How the Uruguay Round Failed." *Journal of World Trade* 25(2):19–22.

Finger, J. M., H. K. Hall and D. R. Nelson. 1982. "The Political Economy of Administered Protection." *American Economic Review* 72:452–66.

Finger, J. M., and Tracy Murray. 1990. "Policing Unfair Imports: The United States Example." *Journal of World Trade* 24(4):39–53.

Finger, J. M., and Andrzej Olechowski, eds. 1987. *The Uruguay Round: A Handbook on the Multilateral Trade Negotiations*. Washington, D.C.: World Bank.

Francois, Joseph F., N. David Palmeter, and Jeffrey C. Anspacher 1991. "Conceptual and Procedural Biases in the Administration of the Countervailing Duty Law." In Richard Boltuck and Robert E. Litan, eds., *Down in the Dumps: Administration of the Unfair Trade Laws*. Washington, D.C.: Brookings Institution.

Frome, E. L., M. H. Kutner, and J. J. Beauchamp. 1973. "Regression Analysis of Poisson-Distributed Data." *Journal of the American Statistical Association* 68:935–39.

Frum, David. 1992. "Dump It." *Forbes*, September, 64.

General Agreement on Tariffs and Trade (GATT). 1980. *Declaration on Trade Measures Taken for Balance of Payments Purposes*. BISD 26 supp. 205. Geneva: GATT.

————. 1985. Trade Policies for a B*etter Future: Proposals for Action* (Leutwiler Report). Geneva: GATT.

————. 1987. Review of Developments in the Trading System: April–September 1987. Geneva: GATT.

————. 1990a. "The International Trading Environment: Report by the Director-General." Geneva: GATT, photocopy.

————. 1990b. Trade Policy Review: United States. Geneva: GATT.

———. 1991. Trade Policy Review: European Communities. Geneva: GATT.

———. 1992. The Dunkel Draft: Draft Final Act Embodying the Results of the Uruguay Round of Multilateral trade Negotiations. Buffalo: William S. Hain.

———. 1993. Final Act Embodying the Results of the Uruguay Round of Multilateral Trade Negotiations: Version of 15 December 1993. Geneva: GATT.

General Accouting Office. 1989. *International Trade: The Health of the U.S. Steel Industry*. Report No. GAO/NS1AD-89-192. Washington, D.C.: General Accounting Office.

Gephardt, Richard. 1988. "Fooling Ourselves About Free Trade." *Wall Street Journal*, April 12, A34.

Gilpin, Robert. 1987. *The Political Economy of International Relations*. Princeton: Princeton University Press.

Golding, Paul R. 1982. *The Effectiveness of Escape Clause Relief In Promoting Adjustment to Import Competition*. Publication 1229. Washington, D.C.: USITC.

Greenaway, David, and Brian Hindley. 1986. *What Britain Pays for Voluntary Export Restraints*. Thames Essay no. 43. London: Trade Policy Research Centre.

Greene, William H. 1988. Limdep User's Manual. New York: William H. Greene, photocopy.

Grilli, Enzo. 1990. "Responses of Developing Countries to Trade Protectionism in Industrial Countries." In Charles S. Pearson and James Riedel, eds., *The Direction of Trade Policy*. Cambridge Mass.: Basil Blackwell.

Haggard, Stephan. 1988. "The Institutional Foundations of Hegemony: Explaining the Reciprocal Trade Agreements Act of 1934." *International Organization* 42(1):91–119.

Hamilton, Carl. 1985. "Economic Aspects of Voluntary Restraints." In D. Greenaway, ed.,*Current Issues in International Trade Theory and Policy*. London: Macmillan.

———. 1986a. "The Upgrading Effect of Voluntary Export Restraints." *Weltwirtschaftliches Archiv* 122:358–64.

———. 1986b. "An Assessment of Voluntary Restraints on Hong Kong Exports to Europe and the USA." Economica 53:339–50.

Hathaway, Dale E. 1987. *Agriculture and the GATT: Rewriting the Rules*. Policy Analysis in International Economics, no. 20. Washington, D.C.: Institute for International Economics.

Hemmendinger, N., and W.H. Barringer. 1981. "The Defense of Anti-dumping and Countervailing Duty Investigations under the Trade Agreements Act of 1979." *North Carolina Journal of International Law and Commercial Regulation* 6:428–61.

Heuser, Heinrich. 1939. *Control of International Trade*. London: George Routledge and Sons.

Hexner, Ervin. 1943. *The International Steel Cartel.* Chapel Hill: University of North Carolina Press.

Hillman, Arye L., and Heinrich W. Ursprung. 1988. "Domestic Politics, Foreign Interests and International Trade Policy." *American Economic Review* 78(4):729–45.

Hindley, Brian. 1980. "Voluntary Export Restraint and the GATT's Main Escape Clause." *The World Economy* 3(3):313–41.

———. 1987. "GATT Safeguards and Voluntary Export Restraints: What Are the Interests of Developing Countries?" *World Bank Economic Review* 1(4):689–705.

———. 1988. "Dumping and the Far East Trade of the European Community." *The World Economy* 11(4):445–64.

Horlick, Gary N. 1990. "Classification of Results of U.S. Antidumping Investigations." Photocopy.

Horlick, Gary N., and Geoffrey D. Oliver. 1989. "Antidumping and Countervailing Duty Law Provisions of the Omnibus Trade and Competitiveness Act of 1988." *Journal of World Trade* 29(2):5–49.

Howell, Thomas R., W. A. Noellert, J. G. Kreier, and A. W. Wolff. 1988. *Steel and the State. Government Intervention and Steel's Structural Crisis.* Boulder and London: Westview.

Hudec, Robert. 1990. "Thinking about the New Section 301: Beyond Good and Evil." In J. N. Bhagwati and Hugh T. Patrick, eds., *Aggressive Unilateralism: America's 301 Trade Policy and the World Trading System.* Ann Arbor: University of Michigan Press.

Hufbauer, Gary Clyde. 1990. "Countervailing Duties." In Jeffrey Schott, ed., *Completing the Uruguay Round: A Results- Oriented Approach to the GATT.* Washington, D.C.: Institute for International Economics.

Hufbauer, G. C., Diane T. Berliner, and Kimberly Ann Elliott. 1986. *Trade Protection in the United States: 31 Case Studies.* Washington, D.C.: Institute for International Economics.

Hufbauer, G. C., J. Shelton Erb and H. P. Starr 1980. "The GATT Codes and the Unconditional Most-Favored Nation Principle." *Law and Policy in International Business* 12:59–93.

Hufbauer, Gary Clyde, ed. 1982. *U.S. International Economic Policy 1981: A Draft Report.* Washington: International Law Institute.

International Iron and Steel Institute, Committee on Statistics. 1991. *Steel Statistical Yearbook.* Brussels: IISI.

International Labour Office. 1987. *The Impact on Employment and Income of Structural and Technological Change in the Clothing Industry.* Geneva: ILO.

Jackson, John. 1969. *World Trade and the Law of GATT.* Indianapolis: Bobs-Merrill.

———. 1988. "Consistency of Export-Restraint Arrangements with the GATT." *The World Economy* 11(4):485–500.

Jerome, Robert W., ed. 1992. *World Trade at the Crossroads: The Uruguay Round, GATT, and Beyond.* Lanham, Md.: University Press of America.

Johnson, Harry G. 1966. "Trade Preferences and Developing Countries." *Lloyd's Bank Review* 80:1-18.

————. 1967. *Economic Policies Toward Less Developed Countries.* New York and Washington: Praeger.

Jones, Kent. 1979. "Forgetfulness of Things Past: Europe and the Steel Cartel." *The World Economy* 2(2):139–54.

————. 1981. "The Political Economy of 'Voluntary' Restraint and the Incidence of Trade Diversion in Steel Import Markets." Ph.D. Diss., University of Geneva.

————. 1984. "The Political Economy of Voluntary Export Restraint Agreements." *Kyklos* 37(1):82–101.

————. 1986. *Politics vs. Economics in World Steel Trade.* London: Allen and Unwin.

————. 1992. "The Income Effect on Product Upgrading Under VER Agreements." Babson Park, Mass.: Babson College, photocopy.

Jones, Rich, Trien T. Nguyen, and John Whalley. 1990. "Computation of a World General Equilibrium Under Bilateral Quotas and an Application to the Analysis of Textile Trade Restrictions." *Journal of Policy Modeling* 12(3):511–26.

Keesing, Donald B., and Martin Wolf. 1980. *Textile Quotas against Developing Countries.* Thames Essay no. 23. London: Trade Policy Research Centre.

Kelly, William B. 1963. "Antecedents of Present Commercial Policy, 1922–1934." In W. B. Kelly, ed., *Studies in United States Commercial Policy.* Chapel Hill: University of North Carolina Press.

Kiersch, Gunther. 1954. *Das Internationale Eisen- und Stahlkartell.* Essen: Rheinisch-Westfalisches Institut für Wirtschaftsforschung.

Kostecki, Michel. 1987. "Export Restraint Arrangements and Trade Liberalization." *The World Economy* 10(4):425–54.

Kreinin, Mordechai. 1984. "Wage Competitiveness in the U.S. Auto and Steel Industries." *Contemporary Policy Issues* 4:39–53.

Krishna, Kala. 1985. "Trade Restrictions as Facilitating Practices." Working Paper, National Bureau of Economic Research, no. 1546. Cambridge, Mass.: NBER.

Krueger, Anne O. 1974. "The Political Economy of the Rent-seeking Society." *American Economic Review* 64:291–303.

————. 1980. "Trade Policy as an Input to Development." *American Economic Review* 70:288–92.

————. 1984. "Trade Policies in Developing Countries." In R. W. Jones and P. B. Kenen, eds., *Handbook of International Economics*, vol. 1. Amsterdam and New York: North-Holland.

Krugman, Paul. 1989. "Industrial Organization and International Trade." In R. Schmalensee and R. Willig, eds., *Handbook of Industrial Organization*, vol. 2. Amsterdam and New York: North-Holland.

Leibenstein, Harvey. 1966. "Allocative Efficiency vs. '*X*-Efficiency.'" *American Economic Review* 56(2):392–415.

Levine, Michael K. 1985. *Inside International Trade Policy Formulation: A History of the 1982 US-EC Steel Arrangements*. New York: Praeger.

Li, Kui Wai. 1991. "Positive Adjustment Against Protectionism: The Case of Textile and Clothing Industry in Hong Kong." *The Developing Economies* 29(3):197–209.

Loeb, Nancy C. 1985. "Antitrust Implications of Domestic Mergers: A Proposal for the Treatment of Imports and Its Application to LTV-Republic Case Note." *New York University Law Review* 60:667–701.

Lowenfeld, A. 1979. *Public Controls on International Trade*. International Economic Law Series no. VI. New York: Matthew Bender.

McDermott, Patrick J. 1988. "Extending and Reach of Their Antidumping Laws: The European Community's 'Screwdriver Assembly' Regulation. *Law and Policy in International Business* 20(2):315–30.

McKinney, Joseph A., and Keith A. Rowley. 1986. "The Economic Impact of the Japanese Automobile Export Restraint." *Atlantic Economic Journal* 14:9–15.

Meier, Gerald, ed. 1984. *Leading Issues in Economic Development*, 4th ed. New York and Oxford: Oxford University Press.

Messerlin, Patrick J. 1988. "Antidumping Laws and Developing Countries." World Bank Policy, Planning and Research Working Paper Series no. WPS16. Washington, D.C.: World Bank.

———. 1989. "The EC Antidumping Regulations: A First Economic Appraisal, 1980–85." *Weltwirtschaftliches Archiv* 125(3):563–87.

———. 1990a. "Antidumping." In Jeffrey Schott, ed., *Completing the Uruguay Round: A Results-Oriented Approach to the GATT Trade Negotiations*. Washington, D.C.: Institute for International Economics.

———. 1990b. "Anti-Dumping Regulations or Pro-Cartel Law? The EC Chemical Cases." *The World Economy* 13(4):.

Moore, Michael O., and Steven M. Suranovic. 1993. "A Welfare Comparison Between VERs and Tariffs Under the GATT." *Canadian Journal of Economics* 26(2):447–56.

Morkre, Morris, and Harold E. Kruth. 1989. "Determining Whether Dumped or Subsized Imports Injure Domestic Industries: International Trade Commossion Approach." *Contemporary Policy Issues* 7(3):78–95.

Mueller, Hans. 1988. "Protection and Market Power in the Steel Industry." *Challenge*. September-October, 52–54.

———. 1992. "U.S. Steel Trade: Facts and Polemics." Submission to the U.S. International Trade Commission. Murfreesboro, Tennessee, July 24. Photocopy.

Murray, T., W. Schmidt and I. Walter. 1978. "Alternative Forms of Protection against Market Disruption." *Kyklos* 31(4):624–37.

New Car Cost Guide (annual). San Jose, California: Auto Invoice Service.

Nicolaides, Phaedon. 1991. "Anti-Competitive Effects of Trade Policy." *Intereconomics* 26(4):173–76.

Organization for Economic Cooperation and Develoment. 1984. *Competition and Trade Policies: Their Interaction.* Paris: OECD.

———. 1986. International Trade and the Consumer. Paris: OECD.

Palmeter, N. David. 1988. "Exchange Rates and Antidumping Determinations." Journal of World Trade 22(2):182–98.

———. 1989. "The Capture of Antidumping Law." *Yale Journal of International Law* 14:182–97.

Patenode, T. J. 1980. "The New Antidumping Procedures of the Trade Agreements Act of 1979: Does It Create a New Non-Tariff Trade Barrier?" *Northwestern Journal of International Law and Business* 2:200–23.

Patterson, Gardner. 1966. *Discrimination in International Trade: The Policy Issues 1945–1965.* Princeton: Princeton University Press.

Pearson, Charles. 1983. *Emerging Protection in the Footwear Industry.* Thames Essay no. 36. London: Trade Policy Research Centre.

Pomeranz, Morton. 1988. "Legal Aspects of International Trade." In Ingo Walter and Tracy Murray, eds., *Handbook of International Business*, 2nd ed. New York: John Wiley and Sons.

Pomfret, Richard. 1988. *Unequal Trade: The Economics of Discriminatory International Trade Policies.* Oxford and New York: Basil Blackwell.

———. 1989a. "Voluntary Export Restraints in the Presence of Monopoly Power." *Kyklos* 42(1):61–72.

———. 1989b. "The Economics of Voluntary Export Restraint Agreements." *Journal of Economic Surveys* 3(3):199–211.

Practicing Law Institute. 1983. *The Trade Agreements Act of 1979—Four Years Later.* Corporate Law and Practice, Course Handbook Series no. 425. New York: Practicing Law Insitute.

Prusa, Thomas J. 1992. "Why are so Many Antidumping Petitions Withdrawn?" *Journal of International Economics* 33(1/2):1–20.

Riedel, James. 1991. "Strategy Wars: the State of Debate on Trade and Industrialization in Developing Countries." In Ad Koekkoek and L.B.M. Mennes, eds., *International Trade and Global Development: Essays in Honor of Jagdish Bhagwati.* London and New York: Routledge.

Rodriguez, Carlos A. 1979. "The Quality of Imports and Differential Welfare Effects of Tariffs, Quotas, and Quality Controls as Protective Devices." *Canadian Journal of Economics* 12(3):439–49.

Rosenthal, Douglas E. 1982. "Antitrust Risks in Abusing the Import Relief Laws." *Swiss Review of International Antitrust Law* 14:31–38.

Santoni, Gary J., and Norman Van Cott 1980. "Import Quotas: The Quality Adjustment Problem." *Southern Economic Journal* 46:1206–11.

Savage, Christopher W., and Gary N. Horlick. 1985. "United States Voluntary Restraint Agreements: Practical Considerations and Policy Recommendations." *Stanford Journal of International Law* 21:281–98.

Schattschneider, E. E. 1935. *Politics, Pressures and the Tariff.* New York: Prentice-Hall.

Schott, Jeffrey J. 1990. *Completing the Uruguay Round: A Results-Oriented Approach to the GATT Trade Negotiations.* Washington, D.C.: Institute for International Economics.

Smith, Alasdair. and Anthony J. Venables. 1991. "Counting the Cost of Voluntary Export Restraints in the European Car Market." In Elhanan Helpman and Assaf Kazin, eds., *International Trade and Trade Policy.* Cambridge: MIT Press.

Spinanger, Dean. 1987. "Will the Multi-fibre Arrangement Keep Bangladesh Humble?" *The World Economy* 10(1):75–84.

Stegemann, Klaus. 1990. "EC Anti-Dumping Policy: Are Price Undertakings a Legal Substitute for Illegal Price Fixing?" *Weltwirtschaftliches Archiv* 126(2):268–98.

Swann, Dennis. 1983. Comp*etition and Industrial Policy in the European Community.* London and New York: Methuen.

Takacs, Wendy E. 1978. "The Non-Equivalence of Tariffs, Import Quotas and Voluntary Export Restraints." *Journal of International Economics* 5:565–73.

———. 1981. "Pressures for Protectionism: An Empirical Analysis." *Economic Inquiry* 19:687–93.

Tarr, David. 1987. "Effects of Restraining Steel Exports from the Republic of Korea and Other Countries to the United States and the European Economic Community." *The World Bank Economic Review* 1(3):397–418.

———. 1989. *A General Equilibrium Analysis of The Welfare and Employment Effects of U.S. Quotas in Textiles, Autos and Steel.* Washington, D.C.: Bureau of Economics, Federal Trade Commission.

Thurow, Lester. 1990. "GATT is Dead." *The Journal of Accountancy* 170:36–39.

Tower, E. 1987. "Comments on Tumlir." *Contemporary Policy Issues* 5(2):13–15.

Trela, Irene, and John Whalley. 1988. "Do Developing Countries Lose from the MFA?" National Bureau of Economic Research Working Paper Series no. 2618. Cambridge, Mass.: NBER.

United Nations, Economic Commission for Europe (annual). 1963–82. *Statistics of World Trade in Steel.* Geneva: United Nations.

U.S. Congress. House. Committee on Ways and Means. 1984. *Overview of Current Provisions of U.S. Trade Law.* WMCP 98–40. Washington, D.C.: U.S. Government Printing Office.

———. 1989. *Overview and Compilation of U.S. Trade Statutes,* 1989 ed. WMCP 191–14. Washington, D.C.: U.S. Government Printing Office.

U.S. Department of Justice, Antitrust Division. 1988. *Antitrust Enforcement Guidelines for International Operations.* Washington: U.S. Justice Department.

U.S. Department of Labor, Bureau of Labor Statistics. 1986. "Consumer Expenditure Results for 1984." Washington, D.C.: Department of Labor. Photocopy.

U.S. International Trade Commission.(annual). 1981–93. *Operation of the Trade Agreements Program (OTAP).* Washington, D.C.: USITC.

———. 1985. *The Internationalization of the Automobile Industry and Its Effects on the U.S. Automobile Industry.* USITC Publication 1712. Washington, D.C.: USITC.

———. 1986. U.S. Imports of Textiles and Apparel under the Multifiber Arrangement: Statistical Report through 1985. USITC Publication 1863. Washington, D.C.: USITC.

———. 1992. *Minivans from Japan.* USITC Publication 2529. Washington, D.C.: USITC.

U.S. Treasury Department. 1975. Annual Report. Washington, D.C.: U.S. Government Printing Office.

———. 1990. Casis Database. Photocopy.

Walter, Ingo. 1979. "Protection of Industries in Trouble—the Case of Iron and Steel." *The World Economy* 2(2):159–87.

Walter, Ingo, and Kent Jones. 1981. "The Battle over Protectionism: How Industry Adjusts to Competitive Shocks." *Journal of Business Strategy* 2(2):37–46.

Ward's Automotive Reports (annual). 1975–91. Detroit, Michigan: Ward's Communications.

Whalley, John, ed. 1989. *The Uruguay Round and Beyond.* Ann Arbor: University of Michigan Press.

Winters, L. Alan, and P.A. Brenton. 1991. "Quantifying the Economic Effects of Non-tariff Barriers: The Case of UK Footwear." *Kyklos* 44(1):71–91.

Wolf, Martin. 1986a. "Fiddling While the GATT Burns." The *World Economy* 9(1):1–18.

———. 1986b. "Handmaiden Under Harrassment: The Multifibre Arrangement as an Obstacle to Development." In H. Giersch, ed., Free Trade in the World Economy: Towards an Opening of Markets. Boulder, Colo.: Westview.

Yoffie, David B. 1983. *Power & Protectionism: Strategies of the Newly Industrializing Countries.* New York: Columbia University Press.

———. 1988. "Mixed Motives, Bureaucratic Power, and Learning: The Past Appeal and Future Evolution of Voluntary Export Restraints." Working Paper, Harvard Business School. Photocopy.

Index